Understanding
PRIMO LEVI

UNDERSTANDING MODERN
EUROPEAN and LATIN AMERICAN
LITERATURE

James Hardin, *General Editor*

volumes on

Ingeborg Bachmann
Samuel Beckett
Thomas Bernhard
Johannes Bobrowski
Heinrich Böll
Italo Calvino
Albert Camus
Elias Canetti
Céline
José Donoso
Max Frisch
Federico García Lorca
Gabriel García Márquez

Günter Grass
Gerhart Hauptmann
Christoph Hein
Eugène Ionesco
Milan Kundera
Primo Levi
Graciliano Ramos
Erich Maria Remarque
Jean-Paul Sartre
Claude Simon
Mario Vargas Llosa
Franz Werfel
Peter Weiss

UNDERSTANDING

PRIMO
LEVI

NICHOLAS PATRUNO

UNIVERSITY OF SOUTH CAROLINA PRESS

© 1995 by the University of South Carolina

Published in Columbia, South Carolina, by the
University of South Carolina Press

Manufactured in the United States of America

Libarary of Congress Cataloging-in-Publication Data

Patruno, Nicholas.
  Understanding Primo Levi / by Nicholas Patruno.
     p.   cm—(Understanding modern European and Latin American
literature)
  Includes bibliographical references and index.
  ISBN 1–57003–026–X
  1. Levi, Primo—Criticism and Interpretation. I. Title
II. Series.
PQ4872.E8Z82 1995
853'.914—dc20   94–18747

Ah l'uomo che se ne va sicuro,
agli altri ed a se stesso amico,
e l'ombra sua non cura che la canicola
stampa sopra uno scalcinato muro!

(Ah, the one who goes forth sure of himself,
a friend to others, and to himself,
and pays no attention to his shadow
that is cast upon a crumbling wall by the scorching summer sun!)

From
"Non chiederci la parola"
by
Eugenio Montale
Michelle Patruno, translator

CONTENTS

EDITOR'S PREFACE

*U*nderstanding Modern European and Latin American Literature has been planned as a series of guides for undergraduate and graduate students and non-academic readers. Like the volumes in its companion series *Understanding Contemporary American Literature,* these books provide introductions to the lives and writings of prominent modern authors and explicates their most important works.

Modern literature makes special demands, and this is particularly true of foreign literature, in which the reader must contend not only with unfamiliar, often arcane artistic conventions and philosophical concepts, but also with the handicap of reading the literature in translation. It is a truism that the nuances of one language can be rendered in another only imperfectly (and this problem is especially acute in fiction), but the fact that the works of European and Latin American writers are situated in a historical and cultural setting quite different from our own can be as great a hindrance to the understanding of these works as the linguistic barrier. For this reason the UMELL series emphasizes the sociological and historical background of the writers treated. The peculiar philosophical and cultural traditions of a given culture may be particularly important for an understanding of certain authors, and these are taken up in the introductory chapter and also in the discussion of those works to which this information is relevant. Beyond this, the books treat the specifically literary aspects of the author under discussion and attempt to explain the complexities of contemporary literature lucidly. The books are conceived as introductions to the authors covered, not as comprehensive analyses. They do not provide detailed summaries of plot because they are meant to be used in conjunction with the books they treat, not as a substitute for study of the original works. The purpose of the books is to provide information and judicious literary assessment of the major works in the most compact, readable form. It is our hope that the UMELL series will help increase knowledge and understanding of European and Latin American cultures and will serve to make the literature of those cultures more accessible.

J. H.

ACKNOWLEDGMENTS

Without the support and assistance of others it would have been very difficult to complete this work.

First my thanks go to Bryn Mawr College and the Pew Charitable Trusts for their support for my research at home and abroad. During my stay in Turin, I enjoyed the hospitality and generosity of my good friends Pasquale and Zaira Liverani. To them, my heartfelt gratitude. They were essential in putting me in contact with others who, in their fondness of and admiration for Primo Levi, shared with me much of what they knew about him.

Dr. Femore, of Campus Bookstore in Turin, was of inestimable help in arranging visits with some of Levi's acquaintances. Dr. Giulio Einaudi allowed me to examine, in the archives of Einuadi Publishing House, all the available material related to Primo Levi and to his works. Dr. Severi of Einaudi assisted me in locating additional material. To all three my heartfelt thanks.

Dr. Giulio Bollati and Dr. Agnese Incisa, of Bollati Boringhieri Publishers, and Renato Portesi, Levi's co-worker at the paint factory SIVA, shared their candid and warm thoughts about Primo Levi the man, the writer, and the chemist. Lorenzo Mondo of Turin's daily *La Stampa* provided me with Levi's most recent writings, a good part of which are not yet published in book form. To them my gratitude.

On this side of the ocean, I thank my students and friends at the Main Line School Night for their patience, comments, and assessments of many ideas in this work. I also wish to thank Christine Flowers, the first reader of the entire manuscript.

Above all, I wish to acknowledge Marianne Ehrlich Naaman, an author in her own right, for her generous help and advice. I am deeply grateful to her for her invaluable suggestions, which helped define and shape the thoughts contained in the pages that follow.

Finally, my thanks go to my family for their support when I needed it the most, especially to my wife Edwina.

CHRONOLOGY

1919   31 July: Primo Levi is born in Turin in a house where he will live for the rest of his life.

1934   Attends public high school Massimo D'Azeglio in Turin.

1937   Enrolls at the University of Turin to major in chemistry.

1938   Fascist government issues the first racial laws. The Jews are forbidden to attend public schools, but since Levi was already enrolled, he is allowed to complete his studies.

1941   July: Graduates from the University of Turin summa cum laude.

    —Finds semi-legal employment in an asbestos cave near Lanzo, in Piedmont. His name is kept off the payroll.

1942   Moves to Milan, where he works for the Swiss pharmaceutical firm Wander.

1943   July: Fall of the Fascist government and arrest and imprisonment of Mussolini. Levi joins Partisan forces in the Aosta region, north of Turin, to fight against Fascist forces.

    —13 December: Arrested with two fellow partisans and, upon admitting to being Jewish, is sent to the concentration camp of Carpi-Fossoli, near Modena.

1944   22 February: From the concentration camp at Carpi-Fossoli, now under the control of German forces, Levi and other prisoners are deported to Auschwitz.

1945   27 January: Levi and other prisoners are liberated from Auschwitz by Russian units.

    —19 October: Returns to Turin.

1946   Finds employment at Duco-Montecatini, a paint factory in Avigliana, outside Turin.

1947   Resigns from his job at Duco.

    —Following rejection by Einaudi publisher, his manuscript is accepted and published by De Silva. Twenty-five hundred copies are printed, most of which will go unsold and then be lost in the Florence flood of 1966.

    —September: Marries Lucia Morpurgo, who will bear him two children: Lisa Lorenza (1948) and Renzo (1957).

	—December: Accepts a position as a chemist in the laboratory of a small paint company, SIVA, outside Turin.
1956	Encouraged by the interest many young people had shown in his experiences, Levi resubmits his work to Einaudi; this time it is accepted for publication.
1958	Einaudi publishes *Se questo è un uomo* (*Survival in Auschwitz*).
1963	April: Publication of *La tregua* (*The Reawakening*).
	—September: *La tregua* receives the Campiello Literary Prize.
1965	*The Reawakening* is translated into English and published under the title *The Truce.*
1966	*Storie naturali,* a collection of short stories, is published under the pseudonym Damiano Malabaila.
1967	Receives the Bagutta literary prize for *Storie naturali.*
1971	Publication of *Vizio di forma,* Levi's second collection of short stories.
1973	Travels extensively to the Soviet Union for work reasons. This experience will serve as inspiration for his book *La chiave a stella* (*The Monkey's Wrench*).
1975	Decides to take early retirement from SIVA but will stay on for two more years as a consultant.
	—Publication of *Il sistema periodico* (*The Periodic Table*), for which he receives the Premio Prato per la Resistenza.
	—Submits for publication *L'osteria di Brema,* a small collection of poems.
1977	Ends his association with SIVA to devote himself full-time to writing.
1978	Publication of *La chiave a stella* (*The Monkey's Wrench*). The book is well received.
	—July: *La chiave a stella* receives the Strega literary prize.
1981	Publication of *La ricerca delle radici,* a personal anthology including writers and works that Levi considers central to his own cultural formation.
	—October: Publication of *Lilít e altri racconti.*
1982	April: Publication of *Se non ora, quando?* (*If Not Now, When?*).
	—June: *Se non ora, quando?* receives the Viareggio literary prize.
	—September: *Se non ora, quando?* receives the Campiello literary prize.
	—Levi returns for a second visit to Auschwitz.
1983	April: Levi's translation of Kafka's *The Trial* is published.
1984	November: English translation of *The Periodic Table* is published in the United States.

1985 January: Publication of *L'altrui mestiere* (*Other People's Trades*), a collection of writings, mostly essays, that had appeared in the Turin daily *La Stampa* between the years 1975 and 1985.

—English translation of *If Not Now, When?* is published in the United States.

—April: Visits the United States to promote *If Not Now, When?* and is invited to lecture at several universities.

1986 April: Publication of *I sommersi e i salvati* (*The Drowned and the Saved*).

—English translation of *The Monkey's Wrench* is published in the United States.

—*Moments of Reprieve,* the English translation of a portion of *Lilít e altri racconti,* is published in the United States.

—November: Publication of *Racconti e saggi.*

1987 April 11: Dies in the house where he was born.

—May: Publication of *Autoritratto di Primo Levi,* Ferdinando Camon's extensive interview with Primo Levi.

1988 *The Drowned and the Saved,* English translation of *I sommersi e i salvati,* appears in the United States.

—*Collected Poems,* English translation of the collection of poems *Ad ora incerta,* appears in the United States.

1989 *Dialogue,* English translation of *Dialogo,* appears in the United States.

—*The Mirror Maker,* an English translation of portions of *Racconti & saggi* and of some additional essays, is published in the United States.

—*Conversations with Primo Levi,* the English translation of *Autoritratto di Primo Levi,* appears in print in the United States, as does *Other People's Trades,* the English version of *L'altrui mestieze.*

1990 May: *The Sixth Day and Other Tales,* an abridged version of the English translation of *Storie naturali* and of *Vizio di forma,* appears in the United States.

Understanding
PRIMO LEVI

Introduction

Primo Levi has emerged as one of the most incisive and candid intellects among those writers who experienced the Holocaust and survived to tell about it. It would be difficult to find anyone who displays the soul of the persecuted Jew with more eloquence. Italian by birth, a Jew by ancestry, and a chemist by profession, Levi was born in Turin, one of Italy's most industrialized cities, on 31 July 1919, the son of a successful electrical engineer. He grew up during the years before World War II in the relative comfort of the middle class at a time in Italy when being of Jewish ancestry had not yet become a cause of segregation and persecution. After graduating from the Lyceum Massimo D'Azeglio, a secondary school noted for its academic excellence and, during those years, its several anti-Fascist teachers,[1] Levi enrolled at the University of Turin in 1937 to major in chemistry. Because he had entered the university a year before the promulgation of the Fascist racial laws, which, along with other restrictions, prohibited Jews in Italy from attending public schools, he was allowed to complete his studies. He graduated summa cum laude in 1941, but his diploma carried the phrase "di razza ebraica" (of the Jewish race). This was his first personal experience of discrimination because of his Jewish origins, though many others were to follow as Fascist dogma reshaped the social, moral, and political atmosphere in Italy. As time and further experience would reveal, however, this discrimination was finally the catalyst in Levi's emergence as one of the most powerful and limpid voices confronting the indignity, humiliation, shame, and lasting guilt associated with the Holocaust. He also distinguished himself through his writings on other topics.

Until his graduation, Levi had little reason to reflect upon his Jewishness. Like most other Jews living in Italy at the time, he considered himself an integral part of his society. He enjoyed the rights and freedoms exercised by the general population and participated fully in the social and political life of the country. In fact, as Vittorio Segre states, after Italy's unification in 1860, the country was served by a Jewish minister of war, two Jewish prime ministers, and one Jewish secretary-general of the Ministry of Foreign Affairs.[2] Many Jews held other cabinet positions during the early years of Italy's love-hate fascination with the Fascist regime. Such representation was remarkable not so much because it occurred in a Fascist-dominated environment but rather because the entire Jewish population in Italy during the middle 1930s barely

1

exceeded 45,000; that is, it was roughly a tenth of one percent of the Italian population.[3]

In late 1943, following the fall of the Fascist government, the Germans created the puppet government known as the Republic of Salò near Lake Garda in northern Italy and placed at its head Benito Mussolini, whom they had rescued from prison. The country found itself divided by a civil war, with the Fascists and the German army in control of much of central Italy and all of northern Italy. It was at this time that the deportation of Jews began.

As a result of the German occupation and collaboration in Italy, nearly 6,400 Italian Jews were deported, mainly to the camps of Auschwitz, Birkenau, and Mauthausen. Of those who were taken away, only a few hundred survivors can be accounted for. Of the 650 prisoners who were taken to Auschwitz with Levi, only fifteen men and eight women returned home.[4] Levi's imprisonment in Auschwitz in February 1944, after someone betrayed him by reporting his partisan activities in the Aosta region north of Turin, made him a witness to one of humanity's darkest moments. Not able to foresee the tragic consequences of his decision, upon capture he chose to admit that he was a Jew rather than own up to his partisan involvement. This confession, he maintained, was made in part because he was tired and worn down emotionally, and partly because he was led to believe that being Jewish would carry a less harsh punishment, but to a great extent because of a sudden surge of pride in his origins.

As prisoner number 174517, Levi had his life proscribed by the most irrational actions of others. But his training as a chemist, which enabled him to be assigned relatively undemanding work in a laboratory at Auschwitz, together with his being in the infirmary with scarlet fever when the Russians liberated Auschwitz in January 1945, took him out of the death camp's mainstream at a most opportune time. He was left behind by the retreating Germans, who, convinced that those in the camp who were ill would perish before anyone could reach them, took with them only the prisoners healthy enough to walk, their intention being to kill them along the way in order to insure their silence. This was one of the Nazis' last attempts to hide any evidence of the monumental calamity they had inflicted on a whole segment of humanity.

Before Auschwitz, Levi admitted that his identification with his Judaic heritage had been so minimal that, he stated half jokingly, he might even have converted to another religion.[5] By his own account, he was shocked into confronting his Jewishness by the wild course of events that allowed the Holocaust to occur. Yet he was also candid in admitting that the experience had the positive effect of awakening in him his sense of identity and an attachment to his long-neglected "cultural patrimony," of which he would be proud for the rest of his life.

While the theme of Jewishness is predominant in all Levi's works, it would be inaccurate to label him a Jewish writer in the narrow, ethnic sense of the word, though that is the first description that comes to mind at the mention of his name. Levi's broad interest in and effective literary treatment of a wide variety of subjects led Italo Calvino, in a 6 March 1985 article in the daily *La Repubblica,* to define Levi as a writer with an "encyclopedic vein."

Educated no differently than other Italians with similar financial means and professional aspirations, and having been schooled in all the traditional literary texts that are the foundation of an education in the humanities and the sciences, Levi could more sensibly be called an Italian writer than a Jewish writer; and perhaps, in the final analysis, it would please him most to be known simply as a writer, without any additional qualification. It is the fusion of Levi's scientific mind with his literary creativity that is the key to his importance as a writer and communicator. His acknowledgment of the importance of communication, not only of one human being with another but also between creative art and scientific disciplines, was seminal to his work. Equally important was his compunction, born of inner experience and his survival of his incarceration, to become the voice that would respond to the Nazis' intention to annihilate the entire Jewish race.

Anyone who survived Nazi imprisonment, Levi believes, did so as a result of "luck." [6] At Auschwitz, Levi quickly learned that to communicate *was* to survive; and as a man of science, who would be inclined to observe patiently and understand, he was able to absorb and then communicate the Holocaust as a didactic event as well as a personal one. This is evident in his approach to writing about it. In his first full-length work, *Se questo è un uomo* (1947, 1958) (*Survival in Auschwitz,* 1987), form and structure, to use Levi's words, were secondary in importance to recording the event in a straightforward manner so that it would never be forgotten. In his first attempts at exploring the survival phenomenon, Levi wrote essentially from a factual point of view to recount arrival at the camp, how one found food or was given work, and how one was chosen or not chosen to live or die. The horror of the camps is heightened by Levi's numbing recitation of the everyday experience. In *La tregua* (1963) (*The Reawakening,* 1987), which is the successor to *Survival in Auschwitz,* he recounted his emergence from the nightmare of Auschwitz and the completion of his circuitous, sometimes picaresque, odyssey of return to his homeland.

After Levi met his need to tell by recording the factual aspects of his ordeal, he went past literal documentation to draw from his creative vein in the stories that appear in *Lilìt e altri racconti* (1981) (*Moments of Reprieve,* 1986), in which he fulfilled his promised "immortalization" of the "human figures . . .

3

friends . . . even adversaries" (*Moments of Reprieve* 10) he encountered at Auschwitz and immediately thereafter by committing their acts and personalities to the written page. In *I sommersi e i salvati* (1986) (*The Drowned and the Saved,* 1989), his last work before his death, Levi, still contending with his sense of responsibility, undertook the risky, painfully incisive psychological and philosophical journey into the entire Holocaust experience. With full awareness that he might never justify to his own satisfaction his continuing existence in the face of such a mass extermination of his fellow Jews, he devoted much effort and time to analyzing the Holocaust phenomenon and attempting to achieve a philosophical rationale that might help to avert a recurrence of that tragic event. Both in his prose and in the thoughts from which it emerged, Levi strove without losing his sense of humility not only to immortalize but to consecrate the millions who died. With the passing of time, Levi found himself at an incontrovertible disadvantage in doing this, because in having survived, he knew he could never fathom the final reality of those who did not. Nor, as he explored at length in his last book, did he ever come to terms with whatever compromises he or anyone else, wittingly or unwittingly, made to survive. He was equally troubled with those, including himself, who failed to take action on the outside, when there was time to do so, to oppose the atrocities perpetrated on the Jews.

In the parable-like 1982 tale *Se non ora quando?* (*If Not Now, When?,* 1985), perhaps Levi's only "true" novel in a conventional sense because it was not created directly from his Holocaust experience, he paid tribute to the Jews of Eastern Europe with his fictional group of heroic figures who have lost all that is dearest to them and undertake a difficult and harrowing journey westward through several countries, finally reaching Israel by way of Italy. But, as we realize after a reading of Levi's complete works, the Holocaust theme was never far from the center of his thoughts and writing.

While the circumstances of his incarceration and liberation served as Levi's initial impulse to write, his literary gift was fueled by a phenomenon that is now clearly recognized and understood, the lingering "guilt of survival," and by his sense of responsibility for providing witness on behalf of those who had perished. He devoted the remainder of his life to meeting his self-appointed obligation, in which, he admitted to Gail Soffer, "to tell the story, to bear witness, was an end for which to save oneself. Not to live *and* to tell, but to live *in order* to tell" (Levi, "Beyond Survival" 12–13). But Levi did not stop here. He wrote competently and absorbingly about other subjects, such as the importance of work well done, a theme that figures in the lively and amusing *La chiave a stella* (1978) (*The Monkey's Wrench,* 1986). He also wrote fantasy tales, many of which border on science fiction, such as the ones included in *Storie naturali* (1966) and *Vizio di forma* (1971). (Many of these stories are collected in *The Sixth Day and Other Tales,* 1990). However, his memories of his agonizing experience were always the ink in his creative pen. Through them his perceptions, productivity, and self-awareness were sharpened and clarified, and his ability to communicate was heightened to new levels of eloquence.

Levi's sober, lean style is reflective of a mind guided by reason and civility. Through his emphasis on clarity, his dispassionate approach, and his accurate observations (honed by his scientific training), he left emotional responses to his readers. He did so because he was wise, not because he was lacking profound passion, pain, and frustration. He dignified himself and the reader by allowing the facts to speak for themselves, and the reader might experience and interpret them within his or her own emotional framework. As a witness and spokesperson, he was neither swayed nor subverted by hatred or by the need for revenge. Neither would he attempt to elicit hatred or a thirst for vengeance from his audience. His magnanimity and moral integrity urge us all to reassess our beliefs and values.

Levi's compelling and ongoing need to address the consequences of the Holocaust was a major factor in his decision to take early retirement and devote himself full-time to writing. Leaving the chemical laboratory, however, did not mean abandoning his scientific legacy. Exploring, exposing, and elaborating the connections between art and science remained a constant challenge to his intellect. Coming from the world of industry rather than the literary or academic establishment, he was able to write with a greater degree of stylistic freedom and with less reverence for established literary norms. To communicate in a constructive manner requires unification of the cultural aspects of science and letters. The moral deterioration that had produced the Holocaust made clear to Levi, as he believed it must have been unquestionably clear to such artistic and scientific worthies as Empedocles, Dante, Leonardo, Galileo, Descartes, Goethe, and Einstein, that for men and women to live in a civilized and compassionate society, science and conscience must coexist in balance, each nurturing the other. He pursued this point in the preface to the 1985 edition of *L'altrui mestiere* (*Other People's Trades,* 1989), a book of essays drawn from sources related to science and the humanities in which he demonstrated the compatibility and interplay of these two disciplines—separation of the two appeared to him absurd and inappropriate.

Levi had great admiration for the early-sixteenth-century French writer-philosopher François Rabelais, who depicted a world of earthly pleasures to explore the transcendence of human life above human misery and whom Levi called "mon maître" (*Other People's Trades* 133). From Rabelais Levi got his belief that the state of misery could and must also contain the potential for a better world. Hence, if the scientific element could be combined with the human one, cohesion and harmony could emerge and a new voice could be created.

Levi found his own "new voice" in *Il sistema periodico* (1975) (*The Periodic Table,* 1984), which many consider to be his greatest work. He achieved in this book his desired synthesis of science and art by placing his insight into humanity's conscience within a scientific frame. He masterfully illustrated the relationship of the scientific metaphor to human behavior, thus demonstrating that he could fulfill his vision as an amalgamator of scientist and writer, element and word.

Levi has been likened to Dante, and no critic has focused on this aspect in more depth and sensitivity than Risa Sodi.[7] Aside from the major difference that Dante lived his experience in poetical terms while Levi lived his in real terms, both were subjected to the vicissitudes of a hell they did not seek, and both, to the benefit of humanity, lived to tell of it. The writer Alfred Kazin considers Levi "one of the two greatest postwar writers Italy has produced," the other being Italo Calvino.[8] Levi's books have been translated into several languages, and all his major works are available in English translation. In the United States, he is certainly among the most widely read contemporary Italian writers. In addition to his novels and short stories, which are the primary focus of this book, Levi wrote two collections of poems (some of which are incorporated into the novels), a large number of essays and articles, and two short plays. He also translated literary works, Kafka's *The Trial* being the best known of them.

In his later years Levi demonstrated a maturity not only of talent and intellect but of worldly acceptance. It is evident that his chosen role of bearing witness to the Holocaust led him into dark corners and alleyways where he found no answers to his questions. Most distressing to him were those voices that, despite the overwhelming evidence, continue to raise doubts about or deny outright the occurrence of the Holocaust atrocities. Yet, through the eloquence of his words, Levi cemented the immortal truth of the Holocaust. Furthermore, in his ability to assimilate his beloved scientific world with the literary challenge, he also succeeded in reinvigorating our thoughts on the trials of human existence and on our human dignity. His spirit, on behalf of all who suffer, was triumphant in the face of harsh adversity.

On 11 April 1987, Primo Levi died at the age of sixty-eight. Many believe it was suicide.

Notes

1. Among these was Cesare Pavese, one of Italy's most prominent writers.

2. *Storia di un ebreo fortunato* (Milan: Bompiani, 1985), 40.

3. These statistics appear in *Discriminazione e persecuzione degli ebrei nell'Italia fascista,* Ugo Caffaz, ed. (Florence: Consiglio Regionale della Toscana, 1988), 64.

4. Statistics from *Discriminazione e persecuzione degli ebrei nell'Italia facista,* 82.

5. Ferdinando Camon, *Conversations with Primo Levi* (Marlboro, Vt.: Marlboro Press, 1989), 68.

6. See interview with Philip Roth, "A Man Saved by His Skills," *New York Times Book Review* (12 October 1986): 40. Levi admits that "in my case, luck played an essential role on at least two occasions."

7. See also Lynn M. Gunzberg, "Down Among the Dead Men: Levi and Dante in Hell," *Modern Language Studies* 16 (Winter 1986): 10–28.

8. In the *New York Times* (17 March 1990): 17.

CHAPTER ONE

Survival in Auschwitz
(Se questo è un uomo)

S*e questo è un uomo* (*Survival in Auschwitz*) appeared in print in 1947, two years after Levi's liberation and return from the concentration camp at Auschwitz. This book was originally published in Italy by De Silva, a small, relatively unknown publisher, following a rejection by Einaudi, a prestigious publishing house in Turin.[1] Although it received favorable reviews, it went virtually unnoticed by the public. Of the original 2,500 copies, close to 600 that had gone unsold and had been stored in Florence were eventually lost in the 1966 flood in that city. In 1956, encouraged by the interest shown (especially by the younger generation) in an exhibition held in Turin on the Italian deportation experience, Levi decided to resubmit his manuscript to Einaudi. This time it was accepted, and the firm published the book in 1958.[2] It has been in print ever since; has appeared in various editions; and has been translated into several languages, including English, French, German, and Dutch. Einaudi's edition is today considered to be the official version. Besides some slight variations of a syntactical nature, it includes the additional chapter "The Canto Of Ulysses," which was absent from the De Silva version.[3]

On the surface, *Survival in Auschwitz* reads as a document in which Levi recounts the experiences and events in which he was a forced participant while incarcerated in the concentration camp of Buna-Monowitz.[4] Levi's role, his self-imposed responsibility in writing this book, is to remind humankind of the Holocaust so that it will never happen again. The book is also his attempt to liberate himself from the psychological burden imposed by having survived this great offense against humanity, which was a constant stimulus to his creativity in fulfilling his compelling need to tell his experiences and make others vicarious participants in them. To designate the book a memoir or diary, as has often been done, is neither totally accurate nor fair. At the core of the book, defined by Stuart H. Hughes as one "of the rare classics in the genre,"[5] and behind its memorialistic facade, is an eloquently expressed ethical and civic message. Levi claims, however, that in the book style takes second place to his urgent need to tell, and he begs forgiveness for the structural imperfections of the text and the "fragmentary character" (6) of the chapters, which, he admits, were not necessarily written in the order in which they appear.

The theme of the work may be found in its short preface, where Levi states, somewhat self-effacingly, that the book adds little if anything to the already well known details of the atrocities carried out in, as he calls them, extermination camps. Nor is it his intention to point an accusing finger at the perpetrators of the Holocaust, even though he makes it clear that he cannot forgive. His purpose in writing is to attempt to synthesize for himself, while at the same time communicating to others, a representation of events that will allow for a sober study of both the destructive and the heroic aspects of the human spirit in the Holocaust.[6] Through this chronicle of observations, at both the physical and the philosophical levels, Levi reveals not only the harsh realities of the daily struggle for survival but the clash between good and evil. The characters are sometimes laudable and sometimes ignoble, but, from a moral point of view, they confirm that the same event can elicit a diverse spectrum of human actions and reactions.

Focusing on what he calls xenophobic obsession in which "every stranger is an enemy," an obsession that he considers a "latent infection" (5) in the depths of the human spirit even though it is rationally baseless, Levi views the *Lager,* or prison camp, system as one without reason and thus a threat to humanity. Its conceptualization and implementation provide specific examples of how individuals or groups have attempted to allay their paranoid convictions that all foreigners are enemies. The emergence of the Lager becomes a drastic, counteractive measure that Levi believes should be understood as an ominous sign, a "sinister alarm signal" (5). It is the Lager experience and all its long-lasting effects that compel him to write, to revisit them over and over, so that the "rest" of us will comprehend the system's unfathomable irrationality. This irrationality is so extreme that, in his preface to this work, fearing the reader's possible disbelief, Levi assures us that the facts are not invented. Moreover, he finds it necessary to apologize, in light of the violence of the subject matter, for his own "immediate and violent impulse" (6) to tell and tell again. But like Coleridge's Ancient Mariner (an image to which he will often return), who is restored to the company of the living, Levi will never tire of telling his story, as his many interviews will confirm. It is only through a constant interface with his recollections that he sees any hope of surviving his survival. In fact, he opens his last book, *The Drowned and the Saved,* by quoting these famous lines from the Coleridge poem: "Since then, at an uncertain hour, / That agony returns: / And till my ghastly tale is told / This heart within me burns."

Following his one-page preface, Levi inserts an epigraphic poem, written in January 1946, which is a loosely paraphrased interpretation of one of the most often invoked Hebrew prayers, the Shemà.[7] Herman Wouk defines it as

9

the creed of the Jew and one of the two most common Hebrew prayers.[8] If the preface and Coleridge's poem provide the framework for understanding the intent of the book, this epigraphic poem defines its theme and gives us insight into its title. The prayer is a powerful call to the reader to contemplate the plight of humanity; and woe to the person who fails or refuses to meditate on this plight. The author assumes, in this case, the austere, poetic, God-like voice to evoke the reader's awareness that while some live in comfortable complacency, others suffer beyond any bounds of human endurance.

Because the poem is a calculated insertion and a help in understanding Levi's frame of mind and his message, a question might be raised about why the current English translation, which has gone through several reprints since the first Collier Books edition of 1961, carries the title *Survival in Auschwitz* while the first English edition appeared under the more accurately translated title *If This Is a Man.* Philip Roth makes the parenthetical observation in an interview with Levi that the American editors should have had the good sense to preserve that title [9]—an observation that, curiously enough, does not appear in the Italian version of that interview.[10] Mr. Roth's sentiments appear to be well founded. Although the title *Survival in Auschwitz* may have more marketing appeal, it is a bland substitute for the original title because it undermines the significance of the epigraphic poem, with its intent of condemnation and remorse and its imperative message and painful admonition. By giving his work the title *If This Is a Man,* the author raises a rhetorical question of conscience whose impact is so powerful that any reply would be superfluous. It is impossible to communicate or understand the rhetorical quality or the pivotal question raised by the original title when it has been changed.

Having set his stage, Levi leads the reader into his story with the ironic phrase "good fortune" to describe his deportation to Auschwitz in 1944. As we contemplate how this could have been fortunate, he clarifies, with less sarcasm, that the year of his deportation was one in which the life span of a prisoner had become somewhat lengthened because of a shortage of labor for the prison workforce. We also know that Levi considered his time at Auschwitz educational, despite the hardship.

The early chapters, which include "The Journey" through "This Side of Good and Evil," read as a direct chronological report of events. In the second and most extensive part, which comprises the chapters "The Drowned and the Saved" through "The Last One," the author spends more time on detailed episodes related to his imprisonment and emerges as a protagonist. Proceeding by way of memory-linked associations, he combines characters and situations to give a more dynamic view of camp life than he did previously. The third and final part of the book is the last chapter, "The Story of Ten Days," in which Levi uses a diary form of narrative to describe the last days he spent in the camp, just before the appearance of the Russian soldiers and subsequent to the flight of the Germans.

On 13 December 1943, Levi, then twenty-four years old, saw the end of his short life as a partisan when he was captured in the mountains of Val D'Aosta and imprisoned in the concentration camp at Carpi-Fossoli, near Modena. His imprisonment was the result of his decision to admit to being an "Italian citizen of Jewish race" (10), which he made in part to avoid what he was led to believe would be the harsher consequences of confessing his involvement in the resistance movement.

On 21 February 1944 Levi learned that all of the more than 600 Jews in the camp would be leaving the following day for an unknown destination. Making a biblical reference, Levi notes that the painful, hopeless exodus, destined to be eternally repeated, was occurring once again. In a moving, lyrical narrative, dignified and subdued in tone,[11] Levi opens his recollections with a description of what takes place during the last night in barrack 6A, occupied by a certain Gattegno and his family. A happy, simple, and pious group who had come from Tripoli with their carpenters' tools, kitchen utensils, accordions, and violins, they will not allow the news of imminent deportation to suppress their dignity. The women busy themselves with tidying up and getting everything ready before they sit on the bare ground in a circle to commence their lamentations, prayers, and weeping, performing the Jewish mourning ritual that commemorates the destruction of the first and second temples.[12] The importance of this scene, we know in retrospect, is that it provides the last actions of human warmth and togetherness the author will experience for a long time.

Levi, who up until this time had lived his life in a world inhabited by "Cartesian phantoms" (9)—that is to say, with aspirations arrived at logically and rationally—will now be referred to as *Stück,* a "piece" of no value. Physical and mental violence will replace all reason. Ironically, what will sustain the group during this trip and afterward are the discomfort, the blows, and the cold they experience in the cattle car, not—contrary to commonly-held belief—any particular will to live or conscious resignation to their fate. This reaction is the first among many Levi describes in which higher-level reasoning is replaced by instinctual action. The assault on human dignity is so irrational that there is no reasoned response to it. In truth, death might have appeared desirable in the face of such dehumanization. Killing the prisoners at this point, however, would have been a rational act of kindness, which the Nazis had no intention of showing. Even the "selection" upon the group's arrival follows no rational pattern.

In a swift, quirky process, those who are judged unfit to work usefully for the Reich are immediately sent to their death. As Levi survives future selections, usually carried out to make room for new arrivals, he begins to realize that it is blind fate that determines who will live. Often the young and the stronger are sent to the gas chambers while, illogically, the old and sick are left to live for at least one more turn. The effect of this, beyond the simple fact of carrying out the grand scheme of eradication, is to create a reaction of shame for having survived and to inculcate a subtle but pernicious disregard for one's fellow human beings in suffering. Old Kuhn, who gives thanks to God for having spared his life, does not care that the twenty-year-old Greek next to him, Beppo, has been selected to die, perhaps in Kuhn's stead. At no other point in this book does Levi give such vent to his anger at the lack of humility and the disregard for the sanctity of life as he does here. He exclaims that were he the god to whom Kuhn's prayer was directed, he would reject it and "spit" it to the ground (118).

Levi's incorporation of Dante, as much for the metaphorical likeness of the experience both writers depict as for the struggle Levi describes to achieve accurate expression of it, is not an act of literary boasting. It is valid in terms of the phenomenon of which he writes and the need to draw a literary parallel. The description of Dante's similar path through hell, although he has taken it for totally different reasons and as an observer with a predestined salvation, has come not without an arduous struggle to describe adequately the horror of the event. Dante's effort is plainly stated in the first canto of *Paradiso* (70–71), where he confesses that "trasumanar significar per verba / non si porìa" (one cannot describe with human terms that which transcends humanity). Levi too admits that his language, and ours, may be too limited to tell adequately of "this offence, the demolition of a man" (22). In fact, a parallel can be drawn between Dante's quotation and Levi's effort to express in human terms that which is inhuman. The word *trasumanar,* intended by Dante in the positive meaning of going *above* and *past* human boundaries, can be replaced, in Levi's case, by the term *subumanar,* which conveys the meaning of going *below* the boundaries of human recognition; thus the title of this chapter, "On the Bottom."

One of the reasons Levi has been called a modern-day Dante in Italy is that he makes many references, implicit and explicit, to the *Divine Comedy,* especially the *Inferno.* Several studies have dealt with this issue; the deepest analysis is by Risa Sodi in *A Dante of Our Time.* Though it is not the intention of this study to point to all of Levi's references to Dante, it is in keeping with the study's objectives to identify his bond with the earlier writer. Even before Levi recounts the arrival of the prisoners at Auschwitz, he makes a reference to the *Inferno* in his description of the soldier who accompanies them in the truck from the cattle train. In the soldier's request that the members of the group turn over to him anything of value in their possession, Levi sees a parallel with Dante's description of Charon, the demon who in the *Inferno* (canto 3) carries the damned in a boat across the Acheron River and who, according to the legend, upon arrival on the other side expects some kind of recompense.

Levi also alludes to Dante in referring to the sign at the entrance to the camp, which reads ARBEIT MACHT FREI (work will make you free), embodying grotesque irony and irrational assault to body and soul. This sign marks the entrance to a modern-day hell and echoes the words written over the entrance to Dante's hell in the *Inferno* (canto 3:9): "Lasciate ogni speranza, voi che entrate" (Abandon all hope, you who enter). The paradox, of course, is that while Dante presents a fictitious world, Auschwitz is real. That Levi has Dante in mind is further accentuated by his observation that the memory of the words on the sign still troubles his dreams many years later. This phenomenon is reflected by Dante's "che nel pensier rinnova la paura!" (The thought of it reawakens the fear!) (canto 1:6).

The words at the entrance of Dante's hell would have applied well to the outcome the Nazis had determined for the Jews in the concentration camps. The Lager proves to be a modern version of Dante's city of Dis, where most of the rules of the world of "the living" are ignored and excessive hunger, thirst, and work are forced on the individual. As in the Malebolge section of the *Inferno*, in which the damned try to get away with whatever they can by using any method they know, in the Lager too one finds characters doing this. Further, pushing satanic perversity to unparalleled heights, the oppressors deceive by raising false hopes where there can be no hope. Freedom can be gained only by death, which is immediate for some but comes to others only after much physical and mental anguish. Auschwitz, this man-made hell, this *anus mundi,* is harsher than the one Dante visits, which is created by Divine Justice and truth. God's hell does not deceive, and the sinners, as they enter, know why they are damned to punishment without hope. The Nazis' hell, on the other hand, deceives, mocks, humiliates, and offends without ever giving reasons— for, after all, there are no reasons to be given, no sins for which the Jews, destined for death, and others incarcerated there are being punished.

Levi recognizes this deception. "This is hell," he writes. "Today, in our times, hell must be like this" (18). As it is suggested in the title of the chapter in which he describes his realization, "On The Bottom," this acknowledgment finds him at the lowest point, where one "cannot think anymore, it is like being already dead" (18). This is only the beginning of the process of dehumanization and the elimination of dignity. Just as a cat victimizes its prey before killing it, the Germans appear to enjoy the slow mental torture and physical abuse of their victims. Those who have been spared an immediate trip to the gas chamber are methodically reduced by the Nazi machine to an animal-like state. Stripped of a name, each captive has a number tattooed on his or her left arm and is eventually dressed in a "zebra"-striped tunic with a red and yellow star. Levi becomes *Häftling* (prisoner) 174517 and, like all the others, is considered by his captors to be little more than an animal. Stripped of clothes and other belongings in preparation for being shorn like animals, the prisoners are forced to abandon whatever remnants they have of their past existence. In the humiliation of laying everything bare, the prisoners are driven by a sense of modesty and instinctively try to cover themselves in the presence of others. Privacy, however, is not allowed, and modesty is useless, for where the Jews are destined to go it will matter little whether or not one can cover one's private parts. The steps that precede the showers and disinfection heighten the mean parody of the shower as a baptismal rite, symbolically cleansing the prisoners of the "sins" they carry from the outside world. This scornful act of disinfection is the ironic requirement necessary for entering a world infested with diseased morality as well as physical filth. This is a further mockery by the demonic mechanism that turns human beings first into *Stück,* nothing, and then into *Häftlinge.*

The pages describing this paradoxical purification are among the liveliest in the book. The fast-paced rhythm, the repetition of words, and the switch from past to present tense all contribute to the successful depiction of the tumult of the action. They capture the newly-arrived victims' state of confusion and fear. Everything is carried out in a tempo suggestive of the well-known German military precision. Orders are blunt and, if they are not carried out with corresponding alacrity, physical force is applied to speed acquiescence. In a short time, the imprisoned men and women have been deprived of their loved ones, their homes, their customs, their clothing, everything. The true meaning of the name "campo di annientamento" (camp of *annihilation*) lies in the fact that it serves as the place of *extermination.*

Among the unpleasant sounds of distorted, confusing, varied languages and the punches, kicks, and blows, the prisoners will now follow orders and execute upon command, ask no questions and seek no explanations, for in the camp "ist kein Warum" (there is no why) (25). They will learn to march in a puppet-like gait to the song "Rosamunda," another of the many grotesque customs of the place. Physical degeneration comes rapidly under such conditions; interaction and communication are fractured; and the Italian prisoners stop seeing each other on Sunday evenings, not only because of the sheer physical struggle involved in walking but perhaps more because of the pain they experience in seeing each other's deterioration and remembering the relative sweetness of their past lives.

In the third chapter, "Initiation," bread becomes a constant obsession, and the word for it is one quickly learned in several languages: *Brot-Broit-chleb-pain-lechem-kenyér.* Bread is also a common means of barter and exchange. Many humiliating deeds are committed for the sake of an additional piece of bread. Among the physical hardships, hunger is the most tormenting.[13] Food becomes the fixation that will intrude in dreams and play tricks on vision. Many prisoners will smack their lips and move their jaws in their sleep in a collective dream reminiscent of the myth of Tantalus, who was condemned not to be able to grasp the food and water within his reach. The prisoners are continually tantalized and then deprived, and this engenders hallucinations such as the one in which they associate the movement of a dredging machine with the act of chewing. They stare at the mechanical jawing, with their lips synchronized to the movement of the machine, their Adam's apples moving up and down as the machine bites into the dirt and then lifts it. The Lager is "hunger," and the prisoners are hunger personified, "living hunger" (67). Hunger is so powerful that at times it makes them forget their other pains. Having reduced the prisoners to docile and obedient animals, the *Kapos,* or guards, sometimes beat them as a farmer beats his horse or donkey, not to do it harm but to prod it to work. The Germans even refer to their food as *Fressen* (animal food).[14] When Resnyk, the hard-working Polish prisoner who shares Levi's bunk and never complains about anything, is ordered to work outside on a cold, blustery day, he observes that he would not even send his dog out in such weather, if he had one.

When the prisoners witness a hanging without evincing any reaction, Levi admits defeat. The Germans have finally succeeded in turning them into an "abject flock" (135) that will remain unresponsive even at such a sight. In the chapter "The Last One," which, as will be seen later, is crucial to understanding Levi's readjustment to normalcy, he witnesses the fourteenth and last hanging.

Occasionally, Levi interjects inferences in his use of numbers or in his recapitulation of their simple occurrence within the framework of events. According to Cirlot's *Dictionary of Symbols,*[15] the number 14 stands for fusion and organization, justice and temperance. By extension, this fourteenth hanging awakens in Levi a sense of responsibility for what is morally unjust. It is on the number 18, however, that the author places heavier symbolic relevance. That number, *chai* in Hebrew, is representative in the Jewish tradition of a "living being." Placing *Null* before a number renders it a negative. The prisoner who is called Null Achtzhen, in the chapter "Ka-Be," is a most dramatic and poignant example of the state of nothingness, short of death, envisioned by the Germans. Null Achtzhen, which means Zero Eighteen, is a nickname given to this prisoner for the last two digits of his tattoo. No one knows his real name, and he is nothing more than a shell of a man. When he speaks, when he stares, he projects a state of hollowness and complete insensibility in which being dead or alive makes no difference. He stands, therefore, as the final and most accomplished product of the Nazis' plan.

Null Achtzhen is the embodiment of the *Muselmann,* or Muslim, in both a physical and a social sense. This is the term the older inmates use to refer to the individual who is destined for quick extinction, usually within a period of three months from the time of arrival.[16] He is the one who has lost the will to survive and either will not or cannot use the means necessary to try to do so. The Muselmann is someone who today would be defined as a loser and is scornfully kept at a distance and at times abused. The prisoners themselves treat the Muselmanner as pariahs in the Lager environment, and such treatment high-lights an aspect of imprisonment more tragic than the treatment prisoners received from the Nazis: that of the relationship of one prisoner to another. To Levi, this relationship is a fundamental, and perhaps the saddest, component of the punishment in the Lager. Whether or not it is planned by the oppressors, the reality is that acts of extreme cruelty were carried out not only by the Nazis but also by some of the prisoners. Levi understands, nevertheless, that in a world where the struggle for survival is without remission and each human being is so "desperately and ferociously" alone (118), such behavior can be expected and even accepted. He sees the camp as being divided between the "drowned," who will soon succumb, and the "saved," who manage in one way or another to survive or are at least able to delay their death. The Muselmann, the type that makes up the core of the camp, is the prime candidate among those who will drown, and the *Prominenten,* those with privileges, will manage to extend their lives. Most of those who hold positions of privilege are political prisoners or outright criminals. A few are Jews who, while not initially favored by fate, manage to survive, often at the expense of others. Levi focuses on these who are in their own ways no less cruel and merciless than their oppressors. They may abuse their own because they want to be noticed by the enemy. More often than not, however, they quickly learn the ironic, albeit somewhat twisted, truth of the Lager that "to he that has, will be given; to he that has not, will be taken away" (80). No hesitation inhibits them from casting aside dignity and ethical behavior. Stripped of material belongings, some allow themselves also to be easily stripped of their moral values. Survival is achieved by any means available, and Levi goes to some length to recreate specific characters who personify these issues.[17]

Pusillanimous, weak little Schepschel, who has survived from one day to the next by executing petty deals, on occasion obtains extra bread by dancing for some Slovak prisoners. He does not think twice of betraying his accomplice, Moischl, to ingratiate himself with the *Blockältester* to get a better job. Alfred L., the self-important, aloof engineer, displays extreme courtesy and self-sacrificing discipline. His reward is a "specialized" position in the chemical laboratory, where he performs in the most rigorous fashion. Elias Lindzin, the dwarf, is feared and respected because of his excessive strength. An indestructible freak of extreme vulgarity, he is hardly understood when he speaks his distorted Yiddish. The Lager environment is not uncomfortable for him. On the contrary, it is a place in which he prospers and rules. His lack of civility, which would have marked him on the outside as someone unable to function in normal social interactions, is to his benefit in the upside-down world of the Lager.

Lindzin is the opposite of Henri, a character who affects Levi greatly. Levi perceives Henri as the most despicable because he is the most calculating, a seemingly civil, intellectual twenty-two-year-old Frenchman who speaks several languages, English and German among them. Levi feels a substantial affinity for him because of his "excellent scientific and classical culture" (90). Talking with Henri can be such a pleasant experience at times that one is almost fooled into believing communication is still possible in the Lager. There is no one, no matter how hardened, who cannot be won over by him. Once he has determined, cynically, that someone is "*son type*" (90), he "cultivates" the person to help himself. Using to full advantage his effeminate features, which remind the author of Sodoma's painting of Saint Sebastian[18] and are suggestive of Henri's willingness to grant sexual favors for gain, Henri knows how to arouse pity in his many protectors and benefactors, who include prisoners, civilian employees, and professionals. He can count on their shielding him from hard labor and, in the end, from the "selections." Levi sees him as a professional seducer and compares him to the serpent in Genesis for the cold and calculating way he sets upon his prey. He knows that Henri survived the camp but, because he knows how he did it, he expressly does not wish ever to see him again, though he would like to see all the other survivors.

Of these "saved" characters, Henri is the one against whom Levi measures his own behavior. The clear cultural affinity between himself and Henri enables him, the scientist by profession and humanist by education, to appreciate the young man's intellect and background. Levi finds it degrading that Henri uses his gifts, which are meant to ennoble humanity, for prostitution and seduction instead. Levi's experience of Henri's manipulation of culture prompts a self-evaluative process that results in his own rejection of deceitful action and a subconscious passion to oppose the will of his oppressors.

With the end of this discourse begins the book's second phase, into which Levi injects a more personal reflection about the Holocaust. Referring back to his initial premise, stated in the book's preface, regarding his need to tell and to make others aware of what has moved him to write, Levi insists that while the facts he presents are not invented, the way and the order in which they appear reflect an internal logic that responds to "an order of urgency" (6) that is better understood if two other points, already raised, are taken into account: the fact that he writes this book to free himself of an internal burden; and the content of the opening poem, which provides the title to the work and asks the basic question "if this is a man."

Since the man about whom Levi speaks is himself, along with all the others like him, he is asking the reader to see how he, the man Primo Levi, has dealt with and responded to the violence of the Lager. That he is able to narrate or recreate the story is not enough; it merely illustrates that he has physically survived. More important to him is to show that his survival, unlike Henri's, was not at the expense of compromises and moral trades-off. Despite the punishment and the horror, it is imperative to him that the reader see and judge for himself if he, Levi, has come through that experience with his dignity largely untarnished. In other words, can he still be called a man? This is the internal burden he wishes to lay bare, and he does so by organizing his chapters in the previously noted order of urgency instead of following a succession that might appear to be more logical based on events or time frames. How could he, after all, presume to have given a logical varnish to something that was illogical by nature? Levi rejects the process of human degradation imposed by the oppressors. He opposes it at first with a kind of "silent resistance,"[19] then with a gradually increasing sense of self-confidence and energy. As these middle chapters progress, Levi becomes a more central figure. He becomes more analytical about his interactions with others, the challenges and situations he faces, and his responses and reactions to them. His resolve to resist and endure, modest and uncertain at first, becomes increasingly sturdier. Evaluating the motives and behavior of others, he is then able to decide whether he wishes to betray his own set of moral values.

The first decision is made when he rejects Steinlauf's advice to stay physically clean and Steinlauf's reasons for keeping clean. Unlike this obedient and decorated Austro-Hungarian army sergeant, who rationally insists that to keep clean is a reflection of one's own dignity and a way to resist the Nazis' will to turn human beings into beasts, Levi feels cleanliness is a superficial issue and refuses to measure his own dignity by it. "There is no more major vanity than to force oneself to swallow whole the moral system elaborated by others" (36), Levi affirms, especially when it is a system imposed by foreigners. How could he accept such indoctrination when at the origin of all his troubles is his active opposition, ill-advised as it may be, to the rigid Fascist rule? Steinlauf's wisdom and virtue may be good for Steinlauf, but they are unacceptable to Levi. In an evil world without a system, it is best not to attempt to initiate or elaborate one.

Perhaps, though this is unknown to him at the time, his oppositional responses to Steinlauf prove to be the philosophical standard by which Levi does survive in the Lager. In the chapter "The Drowned and the Saved" he makes the point that very few survived Auschwitz without having renounced anything of their individual moral positions. Those who did survive with their integrity relatively intact had the fiber either of saints or of martyrs, or they were in some ways assisted by fate. Although he considers himself neither a saint nor a martyr, Levi does see himself as belonging somewhat to this third group. He never attains, and never wishes to attain, the status of the "prominent" ones. If anything, his temperament and character place him much closer to the Muselmanner, for he shares with them the nostalgia for the sweetness of home; unlike them, however, he is able to survive on the strength of his inner character, his abilities, and some luck.

Levi's good fortune appears in the characters of Alberto, Lorenzo, and Jean, who, through their actions and goodness, tend to disprove Machiavelli's belief that humans are evil by nature. It is further enhanced by his falling ill at the right moment and by his educational background and cultural endowments, which, by giving him access to Dante's inspiring words of Ulysses, will remind him that he is still a man.

The first clear indication of a turning point in the author's plight, the emergence of a will to survive, comes in the chapter "Chemical Examination," which in the "urgent order" of development immediately follows the chapter entitled "The Drowned and the Saved." An unpleasant, unnerving, and altogether bizarre encounter, intended to be a personal interview to test the author's competence as a chemist, becomes a confrontation with the prototypical Aryan nemesis in the person of tall, thin, blond Dr. Pannwitz. The exchange that occurs during this interview assures Levi that he is still an intellectually alert, functional human being. The encounter with Dr. Pannwitz is rich in suggestion and meaning. Once again, Levi calls on Dante for his simile. Pannwitz is the devil incarnate; an extension of the devilish power set on destroying an entire people; a modern-day Minos, the one-time king and legislator of Crete depicted by Dante as a hideous demon who judges the sinners and indicates with his curled tail the circle to which, by their acts and deeds, they are sentenced (*Inferno,* canto 5:10–13). Pannwitz disguises his true identity with the modern appearance of a professional to perpetuate the Lager as a hell of our times. Alex, the kapo for the chemical laboratory and a professional hoodlum who gives the doctor's identity away, is compared to one of Dante's frivolous but nonetheless troublesome devils in the Malebolge section of the *Inferno.*[20] Just as these devils assist their master in the physical punishment of the sinners, Alex will serve his master and, as we shall later see, will also commit his act of physical abuse.

More than a test of professional competence, the successful interview with Pannwitz is the vindication of the so-called "inferior" Jew. Although he is painfully aware of his miserable condition and of the absolute control the man on the other side of the desk holds over his very existence, Levi confronts his enemy, timidly at first, then with more confidence, making Pannwitz cognizant of his professional merit. His qualifications may well exceed those of others because, as he does not hesitate to point out, he received his degree summa cum laude (97). He makes his adversary aware that he has mastered his profession by studying and toiling over those same German sources—and in their original language—that are indispensable to anyone who is serious about chemistry, the sources that Pannwitz too has undoubtedly studied. Furthermore, he is able to convey all this in German, even if it is in a somewhat distorted form, in part because of his limited ability to speak the language and partly as a sign of protest and resentment.

As the interview progresses, Levi is somewhat surprised to discover that in spite of all that he has gone through, he is still able to remember and to think. Merely talking about something he loves excites him. He is once again, if only for a short while, in possession of his old logical faculties, those same faculties that made him the envy of his classmates. He grows in stature as he rises to the challenge, holding his own and proving himself to the opposition, who has addressed him in the polite form of the language. Granted, on the human level it is politeness of distance rather than of respect. From a professional point of view, however, Dr. Pannwitz cannot ignore Levi's competence.

More significant than the impression Levi makes on the Aryan is the psychological uplift he gets from this experience. He has faced the evil oppressor and has withstood his test. He has held his own against the most despicable elements of humanity and prevailed. This exhilarates him, making him feel different, if not superior, as is obvious when the examination is over and he goes down the stairs with Alex ahead of him. Alex raises his head to look up at him. This small, unexpected moment of deference will prove to be immensely beneficial to Levi's psyche, even though the harsh and gloomy reality of the camp immediately resumes as Alex then vulgarly wipes his greasy hand on Levi's shoulder. Nothing more than a low-life criminal, Alex has the last say. The devil of this newly created Malebolge, in his "ignorance and stupidity" (100), strikes back because Levi is Italian, a Jew, and an educated man. With this deed, devoid of any hatred or scorn, that "innocent brute"[21] Alex— "innocent" (translation mine) because, unlike Dr. Pannwitz, Alex is "unaware" and does not know any better—gives ulterior proof of being both an accomplice and a victim of the Nazi movement. He demonstrates one more time that Levi, the prisoner, is a thing, a *Stück,* not a man. But in the context of survival and as suggested by that subtle point on the stairway when Levi is looking down at him, Levi feels mostly pity for this creature, who does not know that in the years to come, he as well as Pannwitz and all the others who have offended will be judged, through the words of the author, by the rest of the world on the basis of their ignoble deeds.

In counterbalance to Alex's coarseness and vulgarity, Jean the Pikolo, the Alsatian messenger-clerk whose duty it is to keep a record of the Kommando's working hours and see to it that the hut and bowls are kept clean, is still able, unlike most of the others who hold positions of privilege, to maintain a human relationship with the less fortunate. While Levi reconnected with his intellect in the presence of Pannwitz, it is in his interaction with Jean that the author recaptures the deep-seated humanism and sensitivity necessary to turn the one-sided scientific persona who had stood his ground before the Aryan force into a more complete human being. To confront that force on an equal footing he had to cast aside briefly the balancing element. To remain a human being, however, it is necessary to retain the sensitive, humanistic quality that contributes to the uniqueness of humankind. Jean, who is fittingly a messenger, enters Levi's life to help him do so.[22]

Jean is an anomaly from the start. Without abusing his position of privilege, and while privately conducting the fight for his own survival, this still physically robust, gentle, and friendly man is able to maintain an essentially human relationship with the less fortunate. More than once he has been instrumental in saving prisoners from harsh physical punishment. Thanks to his intelligence, shrewdness and—above all—his ability to persuade, he has succeeded in doing so by capitalizing on the confidence he has gained from

Alex, the kapo, and other superiors. Unlike Alex, who, despite his "pure blood" (100), speaks a coarse German, Jean speaks flawless French and German with equal ease and puts his linguistic ability to positive use, doing for others mainly through his power of speech. Jean's word, "said in the right tone of voice and at the right moment, had great power" (100).

Accompanied by Levi one day on a long walk to the soup kitchen, a walk that is a metaphor for going to the source of knowledge, Jean expresses to Levi his desire to learn Italian. Dante's Canto of Ulysses (*Inferno,* canto 26) comes immediately to Levi's mind as the appropriate instructional tool, triggered as much by Levi's perception of Jean in a context similar to that of the classical hero represented by Dante's Ulysses as by the actual literary content of the canto.[23] From a pragmatic standpoint, to choose Dante's canto as the text on which to base a grammar lesson for a beginner is as unusual as was Jean's request, given the unfavorable conditions of the camp, where acquired language usually did not exceed the most basic and essential terminology. However, the wish to learn a language for the mere intellectual satisfaction—certainly not for any practical application—was unique, meriting a response in kind.

Jean's imposing physical appearance, his persuasive verbal ability, and his vivid intellectual curiosity in a place where there is no support for such qualities are also all characteristics of Dante's Ulysses. Jean, therefore, quickly grasps what Levi communicates, understanding the author's anxiety to seize the time frame allowed by the walk to make a point, reflecting the ever-present concern not just for language and communication but for survival. In reality, Jean will understand much more than Levi will ever hope to teach him.[24] Levi struggles and frequently fails to remember all the lines of the canto. He summarizes some and distorts others simply because he does not remember them or because of his limited ability to translate them into Jean's native French. Jean soon realizes that this lesson is far more therapeutic and important to his teacher than it is instructive to him. With his usual altruism, Jean encourages Levi to go on, to make him feel, sometimes painfully, the impact of the lesson until Levi realizes for himself how much benefit he derives from the process.

At this point, Levi's use of Dante is an example of his belief that literature can help bolster human endurance in suffering and provide uplifting moments that strengthen one's resistance. Dante, having provided the author with a hell to which he can compare his own, now provides him Ulysses, who enlightens him on how to resist that hell. What has begun as mere recitation gains momentum and drama as Levi draws parallels between Dante's Ulysses and his own life situation. The open sea, with its "free, straight . . . and simple" horizon (103), makes him think of the freedom he no longer has; Ulysses' mountain of

Purgatory achingly calls to Levi's mind the mountains surrounding his beloved Turin. And, in recalling Ulysses' exhortation to his companions to follow him ("Think of your breed: / You were not made to live like brutes, / But to pursue excellence and knowledge"; translation mine[25]), Levi synthesizes his own wish to survive, to tell. Jean, who senses the positive effect of these words on Levi, encourages him to repeat them. The brutal reality of the situation is highlighted by the irony of the setting in which the words are recalled—the soup line. How can one think in such sublime terms while struggling for survival? The last line of the chapter replicates the closing line of Dante's canto: "Infin che 'l mar fu sopra noi rinchiuso" (Until the sea closed over us). When this is seen in juxtaposition with the pervasive hunger, which is further emphasized here by the description of the prisoners in line waiting for the soup distribution, one understands their wish to drown in that sea of soup as the only means to satisfy their hunger. They do not collectively, however, have the luxury of savoring Ulysses' eloquence as he pronounces these words. To Levi, Dante's words will serve as the "humanistic" complement to his earlier encounter with Dr. Pannwitz, which was intended as a cold, scientific test of his competence. Similarly, the nobility of Jean's character helps Levi remain in touch with the world of literary allusion, which in turn enables society to respond to human need while preserving a perspective about right and wrong. Levi knows that he was not made to be a "brute," in clear contrast to Alex, or a "beast." His scientific studies and his appreciation of the humanities enable him to resist being reduced to such a state. At this time, Ulysses' words, comparable in impact to those of the book's opening poem, are essential to Levi's moral steadfastness and continued faith in humanity.

Further, the words will find human exemplification in the characters of Alberto and Lorenzo, who supplement Jean's positive influence on the author, each in his own way. Alberto, whom Levi considers his best friend and who is taken away and then killed by the Germans when they evacuate the camp, impresses the author with his moral strength in his refusal to become, unlike most of the other prisoners, wicked and hateful. To Levi, Alberto is a gladiator who entered the Lager with his head held high and will live in it with the integrity of his character untouched by the squalor of the place. With his intelligence and instinct, this strong and yet gentle man will face adversities and fight for his life while managing to remain everybody's friend.

Levi meets Lorenzo, the civilian bricklayer working under contract in the Lager, during the summer and speaks about him in the chapter "The Events of the Summer." It is a most fitting title because, in the Lager, Lorenzo's coming is an unusual "event" in the human warmth and hope he evokes. His presence

23

seems to contradict the statement "When things change, they change for the worse" (106). Miraculously, Lorenzo comes along just when everything seems to grind to a standstill. This static, depressing condition leads the author to admit to himself that for the inmates, for whom the future holds no promise, "history had stopped" (107). Lorenzo is the personification of unconditional goodness, and he will remain one of the author's most memorable figures.[26] His deeds are motivated simply by his desire to help; he expects nothing in return. In this respect, Lorenzo breaks one of the basic codes of the Lager. He will be the most vital single force in Levi's survival. On the materialistic level, because of his civilian status, Lorenzo has an easier time collecting leftover food, which he then gives to the author and to others. He does this fully aware that he could incur physical harm, even death.

It is on the more spiritual level, however, that Levi feels most strongly the impact of this saint-like person.[27] In some of the most moving lines in the book, the author confesses that he owes his life to this man. With his plain and easy manner of being good, Lorenzo shows Levi that there can still be a just world on the outside, that there is still something wholesome, uncorrupted, nonsavage, resolute against hatred and fear. Lorenzo, more than anyone else, prevents Levi from forgetting that he too was a man.[28] Whereas Pannwitz has tested his intellect and Dante challenges him humanistically, Lorenzo tests him through his active and unconditional goodness. Jean, Alberto, and Lorenzo, along with Dante's words, help Levi stay in touch with his humanity and endure humiliations such as that of being called a *Stinkjude* (129) by one of the German girls in the chemical laboratory. These men awaken in him the will and courage to begin secretly jotting down notes about the Lager life and its atrocities. The lessons they provide will strengthen his resolve as he endures the frightful ordeal of another *Selekcja,* or selection, which he describes in the chapter "October 1944." They will give him the strength to lie to his fellow prisoner Kraus, recounting a dream he has made up in which he gives Kraus something to eat and drink and a good bed in which to sleep. Even though Levi is and always will be bothered by this action, he takes it to bring Kraus some solace with at least the illusion of one last good meal and a good rest. Kraus, as far as the author is concerned, exhibits the clear signs of the Muselmann, qualities Levi now begins to understand he has surmounted in himself.

Most important, the models these men provide are vital in enabling the author to regain his place in the rationally functional world, having faced the enemy and survived the encounter and having regained, with Dante's help, the memory and use of the language of an established and noble culture.[29]

In the chapter "The Last Ten Days," which brings the reader to the third and final phase of this work, Levi describes the Germans' withdrawal from Auschwitz with the Russians at their heels. The horrendous Lager machine comes to a halt, and a distinct change occurs in Levi's writing with his adoption of the diary-style narrative, reflective of his reentry into the humanistic world where the self has a value. The diary form also implies the idea of keeping notes on one's actions so that others may know. The last ten days are a reflection of the positive feelings Levi rediscovers about himself and an indication that his hope has been reborn. Though up to this point he has been primarily passive in his attitude, Levi now takes control of the situation. Despite his illness, he rises from his sickbed, actually and symbolically, to become the doer. Through ingenuity, intelligence, strength, courage, initiative, and kindness, and with the assistance of Charles and Arthur, he searches for food and other items that, with inventive modifications or alterations, will be of use to him and to those for whom he has now become the caretaker. He feeds, washes, and clothes the living, and he will bury the dead. He will do what he does because he feels it is his moral duty. Despite his extreme exhaustion, he is, once again, "at peace" with himself and "with the world," sharing with Arthur and Charles the "wonderful warmth" (146) as they sit around the stove, feeling themselves "become men once again" (155). The stove, which they see as their "creation" (146) in their pride in having been able to make it work again, becomes the symbol of that rekindling force needed for the bonding of humanity, a warm feeling that fleetingly recalls the intimacy among the Gattegno family as they made preparations to leave the camp in Italy the night before their deportation.

But the most significant gesture confirming to Levi that his actions are indeed good and kind comes when the other inmates, as a sign of recognition and gratitude, offer to share their bread with him, Arthur, and Charles. Bread, that most valuable nourishment, over which people in the Lager had killed, now becomes once again the symbol of sharing. From being the means of exchange, it returns to being the gift of gratitude. With this offering, one of the Lager's most ignoble axioms—"Eat your bread, and, if you can, that of your neighbor too" (145)—is finally rejected as a result of Levi's actions. With the return to acts of humanity, he is the one who, at this point, has set the example for others to follow.

This change would be less dramatic if it were not understood in the context of one last atrocity forced on the group. In this lies the importance of the penultimate chapter, "The Last One," mentioned previously for its numerical importance in relation to the fact that Levi is forced for the fourteenth time to witness a hanging. The man who is hanged shows his heroism and defiance to the very end with his cry: "Kamaraden, ich bin der Letze!" (Comrades, I am the last one!) (135). While it falls mostly on deaf ears, it affects the author in a way of which he might have been unaware at that moment. Unlike the other chapters, this one opens on an unusually upbeat note, as Levi and Alberto are heartened somewhat by their improved physical conditions, thanks primarily to Lorenzo's assistance with additional food. However, at its closing, as a result of the hanging, the author is overcome by shame. This shame, which can also be perceived as a sense of guilt, is brought about by the author's realization that while he is now "living" in relative comfort and doing little if anything to actively oppose the system, there are those who are willing to give up their lives fighting it and whose courage goes virtually unnoticed.

Shame, however, is exactly what reenergizes Levi. As Gian Paolo Biasin has noted, here shame "is a fundamental glimmer of human consciousness, the indispensable condition for a minimum of solidarity among common men." Shame will become, Biasin goes on to say, "part of the process of liberation, of finding one's humanity again, of restoring responsibility for one's behavior."[30] It is now Levi's self-appointed responsibility to vindicate the cry "I am the last one!" and make sure that it is the last of such cries to go unheeded. Thus the number fourteen, in its suggestion of a sense of justice, has deep significance for Levi. He too feels that he has to do what is morally just. After the dehumanizing, painful, and cruel ordeal to which he and the others have been subjected, what greater reward can there be for a man than to realize that in saving himself he has also helped to save others?

Notes

1. Just before his death, Levi confided to a journalist with the Italian magazine *Panorama* that the writer Natalia Ginzburg, in her role as a consulting editor at Einaudi, had recommended against the acceptance of the typescript. Ginzburg felt that, with the ordeal of the war so fresh in everybody's mind, this type of book would have been ignored by the public.

2. Levi provides this information in the appendix to the 1976 scholastic edition of *Se questo è un uomo.*

3. Unless otherwise stated, all quotations will be from *Survival in Auschwitz,* trans. Stuart Woolf (New York: Macmillan, 1987) and will be noted parenthetically in the text. Where quotations are translated by this author, that will be stated parenthetically in the text.

4. Levi was a prisoner from February 1944 to January 1945 at this ancillary work camp of the Auschwitz complex.

5. Hughes, *Prisoners of Hope* (Cambridge: Harvard University Press, 1983), 77.

6. It should be noted that Levi disapproves of the term Holocaust, which he finds inaccurate. Originally, Holocaust was an ancient sacrificial ritual with religious overtones. The massacre of the Jews was not a sacrificial offering. It was a systematic destruction of unprecedented scale.

7. The sources of this prayer are Deuteronomy 6:4, 6:5–9, and 11:13–21 and Numbers 15:37–41.

8. Wouk, *This Is My God* (New York: Simon and Schuster, 1986), 88.

9. Roth, "A Man Saved by His Skills," *New York Times Book Review* (12 October 1986): 81.

10. Published in the same year in the daily Turin newspaper *La Stampa* under the title "Salvarsi dall'inferno come Robinson," 78.

11. Antonicelli considers it worthy of a Latin poet (in *La nuova stampa,* 31 May 1958).

12. On the Hebrew date of 9 of Ab (the end of July and beginning of August).

13. In the "Afterword" section of *The Reawakening,* Levi admits that, as a result of the Lager experience, he cannot overcome the need to store food away.

14. Levi makes clear reference to this point in the RAI television documentary *Sorgente di vita,* in which he revisits Auschwitz forty years later.

15. New York: Philosophical Library, 1962.

16. Levi discusses this term in greater detail in *The Drowned and the Saved.*

17. This topic is covered in more depth in his last book, which shares this chapter's title, *The Drowned and the Saved.*

18. Giovanni Bazzi, called Sodoma (1477–1549), is known mainly for his painting of Saint Sebastian, now at the Uffizi Gallery in Florence.

19. To borrow Grassano's words in his *Primo Levi* (Florence: La Nuova Italia, 1981), 23.

20. See cantos 20 and 22.

21. The English version translates the Italian *innocente* as "poor" (98). Given the reason for Levi's choice of this word, "innocent" is more fitting.

22. Because of the redeeming role he plays in Levi's life at this moment, Jean can be seen as a kind of God-sent creature.

23. This is canto 26 of Dante's *Inferno.* It bears remembering that Levi adds this chapter in the second, and now official, version of the book.

24. Levi acknowledges this in *The Drowned and The Saved.*

25. In Italian, *virtute e conoscenza. Virtute* has also been translated as "wisdom." "Excellence" or "wisdom" as a translation for *virtute* implies the outstanding qualities that human beings should strive to achieve.

26. Levi writes about Lorenzo again in *Lìlit e altri racconti (Moments of Reprieve).*

27. As a nonbeliever, Levi comes as close as possible to admitting Lorenzo's saintliness when he admits that Lorenzo does not seem to belong to this world (see 111). Levi will name his son after Lorenzo.

28. See 110–11.

29. In *The Drowned and the Saved,* Levi writes at length on how pivotal culture was to his survival.

30. Biasin, " Till My Ghastly Tale is Told: Levi's Moral Discourse from *Se questo è un uomo* to *I sommersi e i salvati*" in *Reason and Light: Essays on Primo Levi,* Susan Tarrow, ed. (Ithaca, Cornell University Press, 1990), 135.

CHAPTER TWO

The Reawakening
(*La tregua*)

Levi began thinking about writing *La tregua* (*The Reawakening*) soon after he finished *Survival in Auschwitz,* but it was not until 1962 that he completed the definitive manuscript, which was published in 1963 by Einaudi.[1] This work confirms his talent as a writer. Critics and readers alike received it favorably, and it was awarded the Campiello prize, one of Italy's most prestigious recognitions for literary work. The first English version was published in 1965 under the more accurate title *The Truce,* and it was reprinted several times for distribution in the United States.[2] Although the British and American editions are the same version, translated by Stuart Woolf, the American edition includes an afterword, translated by Ruth Feldman, in which Levi responds to questions he was asked frequently. Another difference between these editions is the title. *The Reawakening,* the title of the American version, does not correspond to *La tregua,* its Italian title. As he did with *Survival in Auschwitz,* Philip Roth questions the accuracy of the translated title. However, with *The Reawakening* there is evidence that it was Levi who insisted on a different title, perhaps for copyright reasons. Overruling the editor's request to use *Moments of Truce,*[3] the author got his wish in adopting as the book's title that of its last chapter, "Il risveglio."

All this would be of little importance were it not that the title may mislead the reader into believing it was Levi's intention to communicate an optimistic future beyond the time period of the story. However, *The Reawakening* is ironic as a title, as will become evident in the examination that follows. What occurs is a reawakening to the vicissitudes and hardships of everyday life, one that will be marred by the constant memory of the horrors of the *Lager,* or prison, and of the Holocaust. It is not a reawakening that erases the memories and sensations of what has been suffered. The word *truce,* from the title of the first American version, provides a better description of the author's time between his release from Auschwitz and his arrival back at home. It is the period of respite, of relative stasis during which Levi benefits from the opportunity to measure himself against the actions and behavior of others, as it allows him some lighthearted, relatively untroubled time before stepping again into the "normal" life that awaits him in Italy.

This second book is a natural continuation of his first work, *Survival in Auschwitz,* and, in an indirect way, also the precursor of his work written some twenty years later, *If Not Now, When?* Both this earlier work and the later one have as a central theme the return to Italy after a series of trying and sometimes dangerous adventures. In *The Reawakening,* following his liberation from Auschwitz by the Russians, Levi undertakes a journey of almost a year in duration, which brings him back to Italy by way of Russia, Rumania, Hungary, Czechoslovakia, Austria (twice), and Germany.

In *The Reawakening* Levi maintains the stylistic clarity and the rational focus on his objectives that were evident in his first work. He presents his account in a language faithful to the moral tone of the events he describes, rejecting flowery descriptions and "ideological provocations."[4] Levi writes concisely, with a marked preference for the paratactic style. He maintains tight rein over his use of descriptive adjectives. On rare occasions, however, he uses adjectives more liberally to convey the psychological intensity of a character or the character's behavior. Likewise, he is more expansive in structure where he deems it justified to create an emotive mood. On the whole, the prose is clean and concise, and Levi is a skilled storyteller.

There are critics who have noted that *The Reawakening* lacks the compactness and unity of *Survival in Auschwitz.* To take this position indicates a lack of understanding about the essence of the second work. While it is natural to want to connect this book to the previous one, it may be unfair to expect the two books to be alike in style. If we are to take the author at his word, we must remember that his motivation for writing *Survival in Auschwitz* was his need to tell. *The Reawakening* is the continuation of the first work chronologically, but from the standpoint of when and why the author writes it, it is a work more deliberately planned and organized, with specific artistic aims in mind. By the time he wrote the second book, Levi's distance from the actual events had cushioned his painful reactions; thus he could afford emotionally to use his memories to literary advantage. *The Reawakening* is less structurally compact than *Survival in Auschwitz* because its form is designed to enhance an uninhibited description of the changes the author-character undergoes as he reenters society.

The narrative varies in accordance with the psychological conditions to which the author is subjected. The somber and dramatically tense rhythm in the first part of the book reflects the understandable fear that accompanies his liberation from Auschwitz. He uses the lighter tempo of the second part of the story to present episodes that are livelier and more specific to the emotions associated with his growing trust in the actuality of his freedom. Life begins again for the author and his companions at the most instinctual and elemental level. Their spontaneous behavior defies anything that leans toward the analytical. Mirroring his newfound ability and freedom to explore his environment, Levi is creative and diversified. He successfully undertakes the dialogues, the direct discourse, and the use of the challenging *Erlebte Rede* (the indirect free style) and is masterful in his recreation of expressions in Roman dialect enunciated by the character Cesare. Levi's exploration of a variety of moods—the humorous, the ironic, and the good-natured among them—renders this creative experimentation into a therapy to which he gladly submits to overcome his painful experience and reestablish contact with humanity on the most basic level. He accomplishes this through the use of simple language and the depiction of actions that express rediscovery and appreciation of life. The humorous scenes such as the episode of the little hen in the chapter of that name or that of the captain and his motorcycle in "Cesare" are delightful descriptions of his carefree, picaresque adventures at Cesare's side. The accounts of his experience with the Russian soldier in the woods in the chapter "The Woods and the Path" and of comparable incidents indicate his willingness and need to reattach himself to a life that, in order to be lived, must have some levity along with its seriousness.

The apparent lightness of Levi's language seconds the spirit of the vacation period, of the respite he needs and seeks before reentering his former world, the one from which he cannot break away because he is attached to it by tradition and by an ever-present nostalgia. In the world to which he is returning, he must assume a demeanor befitting his professional image. Therefore, the tone of the language in the third part of the story, which describes his arrival in Italy after he has passed through various countries where physical and spiritual destruction are more in evidence, reflects the austerity imposed by the war and is in keeping with the behavior expected of the author at home. The levity gives way to gloom and somberness. The vacation is over, and the language returns to the pensive and worrisome tone of the first chapters, expressive of the sadness and pain of memories with which Levi will have to struggle for the rest of his life.

Levi's extended voyage of return exposes him to events, places, and characters that make this experience an adventurous and relatively relaxing one. This pause, over which they have no say, is not totally welcomed by the survivors, who fail to see at the time that the delay of the inevitable return to their former lives, with all its ups and downs, will prove to be therapeutic. Only later does Levi realize how beneficial and providential this interlude has been in spite of its difficulties and his wanderings on the margins of a war-disrupted world. It is like a gift of fate, never again to be repeated.[5]

This book picks up where *Survival in Auschwitz* ends, with the arrival, on the morning of 27 January 1945, of four Russian soldiers on horseback. They are part of the group that has come to liberate those in the concentration camp as the author and a companion, Charles, are carrying the body of a friend who had died the night before to the site of the common grave. The soldiers are overcome by pity and shame at the sight of so many dead bodies; their shame is that of the just man when he is confronted by unrectified evil, an evil that touches both the perpetrator, through the stigma attached to having been part of the deed, and the victim, who has been the victim of it. It is the shame that the Germans never acknowledge. While these soldiers appear as the "four messengers of peace" (2), bringing with them hope and assistance, their presence is also, paradoxically, "apocalyptic." In it rests the fact that when this small odyssey is over and life returns to "normal," the memory of the past will be a source of frequent torment, and there will be no lingering joy in the hearts of the survivors. Even in liberation, they will be unable to feel happiness. The Lager has contaminated their memory and their conscience. It has convinced them that there is nothing in the future that could be good enough or powerful enough to erase the shameful stain of the past. Total and absolute freedom can no longer be theirs, and Levi underscores this sentiment when he states that the freedom he now possesses, which seemed so distant and unlikely when he was at Auschwitz, has given neither him nor the other survivors access to a Promised Land (26).

Nonetheless, as the title of the first chapter, "The Thaw," suggests, the arrival of the Russians allows the prisoners once again to feel. Along with a thawing in the seasonal sense, there is a thawing of human emotions and sensations. The melting of the snow, the ice turning into a squalid swamp, and the smell of the dead and of garbage make the air thick and unpleasant to breathe. However, as distasteful as all this might seem, it is emblematic of a return to a state of consciousness.

In the "thawing," Levi chooses to focus on the human beings around him, drawing the images of those who have survived, quickly beginning the process of recording and witnessing. Significantly, Levi entrusts to Thylle, an embodiment of the German character, the shedding of the first tears, symbolic of the renewed flow of human emotions. Thylle, a German political prisoner who held a position of prominence and power in the camp, is among the first to benefit from the Russians' presence. The violence and physical abuse he used on the other prisoners reflect the cruelty of the oppressors. Yet he is the first one seen weeping. By describing the emotion of a German first, the author deflates the arrogance of a nation filled with false pride, warped ideals, and misguided superiority. Thylle's reason for crying further heightens the absurdity Levi expresses in choosing him. Rather than tears of shame, his are tears of regret for the political silence imposed on him for more than ten years. Now that he is finally free to express himself openly again, he breaks out into a grotesque and at the same time solemn rendition of the Internationale, the song associated with the communist and socialist parties throughout the world.

The Russians bring supplies, including a cow, which is butchered in a matter of minutes to feed everyone. Some Polish girls arrive to tend to the sick. Those who have survived are taken to the main camp at Auschwitz, "the mother camp."[6] Thus a process in reverse begins: from death the prisoners start to return to life. First, however, the author falls ill again in the main camp and again faces death, this time with an even greater fear awakened by the first taste of freedom and with a fearful nostalgia that makes the idea of loss even more unbearable. Leaving Auschwitz's ancillary camp Buna-Monowitz on a cart, he notices those places in the camp where he has suffered and matured. He sees for the last time the derisive and insulting ARBEIT MACHT FREI sign that welcomed him when he first arrived, and in the square where the roll call took place he observes for the last time the pairing of the gallows with a gigantic Christmas tree, further evidence of the warped, villainous Nazi machinery.

In the "Great Camp," a metropolis in comparison to the satellite camp of Buna-Monowitz, the survivors are once again subjected to a bath, emblematic, like the one they were given on their arrival, of a baptismal rite. However, unlike that first bath and unlike the antiseptic and technically correct one the survivors will be put through later when they pass into the care of the American troops, this bath is devoid of humiliation or grotesque intentions. It is a bath of care and warmth, offered in the spirit of pure assistance. The gentleness with which these survivors are handled by the energetic nurses; the kind words spoken to them; the merciful but unceremonious hands by which they are undressed, washed, and settled in to rest—all are signs of renewed humanity. This is the overt goodness of simple, unsophisticated, wholesome people, mainly peasants, who seem still untouched and uncontaminated by any kind of discrimination.

As Levi is addressing a natural growth process, he initiates his character descriptions with a presentation of the surviving children: Hurbinek, Henek, Peter Pavel, and Kleine Kiepura, all of whom have been deprived of a normal childhood and have become social outcasts. Hurbinek, the youngest, who will die soon after the liberation, is the most tragic. He is "a child of death, a child of Auschwitz" (11), born of unknown parents. In his three years of existence he has never seen a tree, nor has he ever learned to speak. His eloquence lies in his unsuccessful struggle to emit an intelligible sound. In his desperate attempt to express himself he is one of the most memorable and pathetic characters in the book. He exemplifies the annihilative purposes for which the Lager was intended. This child's memory will be kept alive, Levi notes, only through the words he writes (12), and the homage he pays to this unfortunate boy serves as symbolic proof that the oppressors' plan to impose total silence has failed.

Peter Pavel and Kleine Kiepura are two "wild and judicious little animals" (14). In the camp, Peter, a "beautiful‧blond and robust child" (14), made it a point to keep himself meticulously clean and organized and maintained a certain mystery about himself by disappearing early in the morning and returning only to eat and sleep. Kleine, on the other hand, with his very long arms and legs, his excessively protruding jaws, and his long nose—all evocative of a spider's form—is disliked if not feared by all. As the youngest in the camp, he was regarded as its sinister mascot, and as the protégé of the Lager *Kapo,* he took advantage of benefits accorded to only a few. Even though the liberation has deprived him of the protection he enjoyed in the camp and there are no more slaves to whom he can give orders, the corruption he insinuated into that environment is still evident as he continues to speak in the authoritative and crude Lager language of the German guards. He has been infected with the evil of the Lager and, as if willed by some unknown force, to everyone's relief, he suddenly disappears.

Henek characterizes Levi's feelings about "Auschwitz as a university." In a matter of a few months, his strong will to survive helps him grow into a "young carnivore, alert, shrewd, ferocious, and prudent" (13). Of this group of children, Henek interests Levi most. He admires the well-built, intelligent farm boy from Transylvania for his motivation and for the presence of mind he exhibits during difficult times. Levi is also impressed with the maternal care and affection Henek displays toward Hurbinek as he cleans, feeds, and speaks to him. But this deeply human involvement notwithstanding, Henek is cold-blooded and selfish. In fact, his survival in the camp was due largely to his power to select other children for the gas chambers. For him—and this is the oddness in his character—showing kindness to Hurbinek is as easy as selecting the children he sent to their death, an act for which he has no remorse because, according to him, that was the only option he had for his own survival.

In addition to the children, there are adults whose impulses and instincts have been sharpened by the Lager, in some cases to the point of obsession. Such are the two Polish girls Hanka and Jadzia, who introduce the awakening sexual and spiritual facets of life. Both are intent on winning Henek's attentions. Hanka merely shows off in his presence, while Jadzia, sexually driven and impelled to have all men, is more open about her needs. She finds in Noah,

Henek's friend, an obliging partner. He is humorously depicted as a young "Pantagruel, strong as a horse, voracious and lecherous" (17), dressed in colorful clothes.[7] This "friend of all men and . . . lover of all women" (17), in his rounds of collection as *Sheissminister* (minister of latrines and cesspools), would stop in the women's dormitories to satisfy his needs.

Jadzia's emaciation and sickly gray color reflect a state of abandonment and impending death. For Noah, the act of sex is a symbol of revitalization. In consonance with his name, now that the deluge of Auschwitz is over, Noah sees the rainbow past the black clouds and envisions himself as a central agent in a repopulation process. As Noah and Jadzia together symbolize the antithesis of life and death, good and evil factors continuously disintegrating only to come together again, so individually do Frau Vitta, better known among the Italians as Frau Vita, and Olga. Frau Vita, the young widow from Trieste, is oppressed by the many death scenes she has witnessed and by having been forced to carry bodies, or what was left of them, to the common graves. She attempts to cleanse herself of that experience by diving into tumultuous, merciful activity. With a Franciscan-like "simple and fraternal love" (17) for all, she cares for the sick and the children with "frantic compassion" (18) and, in whatever spare time she has after these activities, applies herself with equal intensity to mopping the floors, cleaning windows and utensils, and running among the various dormitories to convey messages, true or imagined. Late at night, however, when work is done, she has difficulty living with her solitude. In a gesture symbolic of life, she jumps from her bunk to dance with an imaginary man she pretends to hold tight in her arms.

Olga, the other woman, is a bearer of death. She arrives in the night to bring the author news that most of his fellow travelers on the train to Auschwitz have died. Levi has been waiting for her for a long time, and though she confirms his fears and anxieties, she also brings him a much-needed sense of resolution. Through her own survival, one understands that life can be resuscitated. Her shaven head is grotesque, but the short gray down on it suggests that there is some hope left, uncertain and erratic as it might be. Her presence marks another one of the many turning points in the author's emotional journey of return as well as his physical one. Olga, a Croatian "of great intelligence and culture, strong, beautiful and with insight" (19), brings in the closing pages of the chapter not only the news of death but also encouragement. As she had attempted earlier to bring comfort to Levi's close friend Vanda, providing her with sleeping tablets to dull her consciousness on her way to the gas chamber, she now inspires Levi to put these figures from the past behind him, to pull himself out of limbo and go forward.

Through the varied assistance of these characters it appears that "the oppression of the past is exposed to a kind of exorcism,"[8] something the author finds necessary as he progresses from a state of impotence to one of new vitality. The coming journey of return will place him in a world of chaos that is in search of a new balance following the disaster of the recent war. The outside world is opposite to the one he has been in; it is a world in which the atrophied emotions of the Lager will now be reversed through the abundance of human encounters and experiences, and the inhuman, methodical organization that ruled the camp will give way to a mostly erratic but human and dynamic atmosphere. His odyssey will provide the author with a period largely free of commitment and responsibility, and though it will not be without difficulties, these will be the vicissitudes of a free man; even when he can have little control over them, he will deal with them with renewed spirit. In some instances he will enjoy the challenges they present and will even be surprised by his discovery of certain aspects of his character of which, until then, he was unaware. In this sense, the book also suggests the author's discovery of himself on a level that is paradoxically deeper—in other words, on a more elementary and primordial level, at which a person needs to interact with others and measure him- or herself against them.

Toward the end of February 1945, as soon as a doctor declares him healthy enough to leave the camp (and not before he is given the doctor's ludicrous recommendation to guard himself against the cold and against hard work), Levi begins his journey as a free man. Yet there are reminders of his recent experience. The first task he is ordered to perform by an ex-Kapo is to shovel snow, something that he is physically unable to do because of his extreme weakness. More important, though, he refuses to do the work imposed on him and gets rid of the shovel, a clear reminder of the hard labor in the camps, by throwing it through a basement window. Following this incident, he finds himself riding with others on a horse-drawn military cart escorted and guided by a Russian soldier. This man is clearly the opposite of the Charon-like German soldier in *Survival in Auschwitz* who, as he escorts the prisoners toward the gloomy camp, asks them to give him their valuables. This time, a reformed Charon sings in a loud and sweet voice in the clear and cold early morning air as he takes the group to the railroad tracks in the middle of a vast, flat, deserted countryside. This is the world of new beginnings, which, in the author's words, seems to have returned to a state of "primeval Chaos"—an image Levi will return to in *If Not Now, When?*—"swarming with scalene, defective, abnormal specimens" and in which "each of them bestirred himself, with blind or deliberate movements, in anxious search of his place, of his own sphere" (22). This is an amorphous and unpressured time, suggested by the author's observation that no one in the group had a watch. Here is the point at which a man can have his new start at his own pace.

One of the most imposing characters in the story is Mordo Nahum, the Greek from Salonika, an exceptional man of about forty with suggestively devilish red hair and red skin and a great curved nose. The two men appear to join forces through mutual need: Nahum's of Levi because of the writer's ability to speak German, and Levi's of the Greek because, as a Greek Jew, Mordo enjoys the reputation, at least in Levi's mind, of having a superior ability in commerce and negotiations.[9] During the unforgettable week they spend together in Cracow and then in Katowice, Levi learns valuable, albeit disconcerting, lessons in survival from this man. Mordo never loses sight of the fact that the game of survival has not changed. He accepts unconditionally the Hobbesian concept that man is a wolf-like predator who turns even against his own, and his solution for survival is to work. Work, to him, is anything, legal or otherwise, that brings a profit without loss of freedom. He will never speak of his experiences in the Lager because its struggle is always present for him. For him there is no such thing as vacation or fun because work is the constant war of life, the only certain thing. His hardened position results from his having learned that life means incessant struggle. "La guerre n'est pas finie" (War is always) (41; translation mine), he will often say, and it is foolish to believe otherwise.

In his rigidity and unwavering attachment to absolute practicality, Mordo is the author's ideological opposite. But even though Levi may find Mordo callous and insensitive, he cannot help admiring him and refers to him as "grande greco" (great Greek), "supergreco" (super-Greek), and "il mio greco" (my Greek).[10] Ironically, this admiration evolves from Levi's aversion to Mordo's principles, which initially seem hostile and harsh to the mild-mannered author. He presents Mordo's rigid, cold, "calculative" characteristics in animal terms: "rapacious . . . like a nightbird surprised by light or a shark outside its natural environment" (24); "the wise serpent" (39).[11]

Mordo accuses Levi of being foolish and lazy: foolish because he has no shoes—an item of the utmost necessity in time of war, even more essential than food—and lazy because he does not share Mordo's work ethic. Mordo believes that no one should expect anything for nothing. This places the two on a brief collision course. Levi is seeking warmth, comfort, and renewal of human contact, while Mordo reprimands him and accuses him of wanting to live off others. Unfortunately, Levi will soon realize that Mordo's cynical view of life is essentially realistic. He experiences this cynicism in Trzebinia when a lawyer presents Levi to an inquisitive crowd not as an Italian Jew but as a political prisoner. The lawyer has no anti-Semitic sentiment; he wishes only to be help-ful, and he explains to the author that he does not identify him as a Jew because prejudice does not end with a war. This fact is, of course, Levi's abiding con-cern and fear. Echoing Mordo's words, the lawyer affirms that, in life, "la guerre n'est pas finie" (41). And Levi will know this to be the sad truth, once back home, as he will contend with the war inside himself for the rest of his life.

At Katowice Levi and Mordo part ways. They will see each other again on two other occasions, and neither will be able to hide a certain fondness for the other. Now, as they part, along with the regret of perhaps never seeing Mordo again, Levi has mixed emotions. This Greek of mythical stature has reawakened sentiments of an unusual kind of friendship, contempt, respect, animosity, and curiosity and has indeed earned the honor of being called Levi's mentor.

Cesare is the other pivotal character in the book. He and Levi first met in the infirmary in Auschwitz, when Cesare was ill with dysentery during the last days in the camp and Levi, fighting off the cold and the smell of feces and death, helped him. From this debased and filthy atmosphere emerged one of Levi's most valued relationships. Cesare more than anyone else helps the author regain a taste for living. A true lover of life, Cesare is therapeutic for Levi. He and Mordo are two sides of the same coin. Their difference lies in their basic warmth, which in Cesare is obvious while in Mordo it is less so. The grayness and single-minded fixation with work that characterize the circum-spect, calculating Mordo yield to a colorful and lively personality in Cesare, who does what he does with an almost childlike excitement and enthusiasm. For Mordo work is an obsession, a sinister confirmation of the self; for Cesare it is simply an "unpleasant necessity" (66), though it might lead to some unex-pected and interesting encounter and thus become a happy occasion. Where Mordo is slave to his own conviction, greedy and strictly rational, Cesare is generous and whimsical. Cesare likes to perform with stylishness and virtuos-ity, to swindle someone for the enjoyment of it and without causing pain. He is motivated more by enjoyment of his own craftiness than by the profit he gains from it.

What Cesare and Mordo have in common is their entrepreneurial spirit. When Cesare works a crowd, he demonstrates his competence as a mime and a skilled charlatan. The reader can sense the enjoyment he experiences in delivering his sales pitch, which includes words and obscene names that he invents on the spot.[12] The scenes he creates around his ability to mimic and his consummate oratorical skill lure Levi into wanting to imitate Cesare's words and expressions as closely as possible through the dialogue and the indirect discourse. This recreation is a unique distinction Levi reserves only for Cesare, whose charm lies partly in his mastery of the colloquial Roman ghetto jargon (rather than conventional Italian), a combination of the Roman idiom interspersed with distorted Hebrew words. Symbolically, this linguistic exercise celebrates the natural harmony between the self and the surrounding environment, indicating Cesare's ability to assimilate everything into his own terms, a most valuable lesson in life. At the same time, by using indigenous language with whomever he is dealing with, he also demonstrates his willingness to communicate on someone else's terms. Thus Cesare returns language to the dynamic and dialectical role it was intended to serve, reviving it from the state of decay to which it had been reduced in the Lager.

Levi honors this man by calling him "child of the sun, everybody's friend" (66). He is described as foreign to hatred or contempt, variable like the sky, festive, "cunning and ingenuous, bold and cautious, very ignorant, very innocent and very civilized" (66). In short, Cesare is a combination of virtues and vices that, taken together, constitute a charming and believable character. He is one of the most delightful and captivating personalities to cross Levi's path.

Furthermore, it can be said that Cesare almost single-handedly forces the author to confront life again by distracting him, however briefly, from the oppressive and horrendous memory of Auschwitz. In short, Cesare "reconciled" Levi with the world and "rekindled in him the joy of living that Auschwitz had extinguished" (66). As much a mentor as Mordo, Cesare is also Levi's savior. His exuberant vitality, contagious throughout the camp, and his unmatched ability to do and to act make him king among these survivors. This may be the reason Levi gives him the imperial name Cesare.[13] Cesare is the hero of this odyssey. This Roman vendor who gained his experience at Porta Portese,[14] who is neither an intellectual nor a member of the affluent middle class that typified the Jewish community of northern Italy to which Levi belonged, takes control of an environment that is closer to his own world than to the author's, and he barters and indulges in all kinds of commercial enterprises with masterful adroitness. He is so good, in fact, that the author often follows him around just to observe and enjoy his artistry. It is a lesson Levi needs to learn in order to recuperate his lost spontaneity, immediacy, imagination, and occasional impudence. Through his interaction with Cesare, Levi reenters the world of social relationships.

Among the many illustrations that provide evidence of Cesare's extraordinary talent—his sale of a shirt with a hole in it and incidents involving a water-bloated fish and a valueless copper ring that he claims is made of gold—none stands out more than the episode in which he acquires the little hen in the chapter called "The Little Hen."[15] Driven by his yearning to eat a chicken, Cesare, with the author as a comical participant at his side, activates an entire small community with words, sounds, mimicry, and gestures. Nowhere else in this book—or in any of his other works—does the author achieve the level of humor present in these delightful and entertaining pages. Figuratively, for part of this journey's duration, Cesare molds Levi into a new man—naturally with many of Cesare's own attributes. The author does not mind, even if it means acting out of his normal character. For Levi's success in extending his embrace of life, Cesare "baptizes" Levi with the nickname Lapè, a word that refers to the new growth of soft hair on a rabbit and suggests, as did Olga's short gray hair, that it is time to look ahead and start anew. As long as he is with Cesare, Levi will feel like a different person.

The word *baptize* appears in the text more than once, and always in connection with name-giving. In this case, however, Cesare's name-giving has a distinct religious connotation. Levi, who often interweaves religious themes drawn with equal liberty from either the Old Testament or the New Testament, always in a secular spirit, makes of Cesare a Christ-like figure. At the beginning of the story, Cesare's emaciated appearance is compared to that of Christ on the cross. The interaction between Cesare and Levi suggests a teacher-disciple relationship. The connection becomes most marked, however, with Cesare's gift of the fish, the symbol of Christianity, to the starving mother and her three children. This is Cesare's most noble, charitable act, one he himself has difficulty understanding because he is troubled by what he perceives as a sign of weakness. To avoid embarrassment, he makes the author promise not to tell anyone what he has done. It is this act, however, that clarifies the abyss between him and Mordo and demonstrates why the author prefers Cesare to Mordo. The ambivalent sentiments the author is left with when he parts from Mordo have consolidated, with Cesare, into warm companionship and affection.[16] Cesare is so central to this work and such an imposing character that using him as the measure for all men is unavoidable and inevitable.

During the several months that Levi spends at Bugicice and Katowice, he encounters a variety of people. Some are representative of the potential for goodness that exists in life, and some are the embodiment of darker motivations. Levi's Russian hosts have a relaxed attitude toward organized discipline. This is a period of respite for them too, prior to the advent of the cold war, and they are happy, sad, and tired all at the same time. Above all, they are appreciative of the food and wine in their possession, which they unselfishly share with the survivors. Compared to the cruelty, the harshness, and the close supervision Levi had to endure in the Lager, the generous behavior of the Russians strikes him as all the more unusual. So fearsome in war, they are now incredibly mild, and their discipline, which stems from harmony and reciprocal love, is completely different from the mechanical and servile character of the Germans.

In the camp at Katowice, Levi has a warm relationship with Marja Fjodorovna Prima, the nurse from Siberia who, because of the similarity of their names, insists jokingly that must be related. His leaving the camp is facilitated by her issuing him the much sought *propusk,* or pass. She also sees to it that he gets better food. Hidden beneath the rough edges of this energetic, unsophisticated, disorganized woman there is a kind human being. She is the personification of active life, dedicated and untiring, indifferent to the past and to the future.

The inner beauty of Marja is matched by the outer beauty of Galina, a carefree eighteen-year-old brunette from the Ukraine. Her presence is stimulating to Levi's burgeoning passions but causes him pain reminiscent of an event he experienced in the presence of the two girls in the chemical laboratory in the Lager.[17] His miserable appearance causes him humiliation and distress, and because Galina's ephemeral presence becomes nothing more than a fleeting glance, she will quickly disappear, "sucked up into the emptiness of the Russian space" (52), and his desire, as before, will remain unfulfilled.

In this group there are also two Italians who catch the author's attention: Leonardo and Rovi. Leonardo is a doctor who had been helped by friends to avoid the gas chamber on three different occasions. Caring for the many in need, he has unlimited endurance, silent self-built courage, and lots of patience. Rovi, an accountant who manages to get himself nominated camp master of the Italian sector, loves power and is thus different from the other Italians, civilian laborers who are for the most part easygoing, hardworking, peaceful, and gentle. His need to give orders and his expectation of being obeyed in a place where order and discipline are not important are anomalous. His obsession with power leads him to declare himself a colonel, and, since no military officer is complete without a uniform, he concocts one that fits his rank. With his heavy Russian boots, Polish railroad hat, medals, pants, and jacket culled from who knows where, his appearance is quite theatrical. The author, in his good-natured way, decides to focus more on this man's comical aspect because he was, after all, neither a tyrant nor an evil person. In fact, Rovi put his pedantry to relatively good administrative use. He shared with the Russian commanding officer a fondness for excessive paperwork. This was enough to put him in good graces with the Soviet Command.

In "The Dreamers" the author looks further into the obsessions, suffering, and despair of his characters. This transitional chapter captures the ambiance of paralysis and frustration, acknowledging that in order to emerge, a person sometimes has to go deeply into the self. There is also the concomitant existential inference that often we become stuck in our misery, with the danger of never extricating ourselves from this state of psychological impotence. The experience of the Lager has frozen its victims into a fixed state; they are obsessed, oppressed, and defeated by the past and unable to drift back into the flow of history. As time goes on, their memories of the past become increasingly dream-like.

Moor of Verona, the dean of the group and one of the most imposing personalities among them, commands respect and fear at the same time with his large size, his rugged appearance, and the profanity with which he vents his anger against everything and everybody, humans and God. Behind and despite his "desperate senile madness" (85) there is a tragic greatness about him that reminds the author of Dante's Capaneous and Shakespeare's Caliban.[18] The austere manner and underlying anger that hide his painful inability to assist his handicapped daughter are sublimations of the apparent nobility in his demeanor and an example of the helpless frustration to which the Lager experience has reduced him.

Others are more openly pathetic. Unlike Moor, they make no secret of their personal dramas. Trovati, fittingly nicknamed Tramonto (Dusk),[19] relives the frustrations of his failed life as an artist by repeatedly enacting, with the assistance of some of the others, the trial for the crime he committed, which precipitated his downfall. Likewise, the mild and gentle Mr. Unverdorben— whose name, German for "uncorrupted" or "uncontaminated," is quite fitting considering the propriety and formality on which he always insists—is a prisoner of his frustrations over an unsuccessful musical career brought to an abrupt end by the accusation of plagiarism for his having taken, literally, one too many bars from someone else's musical composition.

Those who persist in their life of crime are prolonging the stasis of their condition, as is the case with Cravero, the petty thief who leaves his mark on Levi's family back in Italy by taking a bicycle belonging to the author's sister. Others, like D'Agata, settle for a state of trance. This Sicilian bricklayer, obsessed with cleanliness, becomes accustomed to sleeping by day so that he can devote his nights to killing bedbugs.

Victory Day, 8 May 1945, marks the beginning of a new phase in the journey. It is a day on which the disappointment of another delay gives way to exultation, especially for the Italians. From then on there are no more enforced barriers to the group's return except for the actual physical obstacles and bureaucratic procedures. A three-day celebration is held, during which the ex-prisoners enjoy much drinking; a theatrical performance by the Russians, with Marja and Galina acting in it; and an animated soccer match between the Italians and the Polish. Following the match, a deluge causes Levi to fall ill again, this time with pleurisy. This is yet another reminder of the tentative nature of his survival and freedom. But the rain is symbolically purifying, and the illness brings him in contact with Dr. Gottlieb, whose name itself, meaning "God beloved," is suggestive of spiritual healing. By tending to Levi's physical needs and nurturing his intellectual capacities, Gottlieb, whose cultured nature counterbalances Cesare's instinctual personality, will equal the psychological good that Cesare accomplished for Levi.

Gottlieb is fluent in many languages, including Italian, and radiates "intelligence . . . like energy from radium" (83). He is a miracle worker in his ability to heal, and he tells Levi to rise and walk, as Christ instructed the paralyzed man in the Gospel of John. But Gottlieb is more than an excellent physician. He is positive and determined, and he takes impressive charge of the group.

When word arrives at the camp that repatriation is imminent, the plan for return calls for a train ride to Odessa and from there a journey to Italy by sea. There is a joyful outburst among the Italians, who then make a frenzied run into town to spend whatever money they have on necessities for the trip. The author and Cesare decide to celebrate by organizing a "gran pranzo all'italiana" (a great Italian-style dinner), but this turns more realistically into a modest dinner consisting of "spaghetti al burro" (93).

In town, the two men experience the unexpected courtesy of an old German grocer-woman. She is irritable and diffident at first, but upon discovering that they are Italian Jews who have been at Auschwitz, she invites them into the back of her shop and offers them beer. She describes to them in expansive terms her active opposition to Hitler, whom she calls *der Lump* (94), and to the Nazi movement, which resulted in the disappearance and presumed death of her husband. This woman is the voice of the uneducated yet intelligent lower middle class, who saw the danger to society in Hitler's grand scheme and expressed it—in her case, as she tells the two men, directly to "Mr. Adolf Hitler" (94). Her letter, whose only effect was to bring Hitler's brownshirts to her door, placed her in direct contact with the irrationality of Hitler's position. The story embodies the issue of the general inability of concerned human beings to intercede effectively in the Nazi epic. Her mistreatment and eventual exile from Germany provide another small example of what Levi considers the total destruction wrought by the Germans, in which everyone has become a victim and suffered a loss. From this woman, Cesare and Levi learn that there are Germans who were aware of what was happening at Auschwitz. This is the first information the men get from someone who, by nationality, was deemed the enemy. Her openness about her political views gives the author cause to hope that the Germans have recognized the wrong they have committed. Any hope of reconciliation with a repentant enemy would have made Levi's imminent reentry into Western Europe less traumatic.

Dr. Gottlieb accepts responsibility for the group on the trip to Odessa with typical determination and self-confidence and executes his role with guile. He is a Moses-like figure, leading his followers to a Promised Land. In this case, however, it is one at which they do not arrive. And, just as Moses was absent when the Jews reached their Promised Land, Gottlieb mysteriously disappears (though not before healing Levi's pleurisy with a concoction of vodka) and thus ultimately fails to accomplish a miracle, leaving the group to cool their heels in a train station. The message of this turn of events may be that each person struggles alone for survival.

Considering Gottlieb's intentions and the saintly status with which the group has endowed him, the travelers are demoralized by their failure to end up at their expected destination. Where they do end up, however, is in Russia, a place primitive and uncultivated, with people whose instincts are still unspoiled. These people possess characteristics that elsewhere have been destroyed by the atrocities of war. This is Levi's Garden of Eden before the original sin, though his perception of it is colored by the suffering he has experienced. The journey to this place includes hardship and sacrifice; in a symbolic sense, it brings to mind the journey of the sinner heading toward salvation. Upon reaching Italy at last, Levi will realize that it, too, is not the place of which he has dreamed. Indeed, it is a place where he will never completely divest himself of his deep sense of guilt.

At the town of Prokurov, the progression headed "Southwards" toward home suddenly takes an unexpected turn "Northwards," as indicated by the titles of the back-to-back chapters. In the train station, the author encounters two Jewish girls from Minsk. While the two Polish girls, Hankia and Jadzia, were objects of lust and blatant sexuality, these Jewish girls represent innocence and exemplify the goodness that is found in the absence of sin. Looking at them, Levi recalls his own lost innocence and entertains thoughts of seduction. But in the end, it is the girls' candor and inner beauty that seduce him, and he is moved in a way he thought no longer possible. In spite of what these girls have endured, they have not lost their belief in the future or in humanity, nor has their love for life been shaken. Most important, they accept their lot without rancor or regret. Their steadfast faith is something the author needs to continue his journey, and they assist him by giving more helpful advice than the doctor who discharged Levi from the infirmary at Auschwitz. Theirs is quite simple:

take life a day at a time, travel light, and live like the birds of the air that neither sow nor reap—Christ's counsel from Christ's Sermon on the Mount.

The Polish girls are anything but cynical, yet in their simple, unambiguous view of life they perceive that since Levi speaks no Yiddish, he "is not Jewish" (99). Doubts about Levi's ethnic origin because he does not speak Yiddish will become a pivotal concern in his exploration of the irrationality connected with the Holocaust. His recitation of the Shemà, the Hebrew prayer, to prove to them that he is truly Jewish may indicate an insecurity deep within him, attributable to the assault to his dignity during his incarceration, and an underlying discomfort about his spiritual identity. His emotional reaction to the girls is reminiscent of his feelings about the Gattegno family in the opening pages of *Survival in Auschwitz,* as he witnesses their ritual of lamentation the night before the deportation to Auschwitz. The Gattegnos' ritual and the author's encounter with the Polish girls are prefaced by lyrical nocturnal scenes that are strikingly similar. They also share a touch of piety and a solemn mood, occurring at the beginning of a dramatic and indelible experience. The journey to Auschwitz brought the author to a man-made hell. The journey he is about to undertake will bring him awareness of his human spirit without the burden of responsibilities and social duties, permitting him to better assess his condition and future. He is headed to a place of simplicity where, as the girls have told him, "a Jew is a Jew, a Russian a Russian," and "there are no doubts nor ambiguities" (100). In a figurative sense, it is a place of innocence, which, following the austerity and strictness of the Lager, is most welcome.

In this phase of relative emancipation, the first institution to be mocked is the military. This is plainly illustrated by several comical scenes: that of the drunken Russian soldier who repeatedly presents himself to the Russian officers, always saluting very properly; that of the officer who becomes so attached to a motorcycle that he makes a public spectacle of himself as he travels around town; and that of the tap-dancing lieutenant. The author wishes to stress that the Russian army, although fierce in war, never loses its humanity, though it may come off looking a bit odd. These soldiers, unlike the Germans, are not controlled by a strict and unconditional sense of duty and blind obedience. They are not afraid to acknowledge or express their emotions with abandonment and vitality. Their temperament is an extension of the exuberant character of their homeland, a country whose largely ineffective bureaucracy has managed to remain uncontaminated in its zest for life and blind to any kind of class distinction. With the dreadful treatment of Auschwitz fresh in his mind, the author is particularly struck by how the Russians treat people fairly. They will not treat their own any better than they treat the ex-prisoners, as they will not grant any special travel privileges to the Italian civilians and military men of the Bucharest Italian League and the Italian Army in Russia, who wish to be considered with higher regard than the Lager survivors.

On the trip northward, without the capable guidance of Gottlieb, the group is soon reduced to begging. However, through Levi's perception that all human conditions are relative, the material discomfort in which they find themselves becomes clouded by moral overtones. The conditions under which this group is traveling are hardly analogous to the physical and moral squalor of the dozen or so pitiful German prisoners who have been abandoned like animals in the wilderness. Levi notes that the German pride is gone, as is any sign of power and arrogance. The German soldiers' blind obedience to orders has not spared them from becoming emaciated and destitute, without even the will to seek "safety in flight" (105). They too have developed a paralysis, spiritually and physically. Their discolored rags, once the proud uniforms of the Wehrmacht, mirror their disgraced state. Furthermore, they beg for food in Russian, not in their own language. Separation from the authority under which they had been nurtured and had felt superior and infallible has deprived them of their vigor and their language. At one time they enjoyed watching their prisoners perform humiliating and undignified acts; now they are willing to submit themselves to similar acts without objection. They are no longer in command, and their pride has crumbled like a house of cards, as is evident from their willingness to crawl meekly on all fours to get some bread from Daniele, one of the survivors.

Curiously, while the Russians leave the German prisoners unattended and unharmed to fend for themselves, they are much more severe with other Russians who, pressed by need, had "voluntarily" abandoned their homeland and gone to Germany to seek means to stay alive. Russia has no forgiveness for them, as is plain from the way they treat the Ukranian women returning from Germany. Levi, like the other survivors, notes the women's victimization, through which he relives his own journey to the Lager. He is affected by the severity with which these women are treated: forced to return in cattle cars, without luggage; awaited by none and scorned by most; spat upon, insulted, and otherwise humiliated. The Russians fail to acknowledge the suffering, abuses, and hardship these women have endured in order to survive. Ironically, even now that the Germans have been brought to their knees, they still seem to hold the last card. These women are the proof that they have succeeded in corrupting, humiliating, and destroying what had once been wholesome and beautiful. Their compatriots treat them as traitors and, in effect, place on them an implied tattoo that will force them to continue living, as they had in Germany, on the margins of society. Levi recognizes that the inconvenience he experiences is unimportant compared with the harsh future in store for these women.

At the barracks of Slusk, Levi notices vulgar frescoes depicting the German enemy as spiders and vermin. The irony of these pictures is not lost on him, since in the past this was how the Germans had depicted the Jews. Here, under the loose supervision of the good Russian administration, supportive in its benign neglect, those who have come from different parts of the world, young and old, men and women of different religions and nations, blend in apparent harmony. Ethnic identity is unimportant, and for several, being taken for something other than what they are is a saving grace. They have freedom from prejudice and animosity, contentment in the present condition, no need to work, and leisure to enjoy the warm weather and the plentiful food.

Into this becalmed atmosphere, from out of nowhere, Mordo Nahum appears to the author for the last time. Mordo is now in the procurement business, and living up to his earlier description as a "wise serpent,"[20] he tempts Levi, in another scene reminiscent of Adam before the Fall, by offering him one of his women. This temptation serves to point out that sin and evil will always exist, a further confirmation to Levi that the present euphoric state cannot last. With his refusal, Levi metaphorically commits himself to continue, at least for a while longer, his present simple life.

The Red House at Staryje Doroghi is the final destination of the northward journey and the farthest point, for Levi, from the environment that had contaminated and corrupted humanity. Continuing his travels allows him to regain a purity and wholesomeness that he hopes can shelter him from the inevitable shock he knows will accompany his return into "civilized" society. The Red House is the place where he and the others come closest to a carefree experience, a brief period of time during which Levi discards his urban garb and lives a quasi-idyllic existence. The Red House, with its surrounding woods, its stairways leading to nowhere, and its bizarre structure without plan, offers a fairytale atmosphere. People are free to come and go here as they please, and many who have left it choose to return. Here the ex-prisoners are fed relatively well and continue to be treated by the Russians with fairness and without prejudice.

What remains to be seen, however, is whether someone who has been subjected to so much violence and suffering can return to a state of childlike innocence. Furthermore, can a person go back to a state of primitive simplicity after having lived in a relatively sophisticated, intellectual environment? For Levi, the answer is implied by the German book on medicine he finds and absorbs with the keen curiosity he had in his academic life. The reemergence of his interest in the intellectual life indicates that his willingness to continue on his present, somewhat aimless, path will be of brief duration at best. A yearning for his former life is pressing at the edges of his consciousness.

For the time being, however, he chooses to continue on his adventure, which he can do only by altering his personality to fit his circumstances. Eschewing the persona of the straitlaced, civilized man of Western society, he becomes the Lapè Cesare has baptized him. The educated, shy, middle-class Turinese adapts to an environment in which, to interact with types unfamiliar to his knowledge and acquaintance, he has to communicate more by instinct. His remnant sophistication and urbanity give way to mime, gestures, and monosyllabic sounds. As Lapè, he has the ability to mingle with those around him without the guilt or pain caused by his original assimilated status in Italy. Under this different name and persona, he can participate, always at Cesare's side, in the "picaresque" and comical adventures whose details make up some of this book's most delightful and entertaining pages.[21]

The easy conditions at the Red House also cause the visitors to lose perspective on reality and thus arrive at a compromising point from which imagination can easily gain the upper hand, as, Levi seems to imply, it did in the case of the Nazis' arrogance. Levi's encounter with the Russian soldier in the woods causes him extreme anxiety, as the soldier questions him closely and insists on teaching him a few Russian expressions. This is too reminiscent of the dissembled Lager language it was necessary to use in the camp. The encounter arouses such paranoia and fear in Levi that he almost flees. On a different day but at the same time and place of the previous incident, the power of imagination is exemplified in a more dramatic episode, which is rendered all the more striking by the writer's sudden switch to the present tense. This is the episode of the Russian sailor who, carried away by his description of how he fought off and killed the enemy, unsheathes the knife he says he used in this act and becomes lost, as those who have lived through the Holocaust are lost, in his own "dramatic ecstasy" (145). Emerging from the trance-like state, the sailor remains for a few moments gazing at the floor as if surprised not to see his victims and their blood there.

Levi is torn between a growing nostalgia for home and the pleasant life at Staryje Doroghi, but he finally reaches the moment at which he must make a decision. Getting lost in the woods—clearly a metaphorical echo of Dante's opening lines of the *Inferno*—requires a choice of which road finally to take. For Levi, the act of making a choice always has overtones of morality. He sees that the carefree, almost childlike life he is leading can be no more than a brief pause. His ties to Italy and to his former life are too strong to abandon, and his desire to return home prevails. That ever-present "limpid and clean pain" of nostalgia "permits no other thoughts and induces a need for escape" (130). The indolent life and natural beauty of Staryje Doroghi and the whole recent experience of unstructured living are contrary to Levi's sense of essential interaction with life and insufficient to erase his thoughts of home, and this is true too for most of the others. "Getting lost" in the woods is not for Levi. Behind the actual event lies the figurative and deeper meaning. He simply cannot adapt to this kind of life, knows it is an evasion, and feels compelled to return to his former existence. His panic in liberation is the same panic that overtakes him at the thought of being lost and perhaps even dying in those woods. The sound of a train, an object now connected with pain and suffering, becomes, paradoxically, also a symbol of return, which helps to orient him toward an apparent salvation.

Levi acknowledges that he is different from Velletrano or Cantarella or the two German women, for whom this lifestyle is a way of pursuing "virtute e conoscenza" (wisdom and knowledge).[22] Returning to his former life is his expression of fulfillment. He therefore moves himself and his readers closer toward the world after the war by describing several events that take place in the cinema and the theater, settings that imply a world where enjoyment and communication can exist. In the cinema, the group can respond to what they see on the screen, by booing what they perceive to be the enemy and the villain, by cheering those they see as heroes, and at times by imitating the action in a rowdy way. The theater promotes and intensifies an escapist frame of mind in which they can create fantastic renderings of their own dramas. This is a cathartic and sometimes painful exercise.

The satire called "The Shipwrecked and the Spiritless," the tap-dancing act of the aloof and serious Russian lieutenant who performs with a funereal demeanor best fit for a "sacrificial dance" (157), and the scene with Gridacucco, the cook who kills the louse, reflect the memories and consequences of the conditions the group endured as prisoners. The "Three-Cornered Hat," an "obscurely allegorical pantomime" (158) accompanied by a single muted drum, dramatizes through the performers' grotesque deformations the increasing difficulty the prisoners had in standing up straight. This act's impact on the group was so strong that it was "greeted with a silence more eloquent than applause" (159). The audience thus collectively shared something resembling a dream that enabled them to understand that once "work and troubles have ceased, . . . nothing acts as a screen between a man and himself" (159). In its nullity and impotence, life can resemble "the hunch-backed crooked profiles of the monsters generated by the sleep of reason" (159).

The tenuous screen between the worlds of fantasy and reality merges in the satire of the cannibal chief, who is a transparent caricature of the Russian commander in "The Shipwrecked and the Spiritless." A true deus ex machina, he drops from the sky and steps out of his role to announce that the journey home will begin the next day. The next morning, none other than Marshal Timoshenko himself, the real-life hero of the Bolshevik revolution, confirms this news.[23] As the "celestial messenger" (164), tall and corpulent, he comes down to earth in a somewhat tongue-in-cheek way, exiting from a rusty and decrepit Fiat Topolino, the smallest of the Italian cars, to set them off on their journey.[24]

Not without regret, on 15 September 1945 the group of nearly 1,400 leaves Staryje Doroghi. The author is certain that the vast primordial lands and those vigorous Russian villagers who love life will leave a mark on his memory for a long time. In many ways he and the others owe their salvation to these people whose instincts and spontaneity have demonstrated how to grasp life and enjoy it for what it offers. At this moment of departure, Levi articulates the lessons he has learned from this experience when he sees Flora, the gentle, kind-hearted prostitute whose affection both he and Alberto had longed for when they were in the Lager. She was the object of desire that they feared was as unattainable as freedom itself. When Levi sees Flora again, both of them are liberated, and he realizes that while mentally and psychologically he has managed to lift himself from the ordeal of his imprisonment, Flora has not. This is confirmed by her deteriorated physical condition, so changed that the author does not even recognize her at first. The difference between the two of them, as striking as that between a caterpillar and a butterfly, causes the author pain. He is embarrassed even to identify himself to Flora, who is now the slave of a brute who, despite her pregnancy, beats and mistreats her regularly. The world has been turned upside down, and people do not value each other even in liberation.

The return home, a journey accomplished under the indifferent surveillance of seven young Russian soldiers who prefer playing games with Italian children to their duties of supervision, passes relatively smoothly and uneventfully. Notwithstanding his enjoyments since his emancipation, for Levi this has been an odyssey touched by death, cold, hunger, sickness, and, at Staryje Doroghi, the adverse effects of nostalgia and idleness. The author is relieved that time has become real again and he is heading home. His upbeat mood is evidenced in his encounter with Galina, the typist and translator with whom he worked at Katowice and to whom he felt attracted. He had been so humiliated then by his poor physical appearance that he had lacked the courage even to look at her, much less speak. Thanks to the healing aspects of the past few months, he now has the confidence to approach her and the courage to shake her hand, at this point a monumental gesture towards reintegration into normal life.

Unexplained delays, layovers, several sudden changes in direction, and harsh weather lengthen the trip. Lack of supplies and the ongoing hunger of the travelers turn the journey into another nightmare; in contrast to the relative serenity and peaceful coexistence they enjoyed at Staryje Doroghi, they now experience dissension and engage in animated arguments. Ironically, tempers worsen once the group has left Russian soil and is closer to the Western European environment. In Rumania, where the author not only notes the more familiar language but observes that the peasants are strikingly similar in physical appearance and dress to the people of the countryside around Turin, disputes become more vehement. The travelers' boredom and the frustrations they suffer from material inconveniences turn them into destructive creatures. They ransack the village of Curtici, stripping it of all provisions and supplies. Searching for a scapegoat, they find their victim in the carabiniere, a gentle man who, for no valid reason, has to endure their insults and lies. Now that they are free, they fail to see that their conduct toward others parallels the treatment to which they have been subjected. Their reasons for acting this way are as absurd and ill-founded as those that had been used against them. In falsely condemning the carabiniere by attributing to him all the negative characteristics they see in the police force to which he belongs, they fail to realize that, just as the Nazis had done to them, they have stripped an individual of his identity and personal merits. To make it easier to malign him, they have turned him into a faceless stereotype of a larger and more abstract body. Pista, an intelligent and cheerful boy well-liked by the group, befriends the carabiniere and, with his ability to endear himself quickly to everyone, helps the carabiniere wash himself of the "sins" he never committed. As if by process of symbiosis, his friendship with the popular Pista allows him to become once again an accepted member of the company.

Conditions become more depressing when Cesare, the liveliest member of the group, grows so tired of the misery and disputes that he abandons the others in Hungary, leaving a painful emptiness. Wishing to live up to his name, he decides to make a triumphant return to Rome, and so he does, in an airplane.[25]

The ugliness in the group finds an equivalent beyond it as well. The closer the train comes to Germany and the countries that shared its language, the more conspicuous is the human and spiritual destruction all around. Cities and people have been totally defeated. Only charred buildings and human misery remain of the once proud Nazi empire. The sight of Vienna in ruins strikes the author as ironic when it is juxtaposed against the familiar sounds of German, the language of the "master race." Levi and the others experience a sense of consolation, though it is somewhat hollow, when they see a rusty German train filled with musical instruments, swords, guns, images of peace and war from a nation

51

now destroyed as a result of its own evil designs. The destruction arouses the author's pity because he recognizes it as the mark of the irreparable harm the war has done humanity, the repercussions of which will be felt well into the future if not forever.

At the line of territorial demarcation where the ex-prisoners pass from the supervision of the Russian army to that of the American forces, as the West embraces them again, they submit to another bath of disinfection and purification that, despite its necessity, bears striking similarities to the one forced upon them when they entered the concentration camps. Unlike the recent bath given them by the Russians, this one, because of the systematic precision of the "gigantic" (188) American soldiers, is reminiscent of the bath in the Lager; it is without compassion, though free of hatred and prejudice. The Americans carry out their orders with uncompromising objectivity, demonstrated by their stern treatment of the Italian officer who objects to their putting their hands on his woman. Unintentional in their harshness, the Americans also treat the ex-prisoners as *Stücke* as they douse them with insecticide.

This is part of the irony of the "reawakening," a rude process that links the future to the past and offers little hope for improvement in the years ahead. This sad realization comes to the author as the train makes a stop in Munich, also a city reduced to rubble. Driven by the tattoo on his arm, which burns like an open wound, he sets out to confront those at whose hands he had been made to suffer. He believes he is entitled to feel himself the victor in search of justice. He discovers that among the *Herrenvolk,* those lords among people, there are paradoxically "very few men." And among those few, many are lame and in rags. None has the courage to look him in the eye. They remain "deaf, blind and dumb, imprisoned in their ruins, as in a fortress of willful ignorance, still strong, still capable of hatred and contempt, still prisoners of their old tangle of pride and guilt" (191). As long as they lack the humility and courage to admit to their wrong, there is little hope for any positive change.

The only sign of hope arises from the group of young Zionist Jews who, headed to Israel by way of Italy, have taken it upon themselves to attach an extra car to a train.[26] They refuse to ask permission. To them, the old ways have died with Hitler and they feel free and strong, more firmly in control of the world and of their destiny. In contrast, especially considering that they are only slightly younger than Levi, their vigor accentuates the author's premature aging as a result of his ordeal. He can no longer share such enthusiasm and hope as they express. The tattoo on his arm, he feels, has marked him for life; and this is confirmed to him soon after he reaches home, his Ithaca, his Promised Land. There, in spite of all the comforts, the friends, the warmth of a clean bed and a hearty meal, the pride in useful daily work, and the liberating joy of being able to tell a story, the memory of the Lager returns to torment him. The moments of joy he experienced in Russia are now a dream in the past, nothing more than a brief interlude. The anticipated return home is a nightmare in which all of his senses return to the Lager, which becomes the only truth.

The word *Wstawac,* which means in Polish "get up," the feared and awaited wake-up call of the Lager that no one could disobey and that Levi repeats in the book's opening poem, comes to him as a constant abrasion. Now, at the end of the journey, the meaning of that poem can be fully grasped. There is no release from the trauma of the Holocaust. In Levi's nightmare, the Lager has universal significance. As the author explains in the concluding footnote of the Italian scholastic edition of the book,[27] it becomes the symbol of the human condition and is identified with death, from which no one can escape. As life is a mere respite in the inevitable presence of death, in the camp too there was the uneasy nightly rest. Both pauses, however, are nothing more than that—short intervals soon interrupted by a feared wake-up call. The voice that summons the prisoners to "get up" is a voice that leads to death. Death is inscribed in life, implicit in human destiny, inevitable, possessing a power in a way no different from that power it was impossible to disobey on cold mornings at Auschwitz. As much as Levi would have wanted it otherwise, he has to acknowledge that Mordo Nahum, that "wise serpent" of a man whose statement that life is war, had this reality pegged from the beginning. This is the reason Mordo never spoke of the Lager. The Lager is always, constant and eternal. What may change is only the place in which one experiences it.

Notes

1. According to documents at Einaudi, it appears that the title originally contemplated for this work was *Vento caldo* (*Hot Wind*).

2. In 1986 by Summit Books and in the Collier Books edition in 1987.

3. In a telegram sent to Levi on 23 July 1985, Arthur Samuelson, editor of Summit Books, wrote: "I plead with you for *Moments of Truce* as title. I assure you there will be no confusion here. Nothing works better because that is truly it [*sic*] title."

4. Giuseppe Grassano, *Primo Levi* (Florence: La Nuova Italia), 58.

5. *The Reawakening,* trans. Stuart Woolf (New York: Macmillan, 1987), 92. Further references will be noted parenthetically in the text.

6. See Konnillyn G. Feig, *Hitler's Death Camps* (New York & London: Holmes and Meier, 1981), 333.

7. Pantagruel is Gargantua's young giant son in Rabelais's *Gargantua.* He has

enormous strength and is a great eater and drinker.

8. Grassano 48; translation mine.

9. Levi makes several allusions to the unique commercial abilities of the Jews from Salonika in *Survival in Auschwitz.*

10. It is interesting that Mordo Nahum is one of the characters Levi mentions by name in his Pirandellian story "Nel parco" (in *Vizio di forma*). This story is not included in the book's English version, *The Sixth Day and Other Tales.*

11. In fact, Levi calls Mordo *loïco* (logician), a word he takes from Dante's description of Guido da Montefeltro, the man who planned everything "logically," including his own spiritual salvation at his old age. He did not count, however, on the "reasoning" powers of the devil, who claims and gets Guido's soul. The devil mocks the sinner by reminding him that he too is keenly "logico" (*Inferno,* canto 27:123).

12. It is difficult to think of Cesare without thinking of Boccaccio's character Fra Cipolla (in *The Decameron,* tenth tale of the sixth day), who finds enjoyment in making up a story on the spot to explain to a crowd of naive faithfuls how a feather of the Angel Gabriel has miraculously turned into bits of coal gotten from Saint Lawrence's burning at the stake. This connection may be more planned than imagined because, as with Boccaccio's characters, certainly with Fra Cipolla, Levi's intention is to present an individual who has a zest for life.

13. Levi admits that Cesare is Piero Sonnino in *Survival in Auschwitz.* Massimo Dini and Stefano Jesurum, in their book *Primo Levi. Le opere e i giorni* (Milan: Rizzoli, 1992), claim that Cesare's real-life name is Lello Perugia (46).

14. Porta Portese is a section of Rome close to the Tiber and to the area known as the Jewish ghetto. It is noted for its large outdoor flea market, for its shops that often sell illegally obtained merchandise, and, most of all, for the sharpness of its vendors. To be acknowledged as a merchant worthy of Porta Portese means to be a master of the trade.

15. The Italian title for this chapter is "Una curizetta." *Curizetta* is the Italianized or, more precisely, Romanized version of *kuritsa,* Russian for "little chicken." This clearly demonstrates how Cesare incorporates terms from other tongues into his personal language.

16. Grassano 54.

17. In the chapter "Die drei Leute vom Labor" in *Survival in Auschwitz.*

18. Capaneous appears in the *Inferno* (canto 14:64 and canto 25:15). Even though he is in hell and is tormented by a rain of fire, he keeps on blaspheming against Jupiter. Caliban, in *The Tempest,* is the monstrous son of a witch, in constant rebellion against his benefactor, Prosperus.

19. While "dusk" is the literal equivalent of *Tramonto,* it does not convey the full figurative meaning this term has in Italian and in this book. Trovati earned the nickname Tramonto because he used this word to express the early demise of his artistic career. The English "dusk" does not carry the same implication. A more accurate translation in English would have been "eclipse" (or perhaps "faded"). This, however, would have created problems on the literal level, which the translator evidently feels more compelled to follow.

20. Levi compares his cold eyes to those of a "wise serpent" in the incident with the egg. It is evident that at that time the author already had this last encounter in mind.

21. This work has often been described as picaresque.

22. The *Inferno* (canto 26:120). Once again Levi turns to Dante's words of Ulysses to make his point. See comments on the chapter "The Canto of Ulysses" in *Survival in Auschwitz*.

23. Semjon Konstantinovic Timosenko was one of the most able and famous Soviet military leaders during World War II.

24. Literally, *Topolino* means "mouse." It is also the Italian name given to the cartoon figure Mickey Mouse.

25. Levi confirms this in the story "Cesare's Last Adventure" in *Moments of Reprieve.*

26. In an interview with Rita Sodi (*Partisan Review* 54.3 [1987]: 355–56), Levi admits that he had this group of young men and women in mind when he wrote *If Not Now, When?*

27. In the Einaudi series "Letture per la scuola media," no. 3, rpt. 1986, 269–70.

CHAPTER THREE

The Periodic Table

(*Il sistema periodico*)

In a 1963 interview published in the daily *Paese Sera* (12 July), Primo Levi disclosed to the journalist Adolfo Chiesa that he had been thinking for some time about writing a book on chemistry and chemists. The rationale for such an undertaking was Levi's feeling that few people are aware of what chemists actually do, even though the "art" of the chemist derives from cues and stimuli that are important and deserving of exploration. Levi's own exploration, over the ten-year period during which this work was in the making, led to the publication of perhaps his best and most significant work explaining what he considered the importance of the unity between literature and science. *Il sistema periodico,* published in Italy by Einaudi in 1975, appeared in its English version in 1984 with the title *The Periodic Table.* It follows by over ten years his earlier two works dealing with the Holocaust and its aftermath, *Survival in Auschwitz* and *The Reawakening.* During this period Levi also wrote two collections of short stories, both with an emphasis on science fiction: *Storie naturali* (1966), under the pseudonym Damiano Malabaila, and *Vizio di forma* (1971).[1] The literary experimentation in these two works contributed significantly to strengthening Levi's artistic hand and broadening his imaginative capabilities.

Though it is called a novel, *The Periodic Table* is not one in the conventional sense. Levi describes it in the chapter "Cerium" as "my stories about chemistry" and in the last chapter, "Carbon," as neither "a chemical treatise . . . nor an autobiography" but "in some fashion a history."[2] Levi's succinct disavowal of an autobiographical format raises the fundamental question of how one is to interpret this work, which, apart from being a chemical treatise, certainly has the earmarks of autobiography. The author's use of the first-person voice; his references, which are largely based on his personal experiences; and the backdrop of the rise and fall of Fascism, World War II, and its aftermath—all lead the reader to interpret it as autobiography. Levi provides a clue later in the chapter "Carbon" when he writes that this work is "a micro-history, the history of a trade and its defeats, victories, and miseries, such as anyone wants to tell when he feels close to concluding the arc of his career" (224). Readers will be best served, then, if they recognize that Levi's intent is to present a universally applicable drama concealed within his descriptions of his own experiences.

To assert his belief that science and literature are fortified by an interde-
pendence, Levi uses the chemist's periodic table to create a metaphoric interplay throughout the narrative. Each of the book's twenty-one chapters is named
for a chemical element in the periodic table, and each element has a specific
implication within the context of the chapter. The questions to examine are how
each element reflects the characteristics and characters in its chapter and how it
relates metaphorically to them. In some instances the connection is quite evident and in others less so. Each chapter recounts a story or a moment drawn
from the author's experiences over nearly half a century. The book as a whole is
Levi's evaluation of and reaction to his education and preparation for life in the
light of his life's events, some of which are profoundly trying. In a chronological sequence, the author establishes his identity through that of his ancestors
and then focuses on the challenges, conflicts, victories, and defeats he has sustained both personally and professionally. The book covers the period from his
high school and college student days to the time he finished writing it, near the
point of his retirement from the paint factory where he directed the chemical
laboratory. The time had arrived for him to devote himself fully to his writing
and to synthesize the scientific and artistic aspects of his character.

The Periodic Table is unquestionably Levi's most successful attempt at
placing science in a creative context. It is a fitting tribute to the profession that
he always loved and that, besides providing him with the means for a comfortable living, may have saved his life. His experience as a chemist was decidedly
useful in the *Lager,* or prison camp: in the last months of his incarceration, it
enabled him to work indoors in relative comfort. Moreover, his training in chemistry played a critical role in the emergence of his clear and concise writing
style; in his ability to observe and examine; and, as he explains in *Dialogo,* in
giving him access to a "vast assortment of metaphors" (59; my translation),
from which he drew much of his material.

While the influence of Levi's scientific training is unmistakable in the
dispassionate and rational style of his first book, *Survival in Auschwitz* (the
events leading up to and taking place during World War II had shown him the
disastrous consequences of separating science and art), there is no question that
his desire to interweave the scientific process cogently with the creative one
comes to fruition in this work. The two disciplines are blended here to the point
at which the success in one corresponds to the success in the other.

The chapters of *The Periodic Table* are gems of prose, clearly defining
Levi's attempt to create his new metaphors. Cesare Cases noted that in this
work Levi looks at chemistry with romantic eyes.[3] Levi writes of the initial
stages of his career as well as the formative years when, without detracting

anything from the practical side, he approached his work in chemistry with a sense of idealism about what he could achieve. This duality is clearest in the chapter "Hydrogen," in which Levi makes the distinction between the scientific interest of his friend Enrico and his own.

With the passing of time, however, chemistry seems to have lost a certain human dimension for Levi, and he creates his own metaphorical devices to recapture this missing sense. Again his need to tell is important in his writing, as is evident from the opening statement of his book: "Ibergekumene tsores iz gut tsu dertseyln" (Troubles overcome are good to tell). This reflects a change in Levi's psychological disposition, however, since his first two books and *The Drowned and the Saved*. What seems to matter most to him now are the pleasure and the spiritual uplift he gets from writing. This is a critical transition for Levi. His new perspective called for a new focus, one of narrative, literary creativity, in which not only what he writes but how he writes is of great importance. He is not turning his back on his scientific experience but rather he is adding to it. This is a transition envisioned with emphasis on continuity and fluidity, not the abrupt adoption of a new technique or source of creativity.

This work is structured in three sections. The first, which covers the chapters "Argon" through "Nickel," tells of the formative period in Levi's life, from adolescence to his first job. This is a generally positive time for the author, but it also exposes him to the first of the troubles and pain to come. During this period he discovers his ability to listen and the willingness of others to tell him stories. This experience will provide ingredients that encourage him to write. The first phase ends with two stories he had written as a youth, in which he wants to confirm (to himself at least) that he has a talent for writing. The second phase begins with the chapter "Phosphorus" and continues through "Cerium." It covers the period that precedes and includes Levi's loss of freedom and his eventual imprisonment in the Lager. The third phase includes the chapters "Chromium" through "Vanadium" and deals with the postwar period, the time of readjustment in which Levi will no longer view chemistry with romantic eyes. These times demand that he respond to practical needs, thus he has to redimension his values and his vision.

In the first chapter, "Argon," Levi establishes his roots and origins, first genealogically, by focusing on his ancestors and how their heritage has been channeled into his immediate family, and then linguistically, through descriptions of the charming terms that accompany the old Jewish traditions in and around Turin. Levi did considerable research to uncover the language of his ancestors, and he always presents it in "Argon" with humanity and even a touch of humor, while still retaining the language's solemn intonations.

Levi's family, whose origins go back to sixteenth-century Spain or Provence, is no different from most other families. Their problems, difficulties, compromises, and enjoyments are those that most families experience at one time or another during the course of their existence. Levi presents his family members with all their blemishes and virtues, their interesting aspects and their prejudices. What the reader senses most strongly, however, is the author's pride in his ancestors, even though they are far from perfect. Levi's middle-class status is inherent in his family tradition, and from this tradition he takes secure affirmation of his own identity. To him, the family is a noble body whose traits are coincidental with those of the element argon. Whereas argon is an inert or nonreactive element, however, the family has diverged from this characteristic slightly over time in integrating itself into the *goyim* who largely form the Turinese population.

Levi is the last character to be introduced in this first chapter. He is introduced by his father, who remarks to Levi's grandmother that his son is the brightest in his class. Implicit in this statement is the expectation that Levi must fulfill a familial promise to carry on the educational and intellectual tradition of his predecessors. This is an established and significant aspiration for the Jews, who for centuries have been continuously rejected and ejected and, both symbolically and in fact, have never been given an opportunity to put down roots.

Among the many memorable characters in this first chapter, Levi's uncle Barbaricô, a brilliant yet unambitious and unassertive medical doctor, most represents the element argon's characteristic of inertia. He enjoys the simple, quiet life (13), refuses to be forced into a daily routine, and follows his own inclinations. He reads, sleeps, helps out when asked (usually for some favor in return), and generally rejects the ways of civilized society. Levi feels a particular tenderness for this man and an affinity with him, as he is perhaps the only one of the entire family who has not given in to the compromising demands of life. Moreover, Levi may see in him the seeds of his own intellect.

In the chapter "Hydrogen," the author writes of his ideological expectations from his study of chemistry at the age of sixteen: "For me chemistry represented an indefinite cloud of future potentialities which enveloped my life to come in black volutes torn by fiery flashes, like those which had hidden Mount Sinai. Like Moses, from that cloud I expected my law, the principle of order in me, and in the world" (23). These are large expectations, and he realizes he has no hands-on experience: "Our hands were at once coarse and weak, regressive, insensitive: the least trained part of our bodies" (24).

Levi's friendship with Enrico, a fellow student, provides him access to a primitive chemistry laboratory that Enrico's brother has installed in a nearby courtyard. Enrico has limited scientific ability but a strong sense of practicality, and he is determined to carry out his ambitions, which consist mainly of getting from chemistry the means through which "to earn his living and have a secure life" (22). Now eager to put into practice what they have learned, Enrico and Levi conduct an experiment in this primitive lab, in which they make the gas hydrogen. The author parallels his coming into a fuller awareness about life with the explosion he and Enrico set off with the hydrogen in their attempt to move from pure book learning to application. Also implied in the incident is the danger that hydrogen poses when it is used for the wrong purposes. "I experienced retrospective fear and at the same time a kind of foolish pride, at having confirmed a hypothesis and having unleashed a force of nature" (28), Levi writes, humbled by having accidentally unleashed the power of this element. Years later he recalls the event as he questions the competence and maturity of those who have influenced the decision to use hydrogen for destructive purposes. The explosion serves as his frame of reference from which to point out the pitfalls of approaching anything in life without having the proper preparation and readiness to do so.

In the chapter "Zinc," Levi considers the perceived strength of pure matter compared to the relative vitality, durability, and resilience of mixed matter. As a student, he found the compound zinc sulfate, which he was once assigned to prepare, lacking in any imaginative or exciting attributes. But viewing science as in a struggle with the spirit, the author uses the element zinc as the metaphor for examining the Fascist position regarding the Jewish race. In its unadulterated state zinc is resistant to any attack and can therefore be envisioned as representative of the highest form of purity. When it has become blended, or impure, it is not only less noble but also vulnerable to being subsumed. As impurity is often the result of diversity, Levi feels, "dissension, diversity, the grain of salt and mustard are needed: Fascism does not want them, forbids them . . . it wants everybody to be the same" (34). Levi believes that life requires impurity in order to progress, because, "for the wheel to turn, for life to be lived, impurities are needed, and the impurities of impurities in the soil, too, as is known, if it is to be fertile." "I too am Jewish," Levi declares; "I am the impurity that makes the zinc react, I am the grain of salt or mustard" (34). The author does not mind being different. It is impurity which makes him proud.

Levi's shy and charming interaction with Rita develops this hypothesis further. Besides not being Jewish, Rita has none of the qualities of impurity that Levi believes add a spark to life. Nevertheless, he finds attraction and challenge in their differences. He finds her admirable, and through their contrasts he is able not only to discuss the important aspects of Jewish assimilation into Italian society, a long-standing and accepted reality that the rigid Fascist "racial laws" sought to destroy, but he is also able, even though in a minuscule way, to thumb his nose at the whole Fascist paranoia. Levi speaks of the racial laws with resentment but also with great insight when he describes his thoughts about being a Jew in Italy: "I had always considered my origin as an almost negligible but curious fact, a small amusing anomaly. . . . A Jew is somebody who at Christmas does not have a tree, who should not eat salami but eats it all the same, who has learned a bit of Hebrew at thirteen and then has forgotten it" (35–36). Levi's assimilation into the Italian culture superseded his involvement with his own Jewish religious and cultural background. However, the depiction of the stereotypical Jew by the magazine *Defense of the Race,* which had begun to be published around the same time as the events Levi describes in this chapter, is that of a stingy and cunning person. The divergence of views is astounding now, though perhaps it should not be, given our retrospective understanding of the world which promoted statements of this kind.

What takes place at the end of this chapter is quite moving. Following the badly botched experiment, Rita allows Levi to walk her home in blatant disregard of the racial restrictions. Taking Rita by the arm while accompanying her home gives him a feeling of victory, of success. He has not only made, however briefly, a romantic conquest, one of those small but significant events that provide innocent exhilaration in life, but has also shown that the qualities of purity and impurity can indeed go arm in arm.

The fourth chapter, "Iron," is most poignant. It deals with Levi's friendship with Sandro Delmastro at the time when Italy had invaded Albania and Fascist censorship was ubiquitous. This chapter particularly speaks to Levi's achievement as a witness for those who lost their lives during the period of Fascist rule. Sandro's background is different from that of the other students with whom Levi interacts. Levi notes that "the difference in our origins made us rich in 'exchangeable' goods" (40), like the "cation" and the "anion"—a reference to the advantages of diversity and impurity. Sandro, who lost his father, a bricklayer, when he was a young boy, comes from the country. He likes outdoor life, and during the summer he shepherds a flock. His family is paying to educate him more for bringing in earnings that will afford them a comfortable living than for the enjoyment of intellectual pursuit.

Initially, Sandro did not see the moral decay engendered by Fascism, nor did he ever contemplate that Fascism required thinking people to believe without thinking. But Sandro, a good listener and an assiduous reader with an iron grasp, an iron will, and a clear sense of order, pushed himself to test his limitations. His bold physical activities, including mountain climbing, bicycling, and hiking in the woods, were expressions of his preparation for a sturdy, iron-clad future. Sandro lived an isolated life, and Levi, who also felt isolated after the promulgation of the racial laws, was drawn to him. The two began to study together. Levi, who was by all accounts intellectually superior, helped Sandro understand that humanity's nobility lies in conquering matter and becoming its master: "Conquering matter is to understand it, and understanding matter is necessary to understanding the universe and ourselves" (41). Reflected in this statement is Levi's great love of his profession and his view that science is an integral part of the aesthetics of life. To him, Mendeleyev's periodic table is also poetry (41).

While Levi leads Sandro to a higher level of intellectual understanding, Sandro introduces the cosmopolitan Levi to nature and its raw and at times harsh beauty. Sandro, whose affinity with the outdoors and ability to imitate the sounds of animals make him one with nature, teaches Levi to eat "la carne dell'orso" (bear meat; 47)—to survive under harsh and difficult conditions. Since Levi's entire experience at Auschwitz is comparable to "la carne dell'orso," one begins to understand just how profound an effect Sandro had on the author. "I am grateful to Sandro for having led me consciously into trouble," Levi writes, "and I am certain that [these undertakings] helped me later on" (48).

Sandro is the first man to be killed in the Italian resistance, shot in the back by a "monstrous child-executioner" (48). The Fascists leave his body in the road for a long time to make his death a warning to the people who live in the area. Sandro proved himself to be a man of ideals and moral principles, a man of action, a real *Mensch*. The most fitting monument to him is the memory the author preserves through his written words. It is through a metaphorical fusion of science and literature that Levi immortalizes Sandro as a literary figure. As zinc in an impure state, Levi galvanizes the iron embodied by his good friend and preserves his memory. In preventing him, so to speak, from rusting or disappearing, Levi has immortalized him and enabled him to live forever. This immortalization of Sandro is another victory for Levi, the member of an "inferior" race who is able to overcome the barriers and prejudices of the Fascist philosophy with his creative, "impure" spirit.

In 1941 Levi carries out an experiment with potassium, reported in the chapter titled for this element, that causes a fire. Had he done the experiment using sodium, which is almost identical to potassium, there would have been no fire. This episode occurs at the time when Levi is just discovering his need to resist the Fascists, a need delayed by the self-imposed blindness he had adopted as a tactic of survival against the Fascist "Spirit," which he had identified as an adverse force. If one wished not to believe the evidence of premeditated annihilation—and Levi was among those who chose not to—at first "there was . . . no other resource than self-imposed blindness" (51). He cannot long ignore, however, the stories coming from refugees from Eastern Europe about the destruction of the ghettos. Hiding behind the walls of his university laboratory, carrying out his experiments in a science that is now providing fewer and fewer answers to his questions, he has a critical need for a pragmatic approach to his situation. At this point in his life, everything he knows about science leads him to pitfalls and obscures the truth. Even the chemical function of distilling, which Levi finds beautiful, "a ritual . . . in which from imperfect material you obtain the essence" (58), metaphorically betrays him, just as he has been betrayed by the German quest for "purity" of race. In the explosion that results from his substitution of potassium for sodium, he finds himself "contemplating the vestiges of the disaster without seeing them" (59), in a way similar to the way he has adopted a deliberate blindness to blot out his knowledge of the Fascists' intentions. Thus through his misadventure with potassium Levi learns not to have faith in surrogates, no matter how similar they may appear to the real thing.[4]

Nickel means "little devil" in German, and in the chapter named for that element, Levi describes his first job after graduating from the university. This is in a mining operation that he likens to Dante's hell except that it is a happy place, one in which the workers are benevolent, friendly "sprites" with personal stories to tell and lives full of the pungent melodrama and pathos of humanity's struggle to exist and enjoy. The Dantesque connection is furthered by the description of the conical shape Levi ascribes to the mine and by his reference to Antaeus, a giant eventually killed by Hercules, as the characterization of the foreman of the mine.[5] The Fascist lieutenant who informs Levi that the job is available for him is a "mercurial messenger" and later "the annunciatory angel" (62) who comes to Levi's aid when his dying father is unable to provide for his family. It is in this environment that Levi becomes aware that people enjoy telling him their stories and he discerns his special talent for transforming them into artistic expressions. So, as a modern-day Dante, he explores his ability to draw his narratives from the material other people provide him.[6]

Involved in work that he loves, Levi finds his time in the mine a period of fun and challenge. He enjoys his work with his colleagues, to whom he is somewhat mysterious; and because of his success with his scientific work, he finds his writing rewarding and satisfactory also, the two activities always going hand-in-hand. For the first time, he puts to use what he learned in school. Not only is it useful, but it plays a part in determining his professional competence as a chemist. Levi's struggle to extricate and tame the "hidden sprite, the capricious *kupfernickel* which jumps out now here, now there" (74), often leaves him without any concrete evidence of his efforts, yet it obviously bolsters his tenacious will to make his art, producing a creative state that he describes as the "borderline between chemistry and white magic" (78). He explores his involvement from every facet so that its result will confirm his value in defiance of the repression and life-threatening events happening outside the mine.

Levi follows this chapter with the two stories he has referenced in it, "Lead" and "Phosphorus," as though to explain and confirm the relationship between the research and the result. They confirm Levi's early narrative ability, since they were, as he claims, stories he had written at an earlier time. The mood of the stories—though not the style—is that of his science fiction tales. Thus "Lead" and "Phosphorus" set the stage for the science fiction pieces to follow.

Because of its color, heavy weight, and inclination to drop to the bottom, Levi calls lead "the metal of death" (87). It is a "tired" metal, and the whole narrative reads with a certain weightiness that comes from Levi's skill in communicating emotions through his descriptions of the weather and the scenery. The protagonist of the story, Rodmund, is gray, like lead. Rodmund prefigures the characteristics of Faussone, the central character in *Monkey's Wrench,* in his interest and competence in his work. Rodmund is always interested in exploring new lands, and he capitalizes on his consummate expertise in working with lead to pay for his travel.

Rodmund enjoys telling stories about the places he has visited and amuses himself by inventing weird tales. His fascination with the magical, mystic, and supernatural mirrors Levi's attraction to science fiction. Levi needs such escapism to get away from the sadness and pain of the other stories he tells, stories which are weird not because they are far-fetched but because they are too cruel to seem true. On the other hand, he will resort to telling unusual tales to show how the unusual can also be entertaining rather than sorrowful.

"Mercury" is a lighter story, as mercury itself implies weightlessness and elusiveness. It is a tale filled with alchemy, allegory, and erupting volcanoes. Levi even provides a map, which adds to the fairy-tale feeling of the story. "Mercury" is set on a distant, virtually deserted island (the nearest place, St. Helena, is 1,200 miles away) named Desolation by the story's protagonist, Corporal Abrahams. Abrahams leads an uneventful life with his wife Maggie until others arrive on the island. This story is another instance of Levi's Garden of Eden scenario. As soon as others arrive, this scenario begins to twist. Rules are made on the spot, reflecting an arbitrariness Levi often explores thematically in his writing. When Abrahams has his eye on another woman and sees that another man is in love with his wife, swapping mates presents the solution to the problem. Mercury thus becomes the symbol of slippery behavior.

In the chapters "Phosphorus" through "Cerium" Levi continues his autobiographical account, progressing through his experiences with Fascism. Any expression of his love for his work, which was an important part of the chapter "Nickel," disappears in "Phosphorus." Levi's descriptions evoke the same despair as did the physical conditions in the Lager, where a lack of communication and the imposed isolation hampered the expression of feelings. These conditions parallel those of the Swiss-owned laboratory in Milan to which he has come, changing jobs through the help of Giulia, a former classmate already employed in the lab. He is called away from his work in the mine by Dr. Martini, the epitome of an unctuous collaborator. The wily Germans have deliberately sent an Aryan to deal with the Jew; this is an excellent method of keeping their own hands "clean" while creating the appearance that everyone is helping the Jews.

Levi's work, which involves research on diabetes and the production of hormonal extracts, painfully recalls to the reader the biological experimentation done in the concentration camps. In one scene he describes how the factory owner seems to be interested in having Levi work for him, not so much because of Levi's professional qualifications, but because he sees in Levi a potential subject for experimentation. On the premise that diabetes is hereditary, this *commendatore,* following Levi's admission that a few of his ancestors had been diagnosed with that disease or shown symptoms of it in their old age, sees in Levi "an authentic diabetic, of a basically *human race* [italics mine]" (111), on whom to carry out research. The bizarre twist to all this is that Levi would have to place himself in the roles of both subject and tester in his experiments.

Besides the confession here about diabetes in the family, Levi allows readers another rare glimpse into his private life. He describes the few personal items that he chooses to take with him to Milan: Rabelais, *Moby-Dick,* and the *Macaronaeae* are his bedside reading; a pickax, some rope, a logarithmic ruler, and a recorder are his necessities. It is unusual to hear him speak in such concrete terms about himself rather than in his more common philosophical and moral vein.

Levi's description of the laboratory is unquestionably reflective of the Lager. While he finds it well equipped, there are several nit-picking regulations designed to separate him, as a Jew, from the other workers and to prevent anyone from divulging or discovering the research being performed. Regarding his Jewishness, Levi demonstrates that the Aryans are stupid in believing that a Jew cannot see through the imposition of their rules as anything other than a way to cover up their prejudices. As for the second issue, he makes it clear that the measures taken to protect the research were comparable to those the Germans used to prevent any word about what was happening in the Lager from escaping to the outside world.

In Levi's first meeting with Giulia, she divulges that she accomplishes no real research but rather spends her time preparing for her forthcoming wedding and falsifies or concocts research results. No one would know, since no one ever verifies what she does anyway. Levi also finds himself embarked on a futile investigation. His professional sense tells him not to place any faith in the promise of a miracle drug by the author of the text from which he derives his experiments. As a whole, it is work as unproductive as the work in the Lager and as demoralizing, "because to do work in which one does not believe is a great affliction" (120). The rash and unscientific mode of research he is told to carry out, Levi believes, is a direct progeny of the "black magic of the Nazi court" (120).

Phosphorus, "bringer of light," is also Levi's reflection on Giulia, with whom he has fallen in love. She brings Levi light and gaiety; but she also sheds light on the fact that he cannot have her, for this is the reality of the racial laws. Giulia is the forbidden fruit. Worse, Levi finds himself in the position of helping her marry someone else, an act through which he fully fathoms his difference from her and acknowledges the high price he has to pay for being a Jew. In another striking revelation, he confesses that this event, which forced him to confront his inability to relate comfortably to women, would always haunt him and would relegate him to a life "poisoned by envy and by abstract, sterile and aimless desires" (125). Through his depiction of his relationship with Giulia, which lasted as a friendship for many years thereafter, Levi suggests the role that fate and luck play in our lives.

The full impact of the racial laws is exposed in the next chapter, "Gold." In it Levi recounts the story of his capture and the impact of his loss of freedom. The first sentence of the chapter, in which Levi speaks about how people transplanted from Turin to Milan "do not strike root, or at least do it badly" (127), suggests his premonition about his future: the dramatic realization of what it will mean to have lost freedom in a real and physical sense. Levi and his friends lived a repressed existence in Milan, where their exuberance was reconfigured into melancholy poetry and they fought a battle that was already lost. When he could no longer claim ignorance of what was happening around him, with the courage and idealism of youth Levi joined a band of eleven partisans who were subsequently betrayed. Eight of them escaped, while three, including Levi, were captured. Given a choice of admitting he was a Jew or acknowledging his partisan activities, and being informed that the latter choice meant immediate execution, Levi chose to admit his Jewish heritage. He did so primarily "out of an irrational digging in of pride" (134). As it turned out, the racial laws would determine the outcome for him, namely deportation to Auschwitz.

Levi's lack of preparation for what he was about to confront is vividly narrated in his description of hiding his gun following his capture. The gun was almost a toy, certainly not adequate for the fight in which he was about to take part. Waiting in prison, he experienced the Faustian grasping at life of the dying man, making promises to himself of reform and renewal. In his desperation, however, he also had the critical insight that, should he survive, he must focus on actions that would help him experience the essence of life. Not only does Levi express this need, but he reiterates it in the character of an unnamed prisoner who shares with him the secret of where gold can be found and confesses that he mines it in the summer, not because he wants to become rich but because it allows him to live life in freedom. Freedom is as valuable as gold itself. And the prisoner likes the feel of working the gold with his hands, just as Levi will derive satisfaction, if not catharsis, in molding his chemistry into an artistic form that is long-lasting, like gold.

The chapter "Cerium" succinctly depicts what was required of a man to survive in the Lager. Levi's behavior, which he describes and apologizes for in this chapter, is not that of an educated young man of the Italian middle class. The struggle to stay alive made it necessary to subvert morality, short of stealing bread from his fellow inmates. This chapter is in effect Levi's justification, unnecessary though it may be, for what he considers his sordid actions in stealing and trading light flints for bread rations to survive, with his close friend Alberto, the two months before the Russians overcame the Germans.

Beyond stealing, also important to survival is the ability to take risks, which both Levi and Alberto did. By working at night to fashion the rods of stolen cerium into light flints, they risked causing a fire or being discovered in possession of the materials with which to do so. Fear, it appears, was inversely proportionate to the hunger they experienced, so profound, so much more of concern even than death, that they were willing to jeopardize themselves for a piece of bread.

Of course, saving oneself in the camp did not necessarily assure survival, nor was one's behavior necessarily remodified to a moral position once liberation occurred. As evidence of this, Levi describes how, following the disappearance and probable death of Alberto, a fellow prisoner lives for many years on money he garners from telling Alberto's mother heroic though not necessarily true stories about Alberto. The man has no scruples about keeping the poor woman believing that her son is still alive. Levi, on the other hand, takes comfort in knowing that his survival allowed him to preserve the Lager experience as a memorial to those, like Alberto, who perished.

Levi's discussion of his survival and his related justifications, fears, and guilt leads to the third phase of the book, which encompasses the chapters "Chromium" through "Vanadium." This section spans the postwar period, a time of readjustment in which Levi alters his romantic view of chemistry. He now understands that what he had once seen with the idealistic eyes of inexperienced youth is conditioned by practical needs that demand pragmatic actions and revised values. In short, bread is still an issue, though it can now be acquired in an honest fashion.

"Chromium" is the chapter of rebirth. Physically, the element figures in the initiation of a study to determine what went wrong in a simple equation involving commercial paint. Metaphorically, however, it is extended to figure in the examination of what caused a devastating and complex human disaster. In this chapter, questioning certain historically accepted human customs and values allows for the reestablishment of stability and eternal values in a fragmented world. "Chromium" looks back at a time when an acceptable yet simple lack of logic, not only harmless but often comforting, can now safely replace the unacceptable irrationality engendered by Fascism, for stability and equilibrium can result from an inexplicable process.

Coming out of a severe depression after his return, Levi experienced shame for the human race because humans built Auschwitz. The experience of the camp, the death of a woman he loved there, and all the associated guilt he carried rendered him unable to resume his life. At the same time, the experience provided him a compelling raison d'être and the powerful material with which to keep the memory of Auschwitz before the world. His initial boredom was transformed into "nervous gaiety" (157) as he began to experience a satisfaction in his work that stabilized him, freed him from the heavy baggage of his "atrocious memories" (153), and gave him a clearer sense of direction in his life and his writing. His patience and his ability to call on the intricacies of his professional knowledge led him, on one level, to discover the faulty equation that ruined many batches of paint. On a different level, it taught him not to "surrender to the temptation of mistaking an elegant hypothesis for certainty" (157), an understanding that palliated, though it neither explained nor justified, the world's initial fascination with the "elegant" hypothesis of Fascism.

Challenged again by his profession, Levi finds therapy in his work and writing. Combined with meeting the woman who would become his wife, this makes him feel "reborn and replete with new power, washed clean and cured of a long sickness" (153). The source of his rebirth lies in the "atrocious memories." Levi can speak in the same breath about the horrors of Auschwitz and the ludicrous imagery of a "clumsy pyramid of orange livers," both of which he could now "engage in joyous battle" (154). When he conquers the fallacious paint formula, the paint emerges as "completely normal, born again from its ashes like the Phoenix" (158), as Levi himself is reborn. His chemistry has now become his partner in a new love, a new book, and the reestablishment of a life in balance and harmony, at least for the time being, with the past.

The success of this almost therapeutic engagement is evidenced in the two short chapters that follow, "Sulfur" and "Titanium." In these Levi absents himself as the main character and becomes the creative author who draws from his imagination to present two delightful stories. The first plays heavily on his scientific knowledge, and the second on his rich imagination and ability to see the magic in the most simple occurrences of daily life.

Lanza, a fictional character in "Sulfur," resolves an impending crisis at work by figuring out how to avoid an explosion (something Levi had experienced in the early days of his experimental bravado, described in "Hydrogen") and is satisfied with himself for having been able to resist the temptation to seek help. To do so would have amounted to admitting defeat and incompetence, something Levi has always painstakingly avoided. This short chapter praises the challenge of work and the victory of the worker who confronts the challenge in the face of fearful and uncertain moments. It is also a particularly good example of Levi's joining his knowledge of chemistry with his competence as a writer. "Sulfur" strongly heralds *The Monkey's Wrench,* the novel that, with this book, presents Levi's conclusive coalescence of creative prose and science.

"Titanium," the shortest of all the chapters, reads like a fairy tale. It tells about a painter who has a magical touch and a little girl whom he benevolently confines in a circle drawn with white chalk, possibly to prevent her from encountering evil. While the little girl knows that she can physically leave the circle at any time, magical power inhibits her from crossing the chalk line. The implied message is that one's belief in something can make it true, and it can influence our behavior as much as a concrete phenomenon can. When the painter erases the circle, he in no way undoes the enchantment; the magical quality remains in the little girl's mind. Perhaps this conclusion expresses Levi's wish that the innocence of childhood could always remain a part of our adult selves.

When Levi feels tired and unchallenged by his work in the factory, he decides to go into business as an independent chemist with his friend Emilio. Times are difficult, as "six years of war and destruction had brought about a regression in many civil habits and attenuated many needs, first of all the need for decorum" (172). The business will eventually fail and Levi will return to work in a factory. However, this experience of independence gives him the opportunity to meet colorful and interesting people and resuscitates his awareness of the dignity a person can retain.

"Arsenic," Levi's story of the cobbler who unperturbedly accepts evidence that his competitor has tried to poison him by lacing a gift of sugar with the deadly white powder, suggests a most civil way of confronting the corruption and depravity of the world to which Levi has returned. The cobbler is unusual in Levi's gallery, someone outside of the social class from which he usually draws his characters but a person who aptly proves that wisdom and good sense are not limited to any one social class. This man, who feels more comfortable speaking the Piedmontese dialect than he does speaking Italian, exhibits his goodness and understanding by not holding any grudges against the competitor who has attempted to put him permanently out of business. The cobbler understands the economic pressures on his rival. With grace and dignity—and more than a small ulterior motive to show his competitor that he has caught him at his game—he plans to return the arsenic personally and to set the scales straight. The cobbler understands that there are more ways than one to come out on top, and patience and coolheadedness are certainly among them. The cobbler's pride in his work is comparable to Levi's. Nevertheless, Levi experiences discomfort with this person because of the nobility of his character. Dignity, Levi comes to understand, can exist at all social levels, and life is sometimes richest in the absence of material wealth.[7]

Life experience is also the topic of "Nitrogen," in which Levi confronts certain realities with a degree of amusement. Making fun of others, Levi does not spare humor at his own expense. Now an independent "consultant," he has been hired by a sleazy producer of women's cosmetics, "a third-rate actor playing the part of a pimp" (176), to determine through chemical analysis why his cheap lipstick runs. The man's factory is an extension of himself: dirty, disorderly, and cheap-looking, filled with a group of similarly sleazy girls who are employed to receive his kisses eight times a day to test whether or not the lipstick is kiss-proof. Discovering that uric acid is the best medium for making the lipstick stay on the lips, Levi takes off with his wife, with whom he wants to extend the honeymoon made short for lack of money, to the outskirts of Turin in pursuit of chicken excrement, which is the best supply of this commodity.

Following Auschwitz, no chemical procedure can shock Levi. By this point in his life, he realizes that "matter is matter, neither noble nor vile"; "nitrogen is nitrogen" (181). Everything in life, it seems to him, is recycled, emerging sometimes in beauty, sometimes in garbage. He sees in the procedure with the chicken excrement the beauty and mystery of the work of the old alchemists and the irony of deriving "gold from dung" (181) to put on women's lips. But there is nothing romantic about it any longer. His approach is now strictly pragmatic. Auschwitz may have taught him that, too. The meager result of his day's work sifting, refining his gathering, and trying to oxidize it is not gold, of course, but common chicken excrement. The banality of this entire process prompts him to return to his "colorless but safe schemes of inorganic chemistry" (183).

In the lively and pleasant chapter entitled "Tin," Levi recounts the story of his doomed business partnership with his friend Emilio, who convinced him to leave the paint factory and his love affair with varnish to go out on his own. Feeling confined at the factory, possibly in reaction to the circumstances forced on him in the Lager, the author wishes to be independent. In partnership with Emilio he can practice his profession as he sees fit. To be free, however, he also has to accept tasks that offer little or no challenge and professional satisfaction. With his parents' blessing, Emilio has set up in their courtyard a chemistry laboratory whose apparatus and odors literally infiltrate every room in the apartment. Emilio's father, Signor Samuele, is a resourceful elderly man "who still had a preoccupying avidity for experimentation" (185); his mother, Signora Ester, is a supportive, endearing woman who could tolerate the incredible disorder wrought by the boys' invasion of her home. Levi's use of the polite form of address before their given names shows his respect for these two elderly people.

Most of the laboratory work revolves around melting tin, "Jove's metal" (188), to make and sell the stannous chloride used in mirrors. Tin is "a friend" (184) because it marries with iron, a characteristic Levi uses to great effect in his chapter "Iron," in which he tells about Sandro Delmastro. Also, tin "forms alloys with copper to give . . . bronze" (185) and is therefore a productive and useful element. It does its job with humility and without fanfare, which appears to mirror Levi's work ethic. Hydrochloric acid, on the other hand, which they also use in the process, shouts its penetrating odor from a distance and is tricky to work with because it corrodes all metals. Since its odor announces it, at least one has time to take necessary precautions against becoming ill from its fumes.

Eventually the partnership ends because the two are unable to make a living. The opening words of the chapter are significant. "It's bad to be poor" (184), Levi surmises, and one has to do something to change that status. His business venture comes crashing down, however, just like the exhaust hood he and Emilio have carefully constructed in the apartment to carry off the noxious gasses produced as they melt tin. Emilio remarks that he thought the hood would have made more noise when it hit the ground. This reflects his wish that the partnership had been more lasting. Emilio accepts what he considers Levi's desertion, but it is significant that Levi, to whom chemistry has by now become a dull exercise, sees the breakup as almost preordained. It is as if he believes it is part of his destiny as a Jew. This is hinted at by his reference to the proclamation decree of 1785 that he and Emilio come across while they are cleaning out the apartment and dismantling their equipment. Written by the general inquisitor of the Ancona District, the decree states that no Jew was permitted to take dancing or music lessons from Christians.[8] Anti-Semitism, which has prohibited Jews from functioning freely through the ages, reemerges in the men's reading of this old decree and makes the failure of their business venture seem inevitable.

In "Uranium" the author is back working for the paint factory, now as a customer service representative, and he continues to poke fun at his own shortcomings. In this instance, he admits that he is not a good salesperson. Always modest and reticent, he finds himself out of character in the role of salesman and does poorly at it. He performs with hesitation, "compunction and little human warmth" (193). He simply does not have it in him, and his account of how he is handed a badge to wear on his lapel, an impersonal and cold way of establishing an identity, calls to mind the tattooing in the Lager. Any blatant action that singles him out brings back unpleasant memories.

Mr. Bonino, on whom he calls, is "a little round man, untidy, carelessly shaven, and with a toothless smile" (194). He tells Levi a long, boring, poorly recounted story of how he was given a piece of uranium by some German soldiers as thanks for pointing them toward Switzerland. Levi is totally unimpressed with Bonino's storytelling, yet he cannot help being fascinated by the man's imagination. Levi knows that the story is untrue, and he also knows that Bonino is encouraged to go on because he sees the incredulity on the author's face. This only motivates Bonino to try harder to convince him. Levi eventually becomes willing to test the metal, which turns out to be cadmium. Although he is irritated at his gullibility in thinking finally that Bonino might have been telling the truth, he gives Bonino credit for almost convincing him and envies his "boundless freedom of invention" (199).

Bonino's apparent freedom saddens Levi because he believes his own life experience precludes his ever having such emancipated creativity. The burden of the past has determined the author's topic; he is tied to it and unable to "break through the barrier . . . and fly like Superman across centuries, meridians, and parallels" (199) as Bonino has been able to do. It is clear that, in a certain sense, Levi had assessed Bonino incorrectly. Influenced by this man's small, messy desk, which to Levi is the mark of a person of relatively little value to his organization, initially Levi sees Bonino only in connection with his function at work. This prevents him from grasping Bonino's imaginative side, a facet of his character that helps him evade the monotony of his work. The author gets angry at himself for not having acknowledged this about Bonino sooner.

The challenge of testing the metal to see if it is indeed uranium, however, sends Levi flying into the lab, a place in which he infrequently finds himself now because of his job as a service representative. The lab makes him feel young again, longing for adventure and discovery. The thought that the piece of rock in his hands might actually be uranium excites him. He feels he is about to test something different. He undertakes this analysis with the same enthusiasm he had as a youth, particularly when he and Enrico made their flamboyant experiment with hydrogen. As it has done in other chapters, the voice inside him speaks again in the second person, suggesting that the responsibilities of his administrative position have led him to atrophy as a chemist. One also discerns here the intimate connection between science and narrative: Bonino's storytelling leads Levi back to the laboratory, where he is proud to discover that, even though he rarely goes there now, he still has the distinguishing touch of a chemist. His attempt, out of habit, to identify the element by the use of his fingernail or a penknife, by smelling and feeling it, is the traditional approach. The laboratory revisited is still "a source of joy" (198). The reader senses Levi's nostalgia as his scientific reflexes are revived, even for a short while. There is, moreover, the sense of the last hurrah. Levi appears to be signaling to himself that he is about to leave chemistry. For a brief moment, though, he relives its romantic essence as he had longed for it to be. He is thus indirectly grateful to Bonino for having given him reason to return to the laboratory, perhaps for the last time.

In the chapter "Silver," Levi makes another attempt to define his intention for this work to be a "search for events . . . to put on display in a book . . . to convey . . . the strong and bitter flavor of our trade" (203), which he sees as a mirror for life in general. At the same time, though, he is looking at the present with the knowledge he has gained about the struggle in life. In the solitary practice of chemistry is the measure of humankind and of the chemist himself, who confronts matter, as one confronts life, with one's brain, hands, reason, and imagination. Wisdom, however, can temper the enthusiasm of youth, causing people to cling to the past, as does Cerrato, the protagonist in this chapter. Levi admits to having tremendous ambivalence about his own past. He does and does not want to embrace it: he wants to because he knows his values have remained noble and worthy; he is inclined not to because he must then feel the passage of time and youth and his personal losses.

"Honest, clumsy, eager Cerrato, to whom life had given so little and who had given so little to life" (201), highlights the mediocrity that can descend upon us all if we do not constantly strive to rise above it. Cerrato is the counter-balance to Sandro Delmastro, who both gave to life and took from it. Cerrato only reacts to life, and thus, Levi implies, he misses the real meaning of why we are here, which is to struggle against life. Inert, as are Levi's ancestors, but not "shipwrecked," because he never sank to maliciousness or evil deeds, Cerrato simply never committed himself to anything of importance. In his noncommitment, he is the personification of lead. He had not been compromised by Fascism, but neither did he capitalize on the racial laws. His is a character without depth. Furthermore, because he goes on to live in Germany, there is always some question about his motivations and morality, even though Levi tends to trust him because he could trust him twenty-five years before. His reliance on the past is justified when he encounters Cerrato at the reunion dinner and feels him to have aged but not changed. Cerrato's work in photographic chemistry has described his life: the "technicolor years" during his youth in the university and all the others years that were "black and white" (202).

In discussing the lack of understanding about their profession, Levi urges Cerrato to tell him a story that he can use in his writings, a story that would be reflective of what can happen in their line of work. Cerrato chooses the element silver to demonstrate the frustration and groping for answers involved in being a successful chemist. The story is about Cerrato's work in Germany in a department where x-ray paper is manufactured. After distribution, a batch of that paper is found to be defective. The problem is eventually traced to polluted river water used to wash the uniforms of the laboratory personnel who prepare the paper. This story about the factory in Germany, particularly the recounting of the German fixation on order, that "maniacal cleanliness, purity with eight zeroes" (205), activates an unpleasant reconnection for Levi. It brings to his mind not only the sanitary sterility usually associated with the meticulous German mentality but also the issue of his "impure" Jewishness, the validity of which he constantly strives to maintain. It is also reflective of Levi's paradoxical progression toward disillusion as his memories render him less and less resilient to life in the present.

Levi begins to have more respect for this fellow chemist, who proves himself to be a good investigator by finding the cause of the chemical problem and a valid solution to it. Cerrato's discovery of the error in the equation, however, does not come without a sense of guilt for what went wrong in the first place. This is the inexplicable guilt that Levi so often questions, the guilt that exists even when there is no logical reason for its presence. "It's something exactly like original sin: you haven't done anything, but you're guilty and you must pay" (207), Cerrato confirms. And the payment is not in the form of the usual exchange but with the wrenching of one's innards and the continuing guilt.

The promise Levi and Cerrato make to tell each other additional stories that deal with matter as an "evil and obstruction, as if it revolted against the order dear to man" (210), positions them both as protectors. By extension, this may also shed light on Levi's compulsion to write for the purpose of maintaining awareness of the wrong committed, with the aim of preventing such wrong in the future. Cerrato's black and white life, which seems not to hold much promise at first, provides Levi with an important story about serious scientific investigation, a story that is specific in its clarification of individual versus matter, similar to what Levi has accomplished with the telling of "Uranium" and with some of the other elements in the previous chapters. While Cerrato's story lacks the fantasy and imagination of the story told by Bonino in "Uranium," it demonstrates his professional precision and integrity, which Levi admires and respects. The sharing of the story establishes Cerrato as a true colleague with whom he can share the pride and dignity of their profession. The moral here is that people ought to get to the bottom of things, leaving no stone unturned, especially when it comes to exposing those forces bent on doing evil and on creating obstructions.

Cerrato's story leads into Levi's interaction with Dr. Müller in the next chapter, "Vanadium," in which the author more fully reveals his intimate emotions about his captors. On account of another chemical problem Levi enters into correspondence with a person he suspects is the same Doktor Müller who worked with him as a German civilian in the laboratory at Auschwitz. The Dr. Müller at Auschwitz had been kind to Levi, obtaining a pair of shoes for him and arranging for him to get shaved twice a week rather than only once. Levi first suspects that this man is the one he knew earlier because of the way he writes "naptenate" for "naphtenate" (English: naphthene), which he recalls is the same slight mistake of pronunciation and writing made by the Müller at Auschwitz. Levi generally uses deductive analysis to solve the problems he encounters, but in this instance, he works on the "pathologically precise memories of [his] encounters in that by now remote world" (213) to which he also refers as his "previous incarnation" (213). This is an expression hard to overlook for its implication of the line drawn by the Holocaust between the life before, in which many died, and the life after, in which some, like Levi, were fortunate enough to experience a rebirth of sorts. With the help of one of his colleagues, Levi places this Müller as the man he knew at Auschwitz.

In either a confrontational approach or a daring one, Levi, now seeing himself on an equal footing, forwards this Dr. Müller a copy of *Se questo è un uomo* (*Survival in Auschwitz*) with a personal letter. Levi makes it clear that there are two levels of interaction occurring: the professional one and the human one. The men's exchange of letters about the chemical problem continues on a formal basis, eliciting outcomes to the problem that are affected by the more personal correspondence between them. Metaphorically, Levi is suggesting that life is always carried out on more than one level, with each level having an impact on the other, no matter how separate they may appear.

The exchange of letters, which keeps Levi in a state of anxiety about whether or not he will hear from Müller on a personal level, revives all the questions and emotions of the past. When he finally hears, Müller's proposal that the two men meet during the Pentecost is significant because this is a religious holiday observed by both Christians and Jews. While the Christians celebrate the descent of the Holy Spirit upon the disciples the seventh Sunday after Easter, the Jews celebrate Shavuos seven weeks from the second day of Passover, which is also called the holiday of the Giving of the Law, since its timing coincides with the revelation of the Ten Commandments at Mount Sinai. The proposed meeting thus suggests the coming together of the two men before the eyes of a supreme being. It is apparent to Levi, however, that Dr. Müller seeks from the meeting to soothe his conscience without conceding any guilt or admitting any complicity in the evil committed by his countrymen. In planning to meet with Levi, Müller wants "an absolution, because he had a past to overcome" (217). Levi, on the other hand—who cannot forgive, let alone absolve—wants only a "discount on the bill for the defective resin" (217).

As long as Müller has no remorse and no intention of repenting, there can be no real "meeting" between the offender and the offended, either individually or universally. There is no small amount of relief for Levi in learning of the doctor's unexpected and sudden death before their meeting. Levi feels that, had they met, the gentleness of his own personality and the meekness of his own character might have betrayed him and pushed him toward a compromise, something he knows he could not accept because it would profane the memory of those who have given their lives. The memory of the Lager will always return to haunt him, even though, as time passes, he will feel less and less comfortable in speaking for those who died at Auschwitz. Sometimes, as with Dr. Müller, he knows that it is not "sensible" (an important word) to view Müller as "the representative of the butchers" (218). One cannot help hearing in these words, spoken in this particular context and so long after the Holocaust, disappointment that Levi has not been able to sustain the motivating elements that he established as life goals: to witness but not to forgive.

Though he is increasingly disappointed by the weakening of his resolve to witness, Levi nevertheless structures the closing chapter of the book, "Carbon," as a hymn to life, an appreciation of the suffering of the Jews—throughout history and at Auschwitz—and of their ongoing ability to survive. As the metaphor for the Holocaust, carbon is delicately but thoroughly examined in this chapter. In his choice of carbon for his image, Levi has recognized that any element has the potential to serve as an emblem of destiny if one takes the time to discover its mysteries. Speaking of the "future [that] is written in indecipherable characters, [which] become clear only 'afterward'" (225), Levi portrays his realization that only with time and experience do we come to understand these "indecipherable characters" as they relate to the progression of our lives. The words *future* and *afterward* are clear indicators of the demarcation he makes between his life before the Holocaust, when he believed there was goodness, and his life after, which he understands as a time for expressing the emotions his ordeal engendered and for witness and comprehension. As "every element says something to someone" and there are many specifics in life to which we respond, carbon is the element that "says everything to everyone" (225), the universal element that holds the combined experience of our evolution, our history, and our existence. Carbon, which has existed for millions of years and which combines with other elements to create life, seems to take on the significance here of marking the approaching end of Levi's career as a chemist and the beginning of his life as a full-time writer.[9] It is also significant that carbon produces the graphite in pencils, the tools of writing. It is that single cell of carbon that "belongs to a brain, and it is my brain, the brain of the 'me' who is writing; and the cell in question, and within it the atom in question, is in charge of my writing. . . . It is that which at this instant . . . makes my hand run along a certain path on the paper, mark it with these volutes that are signs: a double snap, up and down, between two levels of energy, guides this hand of mine to impress on the paper this dot, here, this one" (232–33).

In the RAI documentary series *Sorgente di vita,* in which Levi revisits Auschwitz forty years after his imprisonment there, he talks about the pervasive smell of coal in Poland, which he will always associate with the Lager.[10] In addition to all the positive characteristics of carbon, the relationship between carbon and the Lager, so associated in Levi's mind with death, may provide literary motivation for a new beginning. The literary quality is evident in Levi's metaphoric story of the discovery of carbon.

For carbon, "time does not exist" (225), just as it did not exist for Levi in the Lager. It lived "congealed in an eternal present" (226) yet within reach of man's "pickax," which, for Levi, is his ability to wield words so that the story gets told. The story, once "immobile," now has turned "tumultuous," as the carbon rises from a chimney and takes to the air, as smoke rose from the ovens and the Holocaust shook the world as Levi knew it. Through a cataclysmic event like the Holocaust, carbon undergoes a chemical change in which it is inserted into the life cycle. This event is so incomprehensible, if "to comprehend is the same as forming an image of a happening whose scale . . . and whose protagonists are in their essence invisible" (227), because there are no words adequate, as Levi has said in repeated frustration, to describe it. Carbon, however, does contains impurities; "thirty times less abundant than argon" (228), that noble, inert element of Levi's ancestors. We have survived, Levi suggests, because the impurities are the "raw material of life," which cannot be daunted. It is their impurity that permits them to survive. Levi speaks of the "atom," which, inserted as part of an architectural structure, is "subjected to complicated exchanges and balances" (229). By this he seems to mean the Jews and their history. They are "dissolved in water" (229) or assimilated, as Levi felt he was in Italy, but are "neither fish, flesh, nor fowl" (229). Nor are they authorized "to take on a higher responsibility" (229), by which Levi suggests the lowest class of citizenship the Nazis bestowed upon the Jews. Levi's description of how carbon is involved in the creation of wine and how it is stored in the human liver to be activated in exacerbated circumstances refers to how the Jews were destined to be abused and, in a sense, kept in reserve for those moments in history when the world needed to lash out at a scapegoat.

Of particular interest is Levi's comment that equilibrium leads to death, signaling that for him, the ongoing struggle is important for survival. Carbon, unlike the human body, has eternal qualities, and it is fitting that Levi should choose it as a metaphor for the end of his career in chemistry and his rebirth as a writer.

Notes

1. Sections of these two works are included in the English version of *The Sixth Day and Other Tales.*

2. *The Periodic Table,* trans. Raymond Rosenthal (New York: Schocken Books, 1984), 139 and 224. Further references will be noted parenthetically in the text.

3. Cases, "Sodio e potassio: scienza e visione del mondo in Primo Levi," included in *Primo Levi as Witness* (Fiesole: Casalini, 1990).

4. Levi also mentions this story in *Dialogo,* where he reiterates that the lesson to be learned from this experiment is not to put one's faith in look-alikes.

5. Antaeus helps Dante and Virgil descend to the bottom of hell to see Lucifer (*Inferno,* canto 31:112–45).

6. This is the approach Levi will use fully in his next work, *The Monkey's Wrench.*

7. This story calls to mind Boccaccio's "Cisti the Baker" (*Decameron,* 6:2), who takes pleasure and pride in doing his job properly and with dignity.

8. Ancona is a city on the Adriatic coast of central Italy, in the Marche region.

9. He retired from his job at SIVA in 1977, two years after the publication of this book.

10. This documentary was produced by the Italian national television network in the early 1980s. He also writes of the pervasive smell of carbon in his essay "Il linguaggio degli odori" (in *Altrui mestiere,* 229). This essay is not included in the English version, *Other People's Trades.*

CHAPTER FOUR

The Monkey's Wrench

(La chiave a stella)

La chiave a stella (*The Monkey's Wrench*) was published by Einaudi in 1978, a year after Levi retired from the paint factory where he worked as a chemist. This book is a delightful narrative departure from the author's previous, more somber Holocaust themes, though he incorporates into it his philosophical concerns about this tragic event as he continues to integrate his art and his science. He also continues to expound on the importance of being able to carry on one's life work with freedom and autonomy as the basis for a creative and productive life. In addition, he develops several subthemes: taking risks, the ongoing possibility of losing power, and interpersonal relationships—the latter particularly in two nostalgic chapters that focus on a father-son relationship.

The Monkey's Wrench is couched in a framework that is subtle, intricate, and more technically experimental than that of many of Levi's works. In blending his literary talent with his scientific training and work, he emulates the "factory worker" genre that had become popular in Italy around the late 1970s and early 1980s.[1] He displays invention and humor through the language he reproduces, which is suggestive of his native dialect, and through skillfully crafted recollections, often shaped as parables. His subtlety, however, does not obscure his intended meaning and morality, which, as he clarifies at the end of the book with a quote from Joseph Conrad, he wishes to express by portraying his life experience through the characters in these stories.

From the uncaptivating backdrop of the world of Libertino Faussone, an Italian construction worker, Levi derives some of his most incisive observations about himself and his art; about the magic that transforms us into creative beings; about his scientific profession and his literary aspirations; and about listening, which he values as "equally ancient and noble" as the art of telling, though it may be less quantifiable.[2] Levi's concept of the technical aspect of being a writer, as told to us by his protagonist, Faussone, involves "grinding," "honing," "deburring" and "hammering" (7) one's ideas and words until a story emerges. Because the world does not operate in an organized and ordered fashion, some form must be imposed on it to make it understandable. Levi accomplishes this by bringing the principles and concepts of scientific thought into his writing.

This book of fourteen relatively short chapters is composed of loosely connected vignettes about Libertino Faussone's travels and challenges as a rigger in international construction. With his "long, solid and quick" (154) hands, Faussone is adept with the tools of his trade: the shovel, the hammer, and the monkey wrench of the title. The vignettes are connected not so much by a story line as by the interweaving of Faussone's recollections and viewpoints with Levi's viewpoints, which he expresses in the role of unnamed companion and patient listener.

We learn in the chapter titled "Beating Copper" that Faussone's father wanted his son to bear the name Libero as a representation of freedom, but circumstances forced him to settle for the name Libertino, unaware that it meant "libertine." The Fascist-controlled bureaucracy made it impossible to speak in terms of freedom. What his father was trying to express in his choice of a name was his wish that Faussone be free not only in a physical sense but also philosophically and politically. As Faussone clarifies in the chapter "The Bevel Gear," "the noun 'freedom' notoriously has many meanings, but perhaps the most accessible form of freedom . . . consists of being good at your job and therefore taking pleasure in doing it" (139).

Faussone is obviously good at his job; he is sought after for his expertise. He loves the sheer thrill of placing huge cranes, stringing long bridges over treacherous spans of water, and installing complex chemical processing equipment that necessitates his crawling through intricate and torturous piping. He is patently a visceral person who also happens to be endowed with an intelligent, quick mind. In this way he can be seen as an extension of Levi, a chemist and a writer.

So too Levi examines life from the perspective of a man who is now free and able to enjoy his work as more than a means of survival. Faussone declares that, for him, "every job is like a first love" (114). There is always the challenge, and frequently the mystery, of not always knowing how things will end up. He acknowledges too that there is something to be said for the comfort and security of repetitiveness. Faussone also reveals, in "The Bevel Gear," that "to live happily you have to have something to do, but it shouldn't be too easy, or else something to wish for, but not just any old wish: something there's a hope of achieving" (139). Moreover, Faussone tells his listener, "It's no accident that I'm in this line of work" (8)—it was the only way for him to fulfill his wish to see the world. He could wait until he got rich enough to be a tourist, or he could become a rigger. In opting for the latter, he can get rich and be a tourist at the same time without having to wait. Thus Levi explores the impact of free choices and their effects on our final contributions in life and our place in it. Time and waiting are anathema to Faussone and perhaps a reflection of Levi's sense, at the time he wrote this work, that life does have parentheses around it, a beginning one in birth and an ending one in death, between which one has to squeeze as much living as possible. One's choice of how to accomplish this is a defining characteristic of each human life. It is possible that Levi might be looking both back and ahead here with some wistfulness about what has filled the space in his own parentheses.

Faussone says, "We can and must fight to see that the fruit of labor remains in the hands of those who work, and that work does not turn into a punishment" (80). This statement gives a clear indication of how he—speaking for Levi— exalts work and berates laziness and lack of pride in one's occupation. This feeling is underscored further in the chapters "Offshore" and "Beating Copper" in Faussone's recollection of how much his father loved his work as a coppersmith and how much he had wanted his son to join him in his trade. These chapters emphasize pride in one's work apart from financial gain, and the importance of cultural and family continuity. Faussone recounts a dream in which he cannot distinguish between himself and his father, perhaps highlighting Levi's own deep feeling of connection with his family roots, from which he draws his strength at times of stress and fear. Likewise, as he points out in the chapter "Without Time," one tends to learn after the fact, and experiencing trouble is the best means of learning how to avoid it.

Levi's skill as a writer is particularly evident in his well-crafted depictions of those minute qualities of each character that convey the character's essence, just as some artists can portray an image with a few deftly drawn pencil lines. As he promises Faussone in "The Bridge," he avoids embellishment, though he may not be able to avoid paring away, "as the sculptor does when he carves the form from the block" (113), to communicate an idea most effectively.

At thirty-five, Faussone perceives himself as "not a great story teller" (8). He often speaks in clichés to insure that he will be understood, as his father often spoke in proverbs for the same reason. Faussone's reliance on this form of expression is evidence of Levi's insecurity: to make certain he will be understood, not just heard, he renders his thoughts and feelings into the simplest and most universal form. Thus he can meet the responsibility he has taken on, as a survivor of one of the most horrible events in human history, to tell the world about that event.

With zoom-lens precision, at the beginning of many of the vignettes Levi catapults the reader into the middle of the intimate discussion taking place between Faussone and his listener, creating immediacy and literary tension.

This technique enables the reader to follow the conversation more closely. Also evident is Levi's skill at reproducing dialogue. His often demonstrated fascination with languages and the effect a command of them can have on one's life is reiterated by his endowing Faussone with enough competence in four or five of them to make him functional in the language of the country in which he is working.[3] Such linguistic ability, as we have seen in Levi's previous writings, is as much an issue of cultural assimilation and communication as one of gaining technical proficiency and an ability to survive. It is clear that a linguistic faux pas that indicates even rudimentary knowledge of a language is better than an exhibition of no knowledge at all. It provides those with whom one interacts a basis of trust, an expression of interest that paves the way for mutual understanding, which is a necessary step in both communication and assimilation.

Frequently stressing his belief in the work ethic and how people can be assessed by their degree of adherence to it, Faussone is proud of his occupation and his proficiency in it; he knows all the tricks of his trade. By endowing him with this prowess, Levi acknowledges that to negotiate life, one has to know the processes that enable one to survive and, ideally, attain a measure of success. In each vignette, Faussone avoids telling the exact locations of his projects because to do so would be to reveal a professional secret. Intrinsic to every line of work, Levi implies through Faussone, are a mystique and a jargon that make it inaccessible to someone not trained in it. This is exactly the wall—a wall raised out of the inability to communicate—at which Levi's literary struggle is aimed. His detailed accounts of Faussone's construction projects are an effort to open up and meld the technical aspects of work into a more humanistic and therefore more accessible composition for the uninitiated.

"Tiresias" is the most pivotal and self-revealing chapter in the book on Levi's thoughts about the differences and similarities between artists and scientists and his doubts about his own artistic abilities. Levi interjects into the listener's account of Tiresias, the blind Greek soothsayer who struggles against the gods, his feelings about his own superhuman struggle for survival in the concentration camp, which, he states, "had changed my condition, giving me a strange power of speech" (52). Moreover, it initiated his struggle to find his expressive voice while being faithful to his profession as a chemist. Levi, who is the listener, is quick to point out that Faussone has not been true to his own stated criteria for a well-told story. The rigger lacks the temperament to hone, burr, grind, and hammer the words into an art form. Being self-focused, he lacks objectivity and tells his stories in such a way as to glorify his own image. He is intolerant of correction from his listener, and he therefore creates not a dialogue but a monologue that "tends to be gray" (46), without much impact.[4]

Faussone admits that speaking about his life has not come easily. In his silences we find his listener acknowledging the power of the absence of words. Intrigued that the listener finds his stories worth recording, Faussone lets his guard down, as though something "had broken through his armor of reserve" (46). Certainly Levi constantly questions his own worthiness to function in the capacity of witness, but in this book he has breached the wall of miscommunication; his reserve is replaced by a gentle new playfulness that makes his thoughts more comprehensible. As Faussone loosens up, so does his listener, and we are allowed to be party to Levi's ideas on the importance of writing. Previously it was his part-time profession, but with this book it has become his central concern, as the reader learns near the book's end. This choice is not made without ambivalence, however, and signs of Levi's doubt are found in Faussone's admission that there "are times when a man loses even his will to work" (47), an occurrence that would definitely cause anxiety for Levi. Invariably, he says, we take "days when everything goes wrong" (47) as proof of our inadequacy. This leads us to question our purpose in life, and it reawakens Levi's guilt over being a survivor.

Levi is also troubled by the sense that no matter how hard we may try to succeed by the rules, all around us we see the rules broken and the outcome of our work and our purpose in life beyond our control. The frustration and helplessness produced by this lack of personal control lead to a feeling of self-defeat and hopelessness. For a writer, this hopelessness is exacerbated by the difficulty of evaluating one's talent. In science and technology, there are concrete measures of one's work. Levi longs for the security of the measurable, the truth in science that exists in the relative objectivity of its interpretation. Literature thrives, conversely, on the variety of interpretations it allows. Despite this difference, though, art and science must lean heavily on each other to be complete. The attempt to separate them can drive creative people in both the arts and the sciences crazy. Further, without trying both, as is pointed out in the "Tiresias" analogy, one is in no position to discuss the merits of the issue. Levi knows that art and science cannot be mutually exclusive, and he points to this through the agreement of Faussone and the listener on the positive things they have in common. Whether in words or in structures, both create something that is likely to outlive the maker and be of use to many. This expresses Levi's reaffirmation of his special ability to survive and to tell.

In "Cloistered" there are further references to the Holocaust and the impact on the individual of the loss of freedom it brought about. On the surface, because of the technical knowledge displayed by the author through Faussone's character, the story seems to be a straightforward account of an attempt to install a truss tower to support a distillation plant. At a deeper level, however, Levi examines one's innate fear of losing one's freedom.

In Faussone's opening comment, in one of the previously noted instances in which Levi propels the reader directly into the action, it is obvious that the conversation between the storyteller and the listener is centered on writing about the Holocaust. The choice of the title of this chapter is interesting in that *cloistered* implies a protected environment, whereas the environment in which Faussone is working, he tells us, is anything but hospitable and protective. In fact, he describes his job as worse than being in prison. In Faussone's comment that "nowadays, to end up in jail, you really have to do something big" (14), Levi alludes to the irrationality of the incarceration of the Jews though they were innocent of any crime. Faussone confesses that he lacks the fortitude to survive the removal of his freedom. At the end of the chapter, in fact, he expresses a distinct feeling of malaise about being in any kind of enclosed environment where he is not in control of his own freedom. Faussone echoes Levi's realization of how valuable freedom is, something about which he has written at length in the chapter "Gold" in *The Periodic Table,* where he recounts his capture and imprisonment for his activities as a partisan preceding his deportation to Auschwitz.

Faussone always speaks in humanizing terms about his work, as if anything he supervises becomes a living being. This reflects the notion that the one who performs work with love sees it as a creation and thus an extension of the self. Levi has Faussone talk this way to make a point about how different work was at Auschwitz, where the lack of respect for the human being found its counterpart in the lack of pride most prisoners took in doing the work imposed on them. With Faussone, work is synonymous with deep personal pride. When something goes wrong in the course of an installation, Levi describes the inanimate machinery in the language of human reaction: in "Cloistered," for example, the plant project becomes "sick" and is like "somebody . . . running a fever and . . . raving" (21). Because Levi considers the rig structure a technological instrument that can be construed, through the functions it will be capable of performing, as having intelligence, it is like "a person in pain, who can't talk" (23). This analogy is also in keeping with Levi's fear that his voice as a witness will fall on deaf ears.

The workmen associated with the plant's construction begin to react to the machinery as they would to a sick person, or, taking a more global view, to a sick society. The workers' eventual denial of the malfunction of the plant, which they perceive to be a judgment of their competence, mirrors the denial that existed during the Holocaust. Further, once the "illness" has been diagnosed and is considered mortal, a "funeral" is necessary to hide the monumental human error that caused the malfunction. Thus the "corpse" cannot repeatedly come back to haunt those responsible for the error. The analogy here is also clear. The Lager played a crucial role in preserving the Nazis' image as a "master race" in history.

There is similar personification in "The Bridge," in which there is guilt in the wake of a disaster as there is "when a person dies, and afterward everybody says they saw it coming" (118). Through Faussone's accounts of how installations go awry, Levi demonstrates how people deny or distort reality or even create fantasies because of fear, a desire to believe in something, or their need for a sense of security. Strongly believing that our ability to work well is influenced by the freedom in which we work, he demonstrates the threat posed to self-esteem by the necessity of working in circumstances beyond our control. The situation becomes even worse when the cause of the flawed work circumstances cannot be identified. Thus Levi describes our delicate emotions, including guilt, and scratches the veneer that precariously shields us from knowledge of our imperfections and provides a basis for our belief in our acceptability.

In two other chapters, "With Malice Aforethought" and "The Bold Girl," the author examines the ability of those not in power to exert control on a system structured by those who are in power. In "Malice" he speaks of collective power, while in "Bold Girl" he describes power as it is experienced between individuals. In the first of these chapters Faussone is confronted with a master-slave relationship in what he implies is a country that represses its work force. At the center of the controversy is the master, Faussone's boss, who, despite his progressive demeanor, denies his workers' requests to have their food cooked in the way stipulated by their religion. The workers' strikes are unsuccessful, and finally they perform a voodoo-like ceremony that, according to the boss's family, brings about the man's death. The story asks the question whether the collective power of a group is such that it can induce, within a structured system, a benevolent or malevolent action. In this case, it asks specifically whether the underdog can overcome its master in a culture insensitive to the religious beliefs of those who play an integral part in contributing to its leader's success. It also examines the impact on the inhabitants of an oppressive culture in which laws are arbitrary and subject to change on whim. When the dispute over the boss's death is submitted to resolution within the system, the conclusion we draw is that the continuation of an argument about who has power is much more important to the existence of our social structure than the argument's resolution would be.[5] This is a pessimistic outlook on life and the world and a perceptive observation on Levi's own experiences.

In "Bold Girl" the balance of power between man and woman and between boss and worker is tenuous; it requires a clear understanding of who has power and responsibility over which aspects of the relationship. Reiterating that the freedom to perform one's work is the key to satisfaction, Faussone takes issue with bosses who cannot delegate authority or cannot resist meddling if they have tried to do so, though they may not know anything about the work being performed. He seeks similar clarity in personal relationships but appears to find the greatest satisfaction not in intimacy itself but in achieving an understanding that allows a relationship to include intimacy. In Faussone's statement "You're quite a guy, making me tell all these stories that, except for you, I've never told anybody" (45), Levi reveals that all relationships, including that of the teller and listener in this story, benefit from a genuine attempt to clarify the roles of the players.

Levi continues his study of human nature in "The Helper." Here he compares the effect of personal commitment (or lack thereof) on the completion of a job to the more instinctive commitment of animals to humans. An ape appears on the work site, evidently separated from his pack because an older, domineering male has prevented any interaction between him and the female apes. Faussone, who also finds himself closed off from female companionship, slips into a "friendship" with this animal more easily than he might with any of his coworkers. A mutual loneliness has brought about a bond between the man and the ape. Faussone can feel empathy for the animal, and this empathy comes through in such a way that the listener feels it too, as do readers of the story.

The ape repeats the actions of the workers. After watching Faussone perform test runs with a derrick apparatus, one night he plays with all its controls, wreaking havoc with the newly finished construction and thus turning humans' work into a monkey's jungle gym. Because Faussone so enjoys the monkey's exuberance and shrewdness, especially when compared to his coworkers' lack of pride and interest in what they are doing, he is willing to take full responsibility for the incident. Levi seems to believe that in some cases animals are smarter than people, more daring and inquisitive, and sometimes even better friends. With the destruction of the rig, whether on purpose or as a result of simple animal instinct, Levi may be suggesting that the work of humans' higher intelligence can often be destroyed by less intelligent but more instinctual actions. This highlights the point that human beings' intelligence is often used more for destructive purposes than for constructive ones.[6]

In "Offshore" and "Beating Copper," Levi allows himself, through Faussone's memory of his father, to reminisce in a rare display of nostalgia about his own father. In addition, he evokes further philosophical thought about the nature of the written word, which he believes can create a fantasy that reality may then shatter. This becomes clear when Faussone says that he has "begun to lose faith in the printed page" (54) because the Alaska where he had worked was in no way similar to the one he had imagined through his reading of Jack London's works.[7] It is also interesting to find Levi admitting, through Faussone, to his inability to be inactive—which is to say, unproductive. Faussone and Levi will take on assignments just to keep busy. It is as though any interruption of the creative process were dangerous to the success of his narrative. Realizing that Faussone is getting wrapped up in the story he is telling, Levi, as the listener, remarks that it is best to let him go on; otherwise he would lose the thread of the tale. (Levi ought to know this well, since, in *Survival in Auschwitz*, it is he who benefits from Jean Pikolo's similar encouragement to go on with the recitation of Dante's "Canto of Ulysses.") Faussone's suitcase is always packed and ready to go. Perhaps this is Levi's expression of his own need to be prepared for whatever creative urge may come his way.

In the last three chapters of the book, "Anchovies I," "Anchovies II," and, between them, the poignant "The Aunts," Levi describes his decision at age fifty-five to relinquish his work in chemistry and devote himself fully to his writing. He is now prepared to take on this responsibility of telling stories, drawn from his own experiences and from what others have shared with him. It is interesting that at this time Levi asks Faussone for permission—and gets it— to retell his stories in a book. This genesis is in stark contrast to that of his previous works, which evolved from his compelling need to create them and involved no other person of whom he would need to make such a request. In these final chapters, Levi reveals himself to Faussone, calling himself a "rigger-chemist" (143, 145). He draws the comparison between himself and the rigger by explaining how his work is similar to Faussone's: the rigger creates things, and puts them together, on a grand scale with very tangible results; Levi deals at the most microscopic level but he too creates tangible if often unpredictable results. Levi's encounter with Faussone's aunts demonstrates fully his thoughts about how people can spend time together without making real contact. Such encounters often resembles a chemical reaction, with attractions and repulsions, "divergence and polarization" (156). As functional objects, he points out, human beings are less than perfect, and often contradictory. In "The Bridge," however, Faussone speaks of the joy he experiences in building bridges because they stretch the boundaries of life and facilitate communication. Levi also perceives himself as a synthesizer, who, through creative expression, brings together science and art, understanding that in life there is nothing simple and that the results of our efforts are often less than perfect. For Faussone's father, "when his work ended, everything ended" (86). If we consider how Primo Levi's life ended, in an untimely and violent fashion, maybe the same can be said for him.

The Monkey's Wrench does presage a significant transition for Levi. Central to the book's closing paragraph is his difficult final decision to leave chemistry and pursue his writing full-time. Faussone's recommendation that Levi stay at his job because he is very good at it confirms to Levi that his proficiency no longer provides him full gratification. It is time to move on and seek more rewarding challenges elsewhere.

The subthemes of connection and growth and Levi's further acceptance of the powerful effects of his heritage, hinted at in this book's poignant disclosures about Faussone and his father and, by extension, about Levi and his own father, demonstrate the author's increasing clarity regarding his Jewishness. They also point to the positive attributes of manual and intellectual quests and to Levi's need to pursue his creative calling. As Levi continues to focus on the learning that occurs through experiencing, he pulls himself closer to the intellectual values of his own father, who had his suits made with extra-large pockets so he could carry books in them. The conclusion to be drawn from this is that often what we refuse from our parents when we are young we end up learning later, sometimes under harsher conditions. Only then do we understand parental love and respect. Levi's reconciliation with his father's intellectual inclinations demonstrates his acknowledgment that, as parents attempt to protect their children from the pains inherent in life, so do children reject their parents, because each generation must learn from its own experiences. Levi explains to Faussone that "certain feats you have to perform in order to understand them" (64). In the struggle to develop our own individuality, we face the difficult task of separating ourselves from our parents. And to allow us to grow, they must find a way to separate themselves from us. This calls to mind Levi's own struggle over the intermingling of his professions as chemist and writer.

This process of separation raises the issue of the continuity of culture between generations, the transmission of knowledge, belief, and family history, which can create a generation gap as the ephemeral is juxtaposed upon what is lasting. Levi realizes that one must make decisions and commitments by which to live and be remembered by others. With this work he does that. The need he feels for continuity causes him not only to cement his relationship with the past but to leave for the future something of himself that is unique.

In the chapter "Offshore," Faussone interprets Compton's fatherly behavior as the man's constant, annoying attempt to impose his beliefs on others. In brushing Compton off, Faussone not only exemplifies the child's rebellion against the adult's attempt to transmit life experiences but also demonstrates the refusal of one human being to accept another, an action that has spawned individual and collective rebellion in many historical contexts. Levi reaches into his past to recall his personal rebellion present in his love-hate relationship with his chosen profession and his family and in his struggle for survival. This is part of the growth process, which results in greater knowledge of oneself, one's work, one's relationship to others, and one's origins. As he assesses his life in these terms, Levi is impelled to make a major change to insure that he can meet his responsibility to himself and to others as a survivor.

Notes

1. Among the works of this genre in Italy, Paolo Volponi's *Memoriale* (Turin: Einaudi, 1981) deserves particular attention.

2. *The Monkey's Wrench,* trans. William Weaver (New York: Summit Books, 1986), 35. Further references will be noted parenthetically in the text. In "Nickel," in *The Periodic Table,* Levi writes that people enjoy telling him stories because he is a good listener. He claims that the absence of good listeners is the main reason there are so few good writers. On this topic see his essay "On Obscure Writing" in *Other People's Trades* (169–75).

3. Significantly, German is not among them. Faussone does not hide his indifference, if not dislike, toward Germany.

4. At other times Levi uses the color gray for positive effects. It can be construed in the best sense when it is a reflection of a story's physical setting or scenery, used to reinforce the writer's message, such as in scenic descriptions in *The Reawakening* and *If Not Now, When?*

5. The activity of ongoing argument is also alluded to in the chapter " The Bridge."

6. This is one of the central points he makes in his book *Storie naturali.*

7. Jack London (1876–1916) was a reporter and a writer of short stories, novels, articles, and poetry. *The Call of the Wild* (1903) is generally considered his best work. *The Strength of the Strong* (1913) and *The Abysmal Brute* (1913) are also among his better-known works.

CHAPTER FIVE

If Not Now, When?

(*Se non ora, quando?*)

S*e non ora, quando?* (*If Not Now, When?*), published by Einaudi in 1982, is Levi's tribute to his Eastern European Jewish brothers and sisters. Written perhaps as an expression of his abiding regret, if not shame, for not knowing more about his own Jewishness, it celebrates the strength, spirit, and resourcefulness of the Jews who fought tenaciously for survival during and immediately after the Holocaust. While raising issues of morality, choice, and the responsibility of one human being for the welfare of another, the interrogatory form of the book's title expresses Levi's frustration at not being able to make sense of the Holocaust. It also signals his deep concern that no one has produced a document that sufficiently describes the effects of the Holocaust on humanity, and perhaps no one ever will.

Levi derives the inspiration for this story partly from reports he garnered after the war about a Yiddish-speaking group of partisans.[1] It comes too from an episode that is told near the end of *The Reawakening,* the book that may be considered this work's direct antecedent since it too recounts the pilgrimage through Central Europe of a group of prisoners, Levi among them, who were liberated from Auschwitz in early 1945. The episode is the one in which a group of young Jews attach a car to the train headed toward Italy, where they board a boat to Israel. Levi states in a note at the end of *If Not Now, When?* that it was his intention not to reproduce a true story but rather to trace an imaginary itinerary of a group of courageous and earthy men and women who have been hardened, but not humiliated or defeated, by years of repression and suffering. These are the survivors of a race struck at its deepest roots by Nazism, men and women whose existence was little known and whose culture was little understood by Levi and many of his countrymen. This partisan group, which Levi clearly conceives as a composite representation of the Jewish race, endured the last years of the Second World War in the eastern sector of Europe, in territory under constant dispute between the Germans and the Russians.

Written during the same period in which Levi was writing *The Drowned and the Saved, If Not Now, When?* also appears to be his attempt to extricate himself from an encroaching sense of emptiness that is revealed particularly in a section of *The Drowned and the Saved* entitled "Stereotypes." In that chapter he attempts to clarify some reasons the Jews did not and could not rebel against their captors. The tenacity of Levi's partisan characters and the driven quality of their acts mirror Levi's own need to come to terms with the ultimate moral failure of a large part of humankind. These are people who retained their dignity in the midst of upheaval. They are characters who fulfill Levi's need for rebirth, reintegration, and the recreation of his own identity after it was so largely negated by his experience during the Holocaust. In his theme of return, he incorporates a return to his Jewishness, which has become an integral part of his survival and which enables him and his characters to return to their homeland, Italy. The book is among several challenges Levi has raised to the world to confront the Holocaust, now and forever, fully realizing that complete understanding of such an event is impossible and that the chance of even a limited understanding is fading with time. To those who have questioned the behavior of the Jews during the Holocaust, this tale of collective and individual heroism and resistance is a powerful response. It is a story about bravery and resilience.

Levi admits that the assimilation of the Italian Jews into Italy's cultural, economic, and political environment left him with little knowledge about his own race. Exalting the thoughts and actions of the characters in this book and the ease with which they meld into cohesive units of human survival, he weighs his own discomfort about his "un-Jewishness" and his lack of facility with Yiddish. The thoughts and conversations of his characters continually reflect an interest in what characteristics identify one as Jewish, and Levi also expresses frequent concern about the stereotyping of all races and cultures. In previous works he has detailed his discomfort, if not embarrassment, about his inability to speak Yiddish. This set him apart in the *Lager,* or prison camp, and invited the distrust of other Jews there. It created disbelief about his background that resulted in his rejection by his fellows as a Jew, and harsher yet, as a man. Vividly and accurately describing the personalities, actions, and accomplishments of his partisan characters, he often touches upon the ability to speak Yiddish as he reconstitutes and affirms his connection with his own Jewishness. By the time he writes this work, he has obviously learned a great deal. As he states in an interview, "The problem of language . . . became uppermost in . . . *If Not Now, When?*"[2] He concedes difficulty in recreating in written Italian conversations that take place in Polish, Russian, and Yiddish, particularly as he knew neither Polish nor Russian and only a few Yiddish words. This deficiency motivated him to study Yiddish, and he did so in earnest for eight months.[3] He implies in his later reflections about language a conciliatory change of heart from his original resentment, which he discussed in *Survival in Auschwitz,* of the debasement that occurred in all the languages spoken in the prison camps and eventually produced a Lager language or, more accurately, Lagerjargon.[4] While emotionally he does not accept the accusation that he cannot be Jewish unless he speaks Yiddish,[5] he feels a moral commitment to learn it now, specifically for communicating with this writing with his Jewish brothers and sisters everywhere.

The action of *If Not Now, When?* takes place over a two-year period between the summers of 1943 and 1945. Levi's use of time spans rather than words for chapter titles gives the reader a sense of emphasis on time and also timelessness. The first paragraphs evoke a feeling of sensory deprivation that comes from not knowing what time it is. This could be an immediate, literal time Levi describes in recounting how the town of Strelka came to have no working clocks, or it could be eternal time, which resembles a primeval, nebulous state out of which life is created. From this timelessness, Levi begins the journey back to the real world.

Describing the series of events that left the village of Strelka "without any time," Levi's protagonist, Mendel, visualizes his village as the original Garden of Eden and comments about the harmony that existed there before the German intrusion. In his rhetorical comment that "God made the Germans: and why did he make them? Or why did he allow Satan to make them?," Mendel is obviously attributing the village's figurative fall from grace to the Germans.[6] Mendel, who was spared when his wife and his neighbors were herded to the edge of a pit and shot, can be identified as Levi, and he stands for the few survivors. The name Mendel, short for Menachem, meaning "consoler," may have been chosen by Levi also to represent his own compulsion, fueled by ongoing guilt and sorrow, to speak for those who can no longer speak for themselves. Responsible for keeping their pain, loss, and destruction before the world, Levi says through Mendel's statement "But I've never consoled anybody" (21) that he has been ultimately unsuccessful in that responsibility.

Mendel is a simple yet intelligent man who has discovered the age-old truth that freedom without structure or purpose can be its own prison. Tired of fighting, and having lost his family and friends, he "no longer felt in his heart the vigor of the young man and soldier, but only weariness, emptiness, and a yearning for . . . nothingness" (38). A watchmaker before the war, he served as an artilleryman in the Russian army but was abandoned or lost his way after a battle in July 1943. He explains to Leonid, another refugee whom he has just met in the woods, that "war . . . most of all is a big confusion, on the field and in people's heads: half the time you can't even figure out who's won and who's lost. The generals decide that afterwards, and the people who write the history books" (27). Individuals have little control over what happens to them, he is saying. This might be understood as Levi's first premise in support of the Jews' lack of resistance to their fate. On the other hand, Mendel's sense of pride leads him to instruct Leonid that while he is no hero, a Jew must be twice as brave around Russians if he does not wish to be tagged as a coward. Leonid, who is nineteen years old, is a bookkeeper by training. At sixteen he was imprisoned in the Lubyanka Prison in Moscow for stealing a watch. This establishes the link between Leonid and Mendel, to whom he says, somewhat jokingly, that they are "practically colleagues" (23). Unlike Mendel, who speaks openly, Leonid keeps his thoughts to himself. Together the two men exemplify Levi's desire to speak out and his simultaneous fear that the world will suffer silently and then remain silent about its suffering.

In a further conversation between Mendel and Leonid, who are evaluating each other and deciding whether to travel together, Mendel looks at Leonid's naked body as they are preparing to take a shower and asks him why he is not circumcised. Leonid, disarmed, asks Mendel how he knows he is Jewish. "A dozen rivers can't wash away the Yiddish accent" (24), Mendel responds. This response makes Levi's point, based on his disturbing personal experience, that the Yiddish language may distinguish a Jew even more than circumcision does.

Following a gentle summer rain, lyrically described as if it were occurring during the most peaceful of times, Mendel and Leonid are confronted by a young girl driving a herd of goats. Now discovered, they have no choice but to leave the hiding place in Brjansk, which has served as Mendel's shelter for several months. This vignette, juxtaposing such a harsh conclusion upon such a gentle scene, is evocative of Adam and Eve's expulsion from Eden. It also portrays a betrayal of innocence and implies that Levi's innocence about his roots has placed him beyond the borders of his homeland, once protective but now no longer so. As Mendel and Leonid set out to join a rumored band of partisans, Levi again shows his connection with his characters through his own partisan experiences in Italy.

As Mendel and Leonid head west, taking care to avoid detection and capture behind enemy lines, Levi intersperses descriptions of the scenery with descriptions of the weather and creates realistic seasonal moods to help the reader visualize the terrain, alternately hospitable and inhospitable, and temperatures that form the backdrop for the emotions and events the characters experience. Their first encounter together is with Peiami Nazimovich, an Uzbek whom Levi endows with language difficulties similar to his own struggles with Yiddish. Peiami speaks Russian "haltingly, with mistakes and with irritating slowness" (34). Also a soldier of the Red Army, he has been "missing" for more than a year and has taken up residence in a downed German plane. Mendel and Leonid, aware that the Uzbek has recognized them as Jews by their conversation in Yiddish, have to decide whether to kill him immediately or to accept his minimal hospitality. As practical men, they quickly resolve the moral issue regarding the Uzbek's life in favor of sharing a skinny rabbit he has caught, justifying their disregard of Jewish dietary laws by claiming that they are "special Jews" because they are "hungry Jews" (36). In a chess game to which the Uzbek has challenged Mendel and Leonid, Peiami plays to win. Mendel realizes that he is not just involved in a game of chess but that, to Peiami, playing and winning symbolize serving "as the champion of something or someone" (42). This can be construed as another of Levi's implications that not all Jews remained passive during the events of the Holocaust. He may be alluding to his own role as witness for those who have died. When the Uzbek eventually loses and stumbles off to sleep, Mendel and Leonid decide that it is best for them to move on. The characteristics Peiami displayed in the competition of the chess game have convinced them that this is not yet the place to be—not now; the question is still when.

Through July and August 1943, Leonid reveals more of his self-doubt, his fear of separation, and an incipient lack of motivation. He is suffering from an emotional paralysis, manifested by his lack of desire "to go someplace or do something" (45). Levi's descriptive prose at this point in the story is heavy, as if the characters are crossing through a dense, debilitating fog. Mendel equates Leonid's inaction with a watch that needs cleaning because of its clogged inner mechanisms. Such images of devitalization are repeated through descriptions of the weather, which turns the ground into a thick mud that impedes movement, and through the appearance of an old horse that Mendel and Leonid commandeer from a Ukrainian they meet on their journey. The animal is so overloaded and lethargic that it can barely move. Throughout the book, Levi emphasizes the bad reputation of the Ukrainians, who opened their doors to the Germans and thus provided them a lifeline in hostile territory.

Although Leonid's passivity disturbs Mendel, it does bring out Mendel's consoling nature and his recognition of the need for patience with a damaged soul. His gentleness is also somewhat self-serving, however, as he examines his own personality through Leonid's silences and intuits them to contain thoughts of family and of accumulated hurts and indignities. He realizes that Leonid is more virtuous than he, something that is confirmed later on by Mendel's betrayal of Leonid. For Mendel, life is a question of making choices and standing firm by them. To choose makes the choice right, and it is important to Mendel to be perceived as being in control of his own actions, especially since there is so little one can control on the broader level. Leonid, however, exposes Mendel's weakness as the pretense it is. "I don't know what I want," Leonid tells him, "but I know I don't know it. You don't know what you want, either, but you think you know" (48). The subtle difference between the two men is the ability to "admit" and the need to "pretend." In Leonid's framework, it is the former act that is more honest. For Levi, honesty and self-delusion are human characteristics that distinguish people. Leonid needles Mendel constantly, reminding him that he lies to himself in pretending to be different from and better than others.

This difference between the two men figures in an incident in which they are refused the hospitality of a village where they hope to sell the old horse and the contents of the cart it was pulling. Leonid blames their rejection on the villagers, who, having recognized them as Jews, give them eggs to salve their shame in place of a bed in which to sleep. Mendel has independently made the decision to continue looking for the partisans. He is still accustomed to functioning alone, without having his choices questioned. Leonid, resentful at not having been consulted, challenges Mendel's authority to plan without considering his wishes and threatens to leave him. The threat is transparent in its expression of Leonid's deep need to be accepted. While outlining his own good qualities, Leonid confronts and berates Mendel for acting as if he knows what he wants, for playing the hero, when his desires can be no different from Leonid's own.

In the midst of this harangue, Leonid switches from Russian to Yiddish and thus puts them on an equal footing as Jews. Mendel maintains the patience that his role as consoler requires, but he makes it clear that he has grasped the meaning of Leonid's words. Mendel also has an equally good understanding of the bookkeeper. Having tolerated being called a "nebbish, a loser, a messhuggener" (54), all insulting terms, Mendel simply reinforces his position that a man "has to weigh his choices carefully. . . . And also his words" (54). Just as the two are falling asleep, Leonid, apparently prompted by his fear that the words he has just spoken may cause Mendel to reject him and leave him behind, suddenly begins to recount his life story. Speaking tersely, with an urgency suggesting that he hopes this sharing will make amends for his previous outburst, he describes his father. When Mendel urges him to tell about his mother, however, Leonid pretends to be asleep. Just as Mendel pretends to know what he wants so that he can feel in control of his life, he senses that Leonid's pretense of sleep is this frightened man's way of controlling his need for silence. The two men have become similar.

After walking for a fortnight, Mendel and Leonid come upon a band of partisans wildly celebrating the end of the war, which they have heard about over the radio that once belonged to the plane in which Mendel and Leonid played the chess games with the Uzbek. Throughout the story, the radio is a symbol of communication and the link to information that is of crucial importance to these bands who have been cut off from normal channels of intelligence. Communication is equivalent to knowledge, and knowledge acquired by way of radio provides a certain status: "A band without a radio becomes a band of bandits" (62). When it is determined that Leonid and Mendel are Russians, not Germans, they are invited to join in. This begins a day-long interlude in which they observe the workings of this particular partisan band, a rather loosely organized group that stereotypes and humiliates Leonid and Mendel as it determines whether to allow them to remain. Eventually, despite their participation in a raid against the Germans, Leonid and Mendel are rejected. Because they are Jews, the leader believes they will hurt the group's morale.

Having heard on the radio that Mussolini has been imprisoned and the king returned to power in Italy, Mendel enters into a dialogue with himself about whether or not there are Jews in Italy. Through this device Levi underscores the degree of ignorance that existed between Eastern European and Western European Jews about each other's existence and raises again the issue of assimilation, which so removed him from a sense of his own Jewishness. "How can you imagine a Jew in a gondola or at the top of Vesuvius?" (67) Mendel asks himself. In other words, how can a Jew be Italian?

As the journey continues, Leonid's mood worsens along with the weather. Mendel fears that Leonid is not someone who can be consoled by words, just as Levi grapples with his feelings of inadequacy in bearing witness for those who died in the Holocaust, and he describes Mendel's guilt "as if he were seeing a man drown in shallow water and, since the man doesn't call for help, allowing him to drown" (69). This also implies a strong indictment of all those who accuse the Jews of not resisting, when people who were actually in a position to help did nothing.

During the fall of 1943, Leonid and Mendel come upon a new camp of partisans, the opposite of the band they have left. While the previous camp was hedonistic, raucous, and disorganized, this one is, in Mendel's description, a well organized "republic . . . a haven, a fortress" (42). The leader awaits the two men at "headquarters." In this camp everyone—man, woman, or child—has specific responsibilities, and Leonid and Mendel are welcomed. In this environment all skills and resources are put to full use. It is understood that, for the group to survive, everyone must contribute, and they must all work together. In certain respects, Levi has recreated a Lager situation here and a depiction of the

97

way the Germans would have wanted the outside world to believe it functioned. Levi's acknowledgment that the Lager was his "university" is reiterated in the words of Adam, the elderly man who is responsible for the children of the camp. Adam had at one time been sent to work on a prison farm, where he had learned which grasses are good to eat. He explains that "even from confinement some good can come" (74). Nevertheless, he admits that, along with teaching the children such helpful information, the adults must also teach them to tell lies to protect themselves from the myriad enemies surrounding them.

Levi juxtaposes current time upon timelessness once again in describing Mendel, who, upon awakening the morning after his arrival in this camp, feels he is in another world and another time. Reality quickly sets in, however, when Mendel meets Dov, the group's leader. Reflecting Levi's sentiments about the safety of his assimilated life in Italy, Dov explains that "this is the safest place a Jew can find within a radius of a thousand kilometers, but that doesn't mean the place is safe" (76). Before, in the midst of the Russians, Jews had to be twice as brave in order not to be looked upon as cowards. Now, to remain safe from the Fascists, they require a more rigorous discipline than that imposed by the Fascists themselves. Dov gives Leonid a chance to prove his allegiance and sincerity by allowing him to take on a special assignment with Mendel. This mission is a test, and the two men's success in it will secure them a position within the partisan band. This situation calls to mind Levi's interview with Dr. Pannwitz in *Survival in Auschwitz* for the position in the Lager's chemistry laboratory.

Leonid appears to accept the mission as a personal challenge, and he views it not only as a means of gaining the trust of the partisans but also as a present for Line. Described by Levi as a woman whose background and childhood endow her with many souls, Line exemplifies self-sufficiency. She was born to parents who were revolutionaries, and she has the passions of a woman, a Zionist, and a communist. Through her, Levi explores to a greater extent than in any of his other works the complex relationship between men and women. As Leonid's involvement with Line becomes more intimate, he shirks his work assignments, and his relationship with Mendel becomes more distant. When Dov confronts Mendel about Leonid's negligence of duties, Mendel, who is also attracted to Line, responds curtly by denying responsibility for Leonid's actions. Yet Mendel questions whether the idea of every man for himself is valid. He wonders if "each of us is Cain to some Abel, and slays him in the field without knowing it through the things he does to him, the things he says to him, and the things he should say to him and doesn't" (83–84). This is another denunciation of those who did nothing to stop the annihilation of the Jews, and these words will take on a poignant and powerful meaning for both men at a later point in the story.

Mendel eventually establishes a companionship with Sissl, a woman who is able to bring a sense of peace and respite to the group but whose calm demeanor is overshadowed by Line's strength of will and, at least for Mendel, her physical magnetism. "Sissl was like a palm tree in the sun; Line . . . a tangled ivy" (128). Line "knows how to want something; maybe she doesn't always know what she wants, but when she does know, she achieves it" (129). This places her in contrast to Leonid, who never knows what he wants, and to Mendel, who lies about what he wants. Mendel, the failed "consoler," sees Line as someone who rescues others, but only to serve her own purposes. To him she is a woman without concern for how her actions may affect others, who believes that each person must watch out for himself. Levi shows Line's self-directed protectionism as yet another facet of the issue of an individual's responsibility for a fellow human being. When Dov asks Mendel to intercede in the relationship between Leonid and Line, which is incurring disapproval throughout the group, Mendel has to contend with his own feelings of jealousy, shame, and internal conflict. Becoming his brother's keeper forces him to evaluate the relationships that have defined his own life. He believes that Line's strength, which some people consider overbearing, is inherently good for Leonid, whom he tends to overprotect. When he admits that he is afraid for Leonid, it is because he already intuits that he has become Cain to Leonid's Abel.

While the mission on which Mendel and Leonid are sent is accomplished, the guide charged with taking them to the position from which they can blow up a German train has deserted. Dov is philosophical about the disappearance when he says that the camp at Novoselki "wasn't a Lager" (89) and that all were free to leave. This defection is the first of several betrayals that eventually sabotage the partisan camp. On the whole, however, the group has become nonchalant about adversity. Life itself is adversity, and one just goes on.

Gedaleh, the respected partisan leader whom Mendel and Leonid are trying to join, finally invites Dov's group to go on a hunt with members of the Wehrmacht on the reappropriated lands of a local count. Dov feels it is important to participate to show the Russians that the Jews also know how to fight. While the hunt is not important, it is dangerous because it will reveal that the partisans are in the vicinity. Dov makes a calculated decision to save his better fighters for the more serious engagements and send Ber and Vadim, "two hopeless *nebbishes*" (94) who are not capable of handling such a challenge. When both men die, Dov faces the reality that he has not been his brother's keeper. The failure of the mission stains his hands with Jewish blood. Mendel, however, takes the view that the two men are perhaps better off dead than having to suffer the living hell in which the rest find themselves. Of additional concern for Dov, the participation of Ber and Vadim in the hunt with the Germans has indeed revealed the partisans' presence, and the Germans engage them in a skirmish from which only eleven partisans come out alive. Levi does not detail the fate of the ones who have perished at the hands of the Germans because it would be too appalling to recount. Dov philosophically sums up the unkind reality of their struggle: "We're fighting for three lines in the history books" (98).

The few survivors now face the full dark winter season ahead, the hardship of which recalls the long incarceration in the Lager at Auschwitz. They are caught up in feelings of endless despair. They fear that the war will last forever, that they will always be fugitives, that the snow will never stop falling, and that daybreak will never come. Everyone seems to have been destroyed in the war, not just the Jews. Human life has been cast into a hierarchical value system that tends to subvert the intrinsic good in everyone to the benefit of those in power. Values are determined by what a someone can do for someone else or by personal whim, so the oppressed become like the oppressors, seeing themselves in the image that the more powerful have created for them. No one is really different; it is simply a question of who has more strength. Levi raises the point that the greatest danger in assimilation is in unwittingly adopting the doctrines, beliefs, and actions of the very group that may become one's enemy.

The group reaffirms its desire for a new life when it decides to seek Gedaleh, a poet and musician whose art, symbolically and literally, has saved his life from the discord and destruction around him. This decision for life marks the inception of their rationale for fighting back. Killing is abhorrent to Mendel, justified only because it is the "only language [the Germans] understand" (111). Yet, while killing is horrible and contrary to one of the Ten Commandments, he feels it is the only act that can convince the Germans of his manhood. When Pavel recounts the story of how the Yeshiva students are able marksmen but are unable to shoot at their enemy when they are ordered to do so, Mendel is quick to grasp the moral point. In response to Ulybin's question to the group about how they would act in similar circumstances, Mendel answers that they are not "*yeshiva bucherim*" (116). This could mean "We can't answer the question," or it could mean "We would shoot." Mendel provides the answer after the group has sabotaged the German telephone line and taken several prisoners. One, a Ukrainian, attempts an escape. Ulybin shoots at him and wounds him in the leg, then hands his pistol to Mendel and tells him "go ahead, yeshiva bucher" (123). Mendel fires.

Pavel Yurevitch Levinski, who insists on being identified as a Jewish Russian rather than a Russian Jew (90), becomes the focus of attention when the group learns from the radio that the Italians have surrendered. He is the only one in the group familiar with Italy. He had toured there with the Moscow Jewish Theater, playing the part of the prophet Jeremiah, who foretold the deportation of the Jews to Babylon. The strong and sensible Pavel, much to the wonderment of the others at his familiarity with the area they are in and his keen sense of direction even in adverse weather, has been able to lead the group to a small hut for shelter. He is the first one out of the hut when they are discovered in it by a vanguard of Gedaleh's men, and he plays a key role in the sabotage of German lines of communication. Levi is inventive in devising and describing subversive actions, displaying a familiarity with the basics of guerrilla tactics that seems remarkable considering the short time he spent as a partisan in Italy. He chooses diversion as a theme for his whole strategy of resistance: diversion of logs on the river, diversion of supplies on trains and planes, and diversion of communication on the telephone lines. To these ends, Pavel's acting experience proves to be invaluable on several occasions. To throw the listening Germans off guard, he imitates a German army officer over the spliced telephone wire, embellishing both the name and the rank of the officer. Later he entertains his companions by reading stolen letters and amateurishly encoded messages in Russian, using a heavy German accent. On another occasion, during a great revel held when Gedaleh's band celebrates its arriving in a safe place, Pavel mocks Hitler, having him speak Yiddish instead of German. He even pokes fun at his own race, imitating a Hassidic rabbi, again playing with the juxtaposition of one language upon another to ludicrous effect. Pavel assumes throughout the book the role of communicator and interpreter for the group.

The absorbing descriptions of the diversion of the German supply planes and the Red Army officer's visit to the partisan camp allow Levi to interject observations about the vanity and superficiality of those who *have* in contrast to the ingenuity and resourcefulness of those who *have not.* There is obvious disdain for the Russian officer who has spent the recent months sleeping in a comfortable bed, with sheets and pillows. There is also disdain for the officer's wife and for what the partisans consider the irrelevant trinkets and luxuries, including chocolate Easter eggs and terra-cotta foot warmers, found among the highjacked German supplies, all "useless, mysterious, ridiculous stuff" (139). Of more use to the men would be some shaving cream to help them keep their faces clean-shaven so they would not be immediately recognizable as partisans. Levi will refer again to the frivolity suggested by these articles at the end of the story when he describes the uncomfortable evening the partisans spend at a party after they arrive in Milan.

To continue their resistance, the partisans must contend with the most numbing assaults upon their motivation and their emotions. Ulybin, Gedaleh's rival leader, is taciturn, removed, contentious, and drunk most of the time, and he finds himself in the incongruous position of being a "commander who no longer had anything to command" (136). He is now in charge of a group of damaged souls with no discernible future but a gnawing longing for homes and families that no longer exist. Exacerbating the widening space between their leader and the group is Ulybin's insulting outburst at Mendel, who took issue with him over sending two inexperienced boys to mine the barracks. Because of their German-sounding last names, Ulybin considers the Jewish partisans half German. This is another of Levi's references to the problems arising out of assimilation. For Mendel, who is affected by this blatant insult, the only retreat from such ranting is to engage in a soliloquy about bearing the sins of the world on his shoulders. In self-accusation, he details all the unlucky events for which he should not be blamed. Levi makes Mendel the Agnus Dei who feels he must deflect the group's problems and mitigate their misery.

Finally Gedaleh appears with a rifle on one shoulder and a violin in hand. Supporting the wounded Dov, who has by this time received medical attention, Gedaleh is reminiscent of Jesus leading Lazarus, risen from the dead.[7] With him is a band of ragged but dignified Jews who have suffered a great deal but have also just successfully attacked a German garrison. A mixture of survivors from various Russian communities, they are scrutinized by Ulybin's group with some misgiving. The Holocaust, however, has created strange bedfellows. The general joy and excitement communicated by Gedaleh's group ignite Ulybin's band. The Germans have received a blow from the Jews; now they too are vulnerable. A sense of renewed motivation emerges out of the despair. Because the partisans have nothing, they also have nothing to lose.

Gedaleh is clearly a leader. With his love of music and poetry, he is reminiscent of David in the Old Testament, and his group is in some ways similar to the group of young Jews that figures in the final pages of *The Reawakening*. Gedaleh's appearance, which coincides with the approach of spring in 1944, is symbolic of the reawakening of hope. His presence, however, also causes a split in allegiance between Ulybin's group, which wants to return—almost to retreat—to the Russian side, and his own, whose plan is to "survive, do the maximum damage to the Germans, and go to Palestine" (160). The story's theme that each man is free to choose his friends and his direction enables the partisans to make their final division, though not without guilt and feelings of loss or desertion. Mendel, always Levi's voice, perceives the final split as demonstrative of the basic differences between Jew and Russian, though later in the story he effects a reconciliation, or assimilation, of the races. Whatever common ground there might be, Levi views it on the level of courage; but there is a difference in how the courage is exercised, and it is based on traditional cultural grounds. The Russian's courage is stubborn and cultivated, the Jew's more instinctive and intuitive.

Even among those Jews who follow Gedaleh, however, there is disagreement about leadership. "Efficient as they were in fighting, the Gedalists were muddlers in making peaceful choices" (175). At this point Levi chooses to define exactly, through Gedaleh's performance of the song from which the book's title is derived, the underlying motives of these partisans. Composed of three verses, the song is one of resurrection and triumph. The poignant story behind it, which is told by Gedaleh, is one of bravery in the face of death. While this story is not an actual event, Levi observes at the end of the book that it could be, since it is based on the true stories of many Jewish poet-singers who met the same tragic fate as Martin Fontasch, this song's composer. The refrain, which contains the wording of the book's title, is derived from the *Pirke Avoth* (The Maxims of the Fathers), a collection of sayings of famous rabbis compiled in the second century B.C. and included in the *Talmud*. Withered by an eternal oppression, it says, the Jews have been reduced to ashes and dust. But those who have survived have the power, by their witness, to strike back. It is no longer a question of being my brother's keeper, goes the refrain, but of taking a stand for each Jew who has suffered, as if I were he. The Holocaust has given the answer about when this stand should occur.

Sung by Gedaleh during a night of celebration and revelation—and here his connection with the Biblical David becomes more obvious—the song is the real turning point in the story. After this night, there is more purpose and direction. One begins to sense the return and reintegration not only in the spirit of the partisans but in Levi's interesting choice to have them make part of the journey by train. This journey is a playful interlude, full of the exhilaration of newfound direction and resolve, and the train symbolizes a return to the current world and time. The past is not easily left behind, however. Pavel's horse, clearly a symbol of the old way of life, must be killed because it falters and injures itself on entering the new world of the living. In a lively exchange, Gedaleh asks Mendel, the watchmaker, to get the train started. "A locomotive isn't a clock, and a clock mender isn't a railway man" (174), Mendel warns. This is not just a statement of insecurity about his skill but a challenge to himself to come from the timelessness of Strelka, his village without clocks, into what Levi calls the inhabited world. "And a man like me isn't a commander, but he acts as a commander (175), Gedaleh retorts, in an exhortation to Mendel to take responsibility for his lot and begin to live again. In one joyous moment of revenge, after arriving in the town of Sarny, Gedaleh and Mendel set the train on a crash course, leaping from it as Mendel murmurs the blessing of miracles. The band is on its way back.

Now that the partisans have reentered the mainstream of life, they have many things to relearn, reevaluate, and reconstruct. The summer months of 1944 bring the group into direct confrontation with a world that has been turned upside down. It is out of synchronization with itself and with its inhabitants. Some of the partisans experience the joy of turning their thoughts from survival back to living, with all of its attendant emotions. At least for the moment, they can relegate the treacheries of life to another time and place. But for others, such as Leonid, whose emotions have been suppressed too long, the newfound freedom is an intolerable burden. The reader is reminded of Levi's previous observation about the prisons inherent in freedom. As the partisans, Mendel and Line in particular, begin to question all dogma and all aspects of morality, they become increasingly aware that the old order cannot exist after the atrocity of the Holocaust. Even Moses "wouldn't think twice about changing the laws," they observe. "Especially if he had seen the things we have" (185). The Talmud, the Jew's most respected book of laws, comes under considerable questioning, particularly the dietary laws and the instruction on women's place in society. Line speaks in defense of women, calling the Mosaic position about men and women reactionary and deriding the idea that a man can own a woman though the reverse is unacceptable. Levi uses this discussion to point out that every culture develops laws that reflect its idealized point of view. Line proposes her idea that love before marriage is free, and marriage is a pact in which two people belong to each other out of respect. Her position clearly answers any question the reader may have later about how she is able to deceive Leonid: they are not married, and he does not own her.

Pavel tells a Talmudic story about chimney sweeps that reveals Levi's acquired knowledge of his own religion and demonstrates the Jewish knack for viewing apparently all aspects of a situation and then coming up with another that has not yet been considered. The story shows that we have a tendency to see ourselves only as others see us; we have no clear idea who we really are because we do not take time to understand ourselves. We also do not take time to understand others, and this creates the topsy-turvy state of the world's affairs. To become a real Jew, Gedaleh counsels, "learn Yiddish . . . and get yourself circumcised" (190). These two criteria continue to have significant and constant bearing on Levi's struggle to recognize himself in the context of his Jewish heritage.

In an atmosphere of renewed hope and liberation, following the discussion about the freedom of men and women together, Mendel experiences a strong yet guilty desire for a woman who can reawaken his passions. His craving is rebuffed in sleep by Sissl, and his semisomnolent thoughts are disturbed by images of his wife and his former life. It is only Line—strong, assertive, and of the present—who can satisfy his lust. Mendel's conscience subsumes his momentary guilt about what he is doing, relegating both Leonid and Sissl, his gentle, quiet companion for several months, into the same timelessness to which he has relegated Rivka, his dead wife. In the repeated invocation of Rivka's memory at moments of strong emotion or important decisions, Mendel's guilt emerges, reflecting not only his reaction to being the survivor but also Levi's hope that memory will in some way play a part in keeping the Holocaust before us. Physical love, however, is for the present. Line, asleep next to Leonid, responds to Mendel's awakening by touching his badly shaven face and the scar on his forehead. When she has removed her army clothing, Mendel discovers her vibrant and challenging spirit in her body, with which he can communicate. In physical love there is a language with all the beauty and pitfalls of spoken languages, and the day's first light reveals the pitfalls. Mendel faces the irrevocability of his action as well as an age-old emotional dilemma. He has created no real bond with Line, and he has betrayed three human beings: Sissl, Rivka, and Leonid, his brother in misfortune.

Leonid becomes suicidal, and Gedaleh and the rest of the group's leaders respond to his bizarre behavior with tolerance. In the past, any action that might compromise the safety of the group, as Leonid's behavior does, would be dealt with expediently and might even result in the perpetrator's death. With Leonid, however, the group is willing to show compassion. The partisans handle his reactions to his betrayal in a more humane way, consonant with the more rational world they are now seeking. There is obviously an understanding that Leonid's behavior is not unprovoked; and his fellows realize not only that Leonid is, as Mendel had called him earlier, "a watch clogged with dust" (206) but that they are all "broken beyond repair" (206). They know how to handle Leonid when they receive a message that the inmates in a nearby prison camp would stage an uprising if they could count on support from the outside. Gedaleh, using the traditional partisan test to allow Leonid to restore his honor among them, chooses Leonid to accompany him and several others because "Leonid has to fight. He needs it the way he needs bread, and the air he breathes" (219). Mendel and Line, haunted by their guilt, speak out vehemently against sending Leonid.

Having arrived too late to prevent carnage at the Lager where the prisoners are rebelling, Mendel expresses the ultimate numbness that the Holocaust produced, a "weariness of a thousand years. . . . Hopeless rage, icy, with no more fire from which to draw warmth and the will to resist. And shame and wonder" (221). For those who have died, it is too late, and those who have survived will "never be able to look one another in the eye again. For them, it'll be better to be dead" (222). This mission is Levi's answer to all those who have demeaned the Jews for not resisting. It suggests not only rebellion against the oppressors but actual support of the rebellion by Jews. On this mission of mercy, Leonid fails to heed Mendel's warning to stay under cover and dies from a single shot. He falls across the threshold of one of the remaining Lager buildings as if caught, helpless to resist, between the terrible forces that have prevailed. Line then disarms his German killer, as if this act will absolve her of her guilt for betraying him. It is also Line who, fearful that the group's act will have no meaning if it is not marked in some way, insists they leave a sign that it was their group who finally overcame the remnants of the German force staying behind to guard the Lager. Mottel writes in large Hebrew letters the phrase "And they will pay back" (226). In Hebrew it is a palindrome, which can be read right to left and left to right, creating a circularity suggestive that "all can give and all can repay" (226). Life is a never-ending circle, as Levi will reiterate at the end of the story. More poignantly, however, Mottel's large Hebrew letters are the defiant partisans' response to the infamous ARBEIT MACHT FREI sign at the doors of Auschwitz.

In the aftermath of these events, Mendel has a dream of frozen and disoriented time, guilt, and traumatic amnesia. Perhaps it is a dream common to those who have survived life-shattering events. The whole group reacts to the support raid with unease, not only because they have killed but because they have done so on the Sabbath. They speak of killing in global as well as individual terms, and, as Line remarks to Mendel, no one thinks anymore about Leonid, though he has just died. This is Levi's prevailing fear about all those who died in the Holocaust. People's refusal to succumb without a fight becomes irrelevant if their struggle is ignored or forgotten by future generations.

In the wake of so much emotional tension, the members of the band try to reestablish normal activity. Isador offers a haircut to anyone who wants one, while Gedaleh takes out his violin to play, softly, a funny song about a rabbi. Speaking quietly together, Line and Mendel can no longer contain their burden. Mendel admits that Leonid was not killed by Gedaleh's forcing him to participate in the raid or by the German who pulled the trigger. What killed Leonid was Line's and his selfish concern for their own needs rather than for the needs of their brother.

In Poland, destruction and chaos pervade the autumn months of 1945. The infrastructure of the war has disintegrated completely by this time. Levi attributes this to the "Nazi destructive genius" (236) that, with its "digging anti-tank trenches in the earth that was waiting to be plowed" (236), has rendered the earth incapable of supporting its inhabitants. The Germans have lost the war, but not before unleashing their massive enmity toward the Jews and churning the sometimes latent but often open hostility of the Eastern European countries into a maelstrom of hate, with Poland taking the brunt from all sides. Gedaleh sums it up succinctly when he says that the Germans have turned all of Europe into a Lager. Mendel perceives the destruction as a debt that grows to such an extent that no one will ever be able to repay it. Edik, the leader of the Polish Internal Army, which has taken the Gedalists into confinement, represents the most disheartening position about the war when he voices to Dov his fear that it will only lead to others.[8] Dov is more optimistic. He believes that the survivors will build a better world for the future. These two positions mirror Levi's fears and desires.

On the last stages of its voyage west, the group is aware of the fragility of freedom and the elusive quality of joy and peace. It is the nature of life that these emotions be cut short, especially for the Jews. Shortly after Mendel agrees to officiate in the marriage of Isador and White Rokhele, Levi has the group spend several days in a bunker, during which its members have ample time for introspection. In a sense, this experience is a prelude to rebirth; it is symbolic that, after it, the group emerges after it from darkness into light. But even after the group has returned to the light, Levi imbues it with what he calls an "undefined malaise . . . no longer at war, not yet at peace" (278). Breaking through a final roadblock in a stolen truck, they have made the last leap to return as Gedaleh yells to the night, "If not this way, how? And if not now, when?" (286). Levi answers the question. The right time is any time human beings struggle for their survival, their dignity, and their right to exist.

The marriage of White Rokhele and Isador serves as an affirmation of the future. But the group still bears the heavy burden of guilt for having survived when so many did not. In the words of Francine, a French pediatrician who was imprisoned at Auschwitz, "At Auschwitz dying was the rule; living was the exception" (294). Guilt over being alive is a phenomenon that Levi understands intimately. He makes the point in several of his works that while many died, nobody killed himself in the Lager; yet many who survived have killed themselves out of shame for having done so. Francine is the first person in the story who states what has actually happened in the concentration camps. She speaks about the gassings, and it is apparent that none of the partisans is aware that such an atrocity has occurred; they do not even know what *gas* means.

Francine is Westernized. Like Levi, she speaks no Yiddish; and she is fond of her native France, just as Levi is strongly attached to Italy. While Francine's revelations about the intended annihilation of the Jews have a Biblical overtone, her name is also an unmistakable reference to Dante (rare in this work), in particular to canto 5 of the *Inferno* (121–123), in which Francesca (the similarity between the names cannot be overlooked) speaks of the sorrow of looking back to happy times when one is pained and suffering. While these words are not repeated by Francine, Levi introduces them in similar form when a benevolent Russian army captain urges all of Gedaleh's confederates to share their stories with him. In the context of the Captain's solicitousness, Levi offers the cathartic Yiddish saying "It's good to tell your past troubles" (300)[9] as representative of the nurturing nature of the captain, who even speaks about wanting to write the partisans' stories so they will not be forgotten. Captain Smirnov's great interest in the group as well as certain of his idiosyncrasies lead Gedaleh and the others to suspect that he is a Jew—a Russian Jew, to recall Pavel's distinction. Why Levi chooses not to reveal Smirnov's background may be the author's implication that some people find enough comfort in assimilation to warrant hiding their racial and religious identity to preserve it. Levi is particularly sensitive to this because, though he never denied his origins, he also never felt completely at home and accepted in Italy.

The group continues its travels, stopping in Neuhaus, a town whose name has a touch of irony. If Levi chooses *Neuhaus* as a name for the town because the word means "new house," which implies a new beginning, it may indeed be another of his signals that the good and the bad in life come mixed together. While the town is a stop on the way to a new existence, there is nothing new in the prejudices exhibited by its inhabitants. In a short, violent clash with the townspeople, Pavel is beaten up, and Black Rokhele is shot and mortally wounded. She dies without speaking any last words, which suggests the possibility that no one will remain to tell about what has happened. Furthermore, in avenging her death in a harsh, quick manner, Gedaleh's cohorts sadly acknowledge, not for the first time, that they have become like their oppressors. The only mitigating consideration is that their revenge is not just for Black Rokhele but for "the account of the millions of Auschwitz" (305) about whom they have recently learned from Francine. The knowledge of this atrocity has increased their feeling of justification in the role they have chosen, but it does not keep them from tasting the bitterness of vengeance. Mendel urges that this be their last fight. Gedaleh wants them to turn their thoughts to the end of the war and to the baby soon to be born to White Rokhele. Nevertheless, they are "unprepared at the threshold of the West and peace" (306), scared and full of sad memories.

Engaging all of his persuasive talents, Gedaleh arranges the use of a railway car for their trip into Italy. The luxury of its roominess, comfort, and speed is in sharp contrast to the deprivations of the long months the partisans have spent in the open country and to the images of the cattle cars making their way to the gas chambers. During the ride, Mendel soliloquizes about his fellow travelers, shaping their individual essences into forms that he intends to carry in his memory. As the train approaches the Italian border, Gedaleh takes out his violin to play accompaniment to their crossing. The music stirs the group to dance, but the violin, forced to its limit, breaks. In a motion of sheer abandon, Gedaleh allows this instrument, which once saved his life by stopping a bullet, to fall to the side of the tracks, hoping that it will carry with it all the pain and anguish of his life to this point. He and his group are about to enter Italy and are encouraged and relieved by what they have learned about the Italians, "good people who have suffered a lot, and who know that those who suffer should be helped" (324).

The group's arrival in Milan is an ending but also a beginning. While the country has been damaged extensively by the war, it is still, unlike other places the group has recently passed through or lived in, a hospitable and civilized country whose inhabitants are not labeled as Jewish or Russian or Catholic or anything else but Italian. The partisans, though, do stand out in this civilized environment as what they are, a feisty band of survivors whose heroism and valor are yet to be celebrated or commemorated in writing. Nor do they immediately assimilate, as is obvious in Levi's description of the difficulty they have in communicating in Italian and of their discomfort at the party they attend at the invitation of the assistance center volunteer, who views them as interesting specimens to show off to her friends. Even their rough clothing sets them apart from Signora Adele's sleek, sophisticated acquaintances. Mendel's feeling at this event is that he is being used in a game beyond his comprehension, as his race has been used and abused in the incomprehensible Holocaust.

The impending birth of White Rokhele's child gives the partisans an excuse to leave the reception and go to the hospital, where, huddled together in the sterile environment, they experience the anxiety and elation of watching a new life begin. Mendel contemplates the new beginning of his own life. In preparation for the separations that must now occur, he realizes that we carry life's experience inside ourselves so that nothing is lost to us but what we do not remember, sometimes by choice. The past is carried in the arms of the present. In placing the birth of this baby on the same day the atomic bomb is dropped on Hiroshima, Levi reflects his belief that life is a cycle in which at best we struggle against oppression and at worst we become the oppressor. Either we survive or we succumb. Moreover, there is always the ominous possibility that we will not be able to choose between these options and determine our fate.

Notes

1.   Information he received from his friend Enrico Vito Finzi, who, in 1945, worked in Milan in an agency that provided assistance to refugees from Eastern Europe.

2.   Ferdinando Camon, *Conversations with Primo Levi* (Marlboro, Vt.: Marlboro Press, 1989), 64.

3.   See *Autoritratto* 67–68. Because of his sincere effort to learn Yiddish, which he studied for eight months, Levi was disappointed when, during a visit to the United States, rather than having his efforts appreciated it was instead pointed out that his Yiddish was less than accurate.

4.   Levi addresses this specifically in *The Drowned and the Saved,* as will be seen in the discussion of that book.

5.   This is evident in the chapter "Southwards" in *The Reawakening,* particularly p. 99.

6.   *If Not Now, When?* (New York: Summit Books, 1985), 19. Further references will be noted parenthetically in the text.

7.   John 11:1.

8.   The statement of Mordo Nahum in *The Reawakening* surfaces again: "War is always."

9.   It is also the epigraphic proverb that appears in *The Periodic Table.*

CHAPTER SIX

The Drowned and the Saved

(*I sommersi e i salvati*)

While Levi seems to have written *I sommersi e i salvati* (*The Drowned and the Saved*) to satisfy his need to come to terms with the Holocaust, the work may also emerge from his desire to respond to what can be perceived as a challenge posed by the Austrian political prisoner of the Holocaust Hermann Langbein, a writer whom Levi calls the historian of Auschwitz and with whom he obviously feels a tremendous affinity.[1] Langbein suggests that there has been no dispassionate analysis of the human reaction to the extremes of the Holocaust.[2]

The Drowned and the Saved, the last book Levi completed before his death, is perhaps the most psychologically incisive of all his Holocaust works. It is in several ways a continuation of *Survival in Auschwitz,* but it supersedes the more descriptive text of that first work with a greater analytical, more penetrating approach. Whereas in that first book's preface Levi stated that he was abstaining from judging the behavior of the Germans during the Nazi era, he is now ready to go beyond witnessing, as a survivor of Auschwitz, to examine the Holocaust fully, to accuse, and perhaps even to pass judgment. Here he explores complex, often ambiguous relationships between oppressor and victim, between those who died and those who survived. In penetrating essays on shame, identity, morality, power, conflict, and resistance, he reveals the quiet but powerful emotions of those who survived the Holocaust and thus bear the responsibility to speak for those who did not.

Originally published by Einaudi in 1986, *The Drowned and the Saved* is a two-hundred-page collection of intensely probing essays on the *Lager,* or prison camp, "revisited." Its title is the title of one of the chapters in *Survival in Auschwitz.* Levi interrupted the writing of *The Drowned and the Saved* to write *If Not Now, When?,* in which he also considered the lingering effects of the camp experience but which proved insufficient to satisfy his intellectual and spiritual need to recount. He thus resumes work on *The Drowned and the Saved* to address his experience again, returning from the vantage point of forty years' distance to the recurrent theme in "The Rime of the Ancient Mariner" and validating that even this much later the "agony" endures and the need to tell the "ghastly tale" engages his creative abilities. In a cogent, concise style, Levi unearths his painful past with the hope of achieving a final surcease from his struggle. "This book is drenched in memory" he realizes; "what's more, a distant memory. Thus it draws from a suspect source and must be protected against itself. . . . Furthermore, the data it contains are strongly substantiated by the imposing literature that has been formed around the theme of man submerged (or 'saved'), also through the collaboration, voluntary or not, of the culprits of that time."[3] Now he distinctly points a finger and, while hesitating to call it an open conspiracy, he is of the opinion that those in and out of the camps who could have and should have spoken against the horrors failed to live up to their moral responsibilities. They chose to ignore the tragedy by not accusing its instigators and not telling about it. He sees in their behavior an illustration of the "cowardice to which Hitlerian terror had reduced them: cowardice which became an integral part of mores and so profound as to prevent husbands from telling their wives, parents their children" (15).

Reflecting on the perverse mechanisms employed by the Nazis to debase and destroy the human personality, Levi raises in this book the much debated and perhaps still unanswered question of how much responsibility the Germans must bear for the Holocaust and what has been done to prevent such an event from recurring. Barring some unexpected occurrence in the future and taking into account other genocidal atrocities of this century, Levi contemplates that because of its technological efficiency and its harsh cruelty, history will record the Holocaust as one of the most heinous acts ever perpetrated against humanity. Unfortunately, Levi says, the experience of the Lager still has not had sufficient impact on humankind to prevent a recurrence of such a happening. Saddened and disappointed that this horror has not served as a persuasive force against the various forms of fanaticism and violence that continue to plague humankind, not least among them the possibility of a nuclear calamity, Levi advances the idea that the phenomenon continues to raise serious questions, which he addresses through the essays in this work.

While his desire to cry a warning and foster awareness provides, to paraphrase Lorenzo Mondo, the external motivation and "pedagogical" intent of the book,[4] there is a deeper, more painful and personal need that drives Levi. It is his guilt over surviving, which has become more burdensome and oppressive to him with the passing of time. Mystified and troubled that he has survived while many others have died, he finds it increasingly difficult to accept the idea that some unknown power has willed that he live so he can tell the story.[5] His agnosticism makes him skeptical, and his rational self offers him no answers. He questions his right to speak for those who cannot. How can he, who has not experienced the worst outcome of the atrocities of the camp, truly express the experiences of those who were not spared? Not having made the ultimate sacrifice, he must now make the ultimate effort to examine the evil source of the Holocaust more closely. Through this effort, he hopes to regain his confidence and be united with those on whose behalf he is speaking.

To achieve this end, along with healing and self-redemption, Levi returns to the Dante-like abyss. He understands that he must reconnect with this past horror before he can accuse, and because of his rigorous impartiality and his dislike for sweeping generalizations, he must explore the issue fully regardless of the pain this probing may cause.[6] What is important to him is that all be weighed with the dispassionate judgment Langbein found missing in previous accounts. This must begin with one's own memory, which, as Levi has stated, is the only tool the survivor has at his disposal, imperfect and unreliable as it may become with the passing of time. Having drawn these conclusions, Levi hopes that through his memories and his ability to reason, he can reawaken society to an awareness of the risks inherent in remaining oblivious to the danger signals emanating from the Holocaust. Much of what is known about the atrocities of the death camps comes from the memory of those survivors who have had the courage to speak about it. The "best historians of the Lagers emerged from among the very few who had the ability and luck to attain a privileged observatory without bowing to compromises, and the skill to tell what they saw, suffered, and did with the humility of a good chronicler" (18). Humility and refusal to compromise are the two characteristics most important to Levi in his writing and also in his life after the Holocaust. Because of the importance he places on memory as a tool, Levi begins this series of recollections with the essay "The Memory of the Offense."

"Human memory," he writes, "is a marvelous but fallacious instrument. . . . The memories which lie within us are not carved in stone; not only do they tend to become erased, as the years go by, but often they change, or even grow, by incorporating extraneous features" (23). In other words, memory plays tricks. It may be distracted by other, more powerful memories of "extreme experiences" (24) in which injury was inflicted and suffered; it therefore needs to be questioned, and its conclusions should be arrived at with skepticism.

Levi focuses on these extreme experiences in the context of the "paradoxical analogy" between oppressor and victim, both caught in the same trap—the oppressor wanting to erase the memory of perpetration to alleviate guilt and the victim wanting to escape from the remembered terror of it. Because the tormentor wants to forget, it inevitably falls to the victim to keep the memory alive long after the offense. "Anyone who has been tortured remains tortured. . . .

Anyone who has suffered torture never again will be able to be at ease in the world" (25). While the oppressor deserves punishment, no matter how one might understand the context of the actions, the victim surely deserves help and pity, because "both, faced by the indecency of the irrevocable act, need refuge and protection . . . and often for their entire lives" (25). Both Nazi perpetrators and "privileged" prisoners (the *Prominenten* discussed in the chapter " The Drowned and the Saved" in *Survival in Auschwitz*) often preferred to keep quiet to protect themselves from admitting to and thereby reexperiencing the pain and shame they felt over the moral compromises they made to survive. Perhaps retelling was too painful.

Levi insists, however, that as much as both victim and oppressor seek defense and refuge, their roles must not be confused. Further complicating the issue, the Nazis had in essence declared war on memory, as much for their followers as for their victims and the outside world. They understood that memory, susceptible to all kinds of psychological and physical influences, is neither reliable nor useful as convincing evidence. The Nazis could act with assurance, then, because even if there were survivors to tell—whether supporters or victims—evidence based on their memories would be accepted only with considerable skepticism. The pain of the memory, then, is exacerbated by the fact that no one on the outside will believe what seems unbelievable.[7] Moreover, since a large amount of documentary evidence that could have served as proof was destroyed, it became all the more difficult for any survivor to substantiate the accusation against the Nazis. Thus an additional punishment is placed on the survivor. Once again the victim suffers alone because there is little to corroborate the reason for the suffering.

Memory does, however, help the victims in one way: just as the oppressor can distort reality, so can the oppressed. But while the oppressor does so with the deceitful intention of covering up his evil deeds, the victim does so to defend himself from unbearable pain. "Anyone who lies in good faith is better off " (27), Levi writes, implying that in the irony of these specific circumstances a good lie is more acceptable than the truth. This defense mechanism may be of comfort, and it is certainly understandable, but it also elicits unease and sadness in the author because he perceives that, to deliberately create a distortion, the speaker must be in a demeaned state in which he behaves illogically. Sustained by his scientific training, Levi cannot conceive of human nature detached from the rational self, so he is saddened, although not surprised, when his close friend Alberto, upon his father's being chosen for the mass executions in the gas chamber in October 1944, falls victim to "consolatory illusions" (33). Alberto too is a scientist. Yet, in the painful reality of his father's death, he finds the objectivity of his scientific training useless and erects the very defenses he has criticized in others, believing that things in the camp are about to improve drastically and that his father will survive. Later, Alberto's mother will not accept the reality of her son's death when Levi tells her about it; she is convinced that his return has been temporarily delayed by minor obstacles.

Levi sees a transformation of the "consolatory illusions" of the victims into a "convenient reality" (27) in the case of the persecutors. He finds revolting the banality of the explanations to such questions as "Why did you do it?" and "Did you know you were committing a crime when you did?" In view of the severity of the crimes, Levi finds those who justify their actions as "simply following orders" audacious and considers it bizarre and immoral when the oppressor perceives himself as a victim. More than anything else, Levi believes these answers display dishonesty and bad faith. As time goes on, the perpetrators put their sins behind them and are totally convinced that the lie they have created for themselves is the absolute truth.

Such is the case with the former commissioner of Jewish affairs in the Vichy government, Louis Darquier de Pellepoix, whose long, undisturbed life in Spain, despite the active role he played in the deportation and death of seventy thousand Jews, offends Levi. He views Pellepoix as the epitome of those who played a role in the decimation of the Jews during the Holocaust, "someone who, accustomed to lying in public, ends by lying in private, too, to himself as well" (28). Besides questioning the accuracy of the number of Jews who died, Pellepoix has convinced himself that the gas chambers at Auschwitz were used to kill lice and that all this activity occurred after the war.

The Eichmanns and the Hesses, who defended themselves, Levi writes, on the basis that they were forced by their ingrained respect for hierarchy and nationalism into absolute obedience, completely suppressed their evil deeds by enclosing themselves in a comfortable state of amnesia. The use of euphemistic terms such as *final solution* and *special treatment* served not only to rationalize actions but also to block unpleasant memories. These terms were used not just to deceive the victims but also to hide from the German people and from some of the branches of the armed forces involved in unrelated tasks what was actually happening in the occupied territories. Whether or not these people successfully obliterated their memories remains to be evaluated and may never be fully understood. The totalitarian system in which they functioned allowed no one to act autonomously and conveniently sheltered them from remembering that they were educated before the period of the Third Reich. Their choice to join the Nazi party was motivated more by opportunism than by nationalistic enthusiasm. In their own minds, they had committed no crime. Ignorance in the outside world was bliss for the Nazis.

In "The Gray Zone," the second chapter and the longest essay in the book, Levi dissects issues that emerge from the human social need to be in a state of conflict rather than one of harmony.[8] It is a state of opposites, one he calls the We/They, Vanquished/Victor, Good Guy/Bad Guy situation, a construct by which he explores the ability of power to corrupt and tries to come to grips with the interactive, dependent nature of power itself. Within the camp, the Nazis structured a hierarchical system in which the prisoners, although always slaves of the Nazis, also became the oppressors of their fellow inmates. There were groups within groups, in other words—oppressors among victims, victims among oppressors. This intriguing and confusing situation is one not often considered in Holocaust discussions. It is the Gray Zone, the place that throve on ambiguity and compromise and encouraged the "ascent of the privileged . . . where the two camps of masters and servants both diverge and converge" (42).

The Gray Zone was a network deftly formed by the oppressor to engender submission and collaboration of the most evil sort: "establishing a bond of complicity so that they can no longer turn back" (43). The ultimate goal of this bond was to "consolidate established privilege vis-à-vis those without privilege" (43) and create a structure that, in later memory, would be unassailable. This structure was something the *Zugang,* the most recently arrived inmate, discovered as soon as he set foot into the camp. The "network of human relationships inside the Lager was not simple," Levi elucidates; "it could not be reduced to the two blocs of victims and prosecutors" (37). Unprepared as the new prisoners were, and not having any model as a base of comparison, they expected a "terrible but decipherable world" (38). They soon discovered that the world into which they had been propelled was not only terrible but also indecipherable. It was a world that disabled one's will to withstand the calculated assault. What they did not expect was the mistreatment that awaited them at the hands of other inmates. As Levi reiterates, "it is difficult to defend oneself against a blow for which one is not prepared" (38). Virtually all survivors who have written about the camp have expressed the shock of being met by unpleasantness and hostility rather than a spirit of collective nurturing that would promote survival. The hostility of the first encounter was usually followed by other acts of cruelty, by derision, pitiless pranks, and resentment. Perhaps the harsh treatment given newcomers stemmed from the sordid counteractive solidarity that is created among those who, having forged a bond from the longer period of confinement they shared, saw themselves as the "we" against all others, pointing to the possibility that the longer one survived, the better chance one had to continue surviving.

Privileged prisoners, Levi points out, were a minority in the camp but clearly in the majority among the survivors. These were prisoners selected by the Nazis to carry out duties and responsibilities in the daily operation of the camp. Selections of these prisoners were made not with the intention of singling out someone for a more fortunate circumstance. In the interest already mentioned of creating an obedient and tractable network, the Nazis duped these prisoners into becoming accomplices in their evil deeds and tainted them with their own sins. With the Nazis' permission, they developed a "corporate mentality and energetically defended their 'job' against anyone from below or above who might covet it" (44–45). By forcing the privileged prisoners to carry out their duties, especially those involving brutality and death, the Nazis alleviated their own sense of guilt. Through this means, they degraded their prisoners by a malicious process of assimilation. While there were prisoners who did not particularly mind doing this kind of dirty work—and this was especially true of the sadists and the common criminals in the camp—most others accepted this duty to improve their chances of survival. For carrying out their assignments, they received a little more food and perhaps other kinds of favoritism. Because of the high stakes involved, they performed their roles well. This situation became all the more contemptuous, at least superficially, when these privileged prisoners were Jews themselves. Here Levi has the extremely difficult task of trying to explain to the outside world—the world that prefers to have simplified (and inaccurate) explanations—how certain actions can be understood, if not justified, in context of the circumstances. Strangely, what may at first appear to be a privileged position sometimes turns out to be not privileged at all. Levi's section on the *Sonderkommados,* the euphemistically named "special squads" whose job it was to implement the exterminations, is shaded in anguished compassion. The Sonderkommando squads were made up mostly of Jews, especially at Auschwitz, where, after 1943, Jews comprised almost ninety-five percent of the population.

In conceiving and implementing the system of the squads, Levi believes, the Nazis committed their most demonic crime. It placed the onus of guilt on the victims, depicting them as traitors to their own, the stereotypical image of the betrayal of Jesus Christ. Thus the Nazis destroyed not only their captives' bodies but also their souls. Ironically, it was through this perverted process that the oppressors approached a closeness with their victims. They had succeeded in reducing the privileged prisoners to their own moral level, and at this point there could be some kind of exchange. This is illustrated by the soccer match, one of the most memorable episodes in the book, between the Nazis and the Sonderkommandos. Such interaction would have been impossible under any

117

other circumstance, but now that both had the blood of the same victims on their hands, there was more of an equality, however perverse. Now that the Nazis had turned some of their prisoners into Cains and dragged them down to their own level, they could "play together" (55). The subjugation had been accomplished.

Because of their work, this privileged group was also marked for certain death. If there was a group that the Nazis could not allow to escape, it was this one. To prevent them from telling about what they did was so important that even in the camp they were confined to special quarters. Levi defends these people against those who would accuse and condemn them. Many of the privileged prisoners were selected as soon as they got off the trains, and refusal would have resulted in their immediate execution. In contrast, a Nazi official's refusal to carry out an execution order would have resulted only in a reprimand, a transfer, or—at worst—a demotion. Furthermore, Levi adds, it should not be forgotten that there were those who did take their own lives and those who did revolt and fight back, even though they knew they would be killed.[9] "No one is authorized to judge them" (59), he states, unless one is fully familiar with all the circumstances surrounding the camp experience, and that is something that not even those who were in the camp can honestly claim, let alone those who were not. They did what they did because they too were driven by the desire to survive.

As brutal as these privileged prisoners might appear in their role, Levi adds, they had their humane moments, as illustrated by the memorable and moving incident of the girl who had miraculously survived the gas chamber and whom they attempted to save. Levi does not deny that one needed an extraordinarily hard makeup to perform as a Sonderkommando, but sometimes within even the hardest soul there can be room for pity and tenderness. The contrasting unbending Nazi attitude is demonstrated when Mushfeld, a *Schutzstaffel* (SS) man later to be hanged in Krakow, decides that the girl must die. She is a witness, and her voice must be silenced.

Chaim Rumkowski's story, the last in this chapter, shows the Nazis' ability to capitalize on the desire for power, which is depicted here as addictive. Power can render everything else secondary and can make a one blind to one's own suffering, let alone that of others. In this sense, it serves as a means of forgetting. The corruptive way it was handled by the Nazis prompted people to forget their sense of morality. The corruption that attended power went beyond the question of oppressors and oppressed, of Germans persecuting Jews. It was an integral part of human nature, and to illustrate it there could be no better example than that of Chaim Rumkowski, "the king of the Jews" (66).[10] In this troubling story within a story, Levi presents a man who sees himself as lord of the ghetto of Lodz and who is, in most instances, oblivious to the humiliations and ridicule of the Germans. In his pathetic way, this failed businessman envisions himself in the likeness of another Hitler or Mussolini as he travels about the ghetto in his carriage drawn by a skeletal nag, ruling with an iron hand and surrounded by the usual flatterers and henchmen. His vanity leads him even to have special coins made with an inscription dubbing him "der alteste Der Juden" (the elder of the Jews). He is intoxicated by the power he has been able to grasp and becomes ruthless against his fellow Jews in an environment where one is lucky to stay alive. It is presumed that he too, however, finally dies in a concentration camp, like most of the others in the ghetto.

Levi tells this story neither to be critical of Rumkowski nor to exonerate him. Once caught in the web of power, he simply followed his instincts, as the privileged inmates did; the instincts are not to be judged differently because of the place where they were exercised. Levi insists that Rumkowski and the prisoners are nothing more and nothing less than a reflection of the universal desire for social prestige. He observes that it is very easy to be "dazzled" by power and prestige and, as vulnerable as we all are to being entrapped by them, we tend to forget our "essential fragility" (69). In this sense, then, we are all creatures caught in the ghetto, and sooner or later there will always be another threatening power on the outside with which we must contend.

The essay "Shame" is an analysis of the origin of the lasting shame and guilt of the survivors, which are reinforced by a conventional thought process that tends to override the truth. The author examines the most painful emotions of many if not most of those who have survived the Lager, and he reflects on the mechanisms that enabled the perpetrators to delude themselves into a denial of the Holocaust while its survivors struggle to perpetuate its memory so that the truth might prevent a recurrence.

Contrary to what most may believe and to the romantic notion that regaining freedom brings a sensation of relief and joy, the survivors of the Lager experienced quite a different feeling: a constant and unchanging sense of anguish, a "shame of incapacity" as Levi calls it, that brings into question the survivors' morality and their actions on behalf of their fellows. Referring to one of the opening passages of his earlier book *The Reawakening,* Levi discusses the widespread similarity of reaction to the Holocaust, as exemplified by the Russian soldiers liberating Auschwitz, who reflected "the shame which the just man experiences when confronted by a crime committed by another, and he feels remorse because of its existence" (72–73). Speaking of the words he had written many years earlier, shortly after the liberation, in his initial attempts to describe survivors' and observers' reactions to the Holocaust, Levi confirms that there is nothing he would want to add, delete, or modify. His implication is that what was valid forty years ago is still valid, and it justifies his ongoing effort to keep the reality of the Holocaust before the world.

On a rational level, there is no reason for those who were imprisoned to bear any guilt or shame for any of their actions. In view of the animal-like conditions to which the prisoners had been reduced, afflicted by hunger, filth, cold, hard labor, and corporal and mental punishment, it should be hard for anyone else to blame them. Yet the feeling of shame has haunted many survivors, the author among them, perhaps even to the point of suicide. Not for the first time, Levi addresses the issue of suicide here in a remarkably straightforward manner. Taking as a point of departure the initial emotional reaction that he calls a "vague discomfort which accompanied liberation" (73), he raises the question of whether or not those who have been so devastated can feel joy. Related to this, perhaps, is the fear that, having been liberated, one may somehow have this new liberty taken away before one has been able to grasp it fully. Each survivor, Levi continues, has survived through individual resources, and each is tormented by an ongoing regret for something that he or she may have done or failed to do. In such an animal existence, which is beyond people's control, the collective morality changes. For instance, stealing something like bread from an inmate friend is justified on grounds of the dissolution of such institutions as family, country, and culture.[11] The memory of these institutions, which previously were central in determining morality, brings the prisoners immense pain because their dissolution in the camp, Levi notes, "gave us the opportunity to measure our diminishment from the outside" (75). The abject condition to which they had been reduced distanced them further from reality and sanity.

Paradoxically, the loss of morality played not so subtly upon those returning to the rational world, perhaps contributing to the high incidence of suicide among survivors, which was rare during incarceration. Levi believes this to be the case, observing that the Nazis had concocted a system so arduous that it left no time for the prisoners to contemplate suicide in the camp. Suicide is an act of choice that evolves through a thought process, and Levi suggests that the animalistic environment in the camp was not conducive to such thinking, since prisoners had too many basic needs on which to focus their physical and mental energies. Additionally, Levi proposes that suicide is the response to a deep sense of guilt about surviving that no punishment can ease. The prisoners' daily suffering in the camp should have expiated any guilt they might have had about surviving. Once they were liberated, however, they experienced a deep sense of guilt. Some survivors who had integrated themselves into the camp system found it unbearable to confront their complicity. This is a recurrent theme of Levi's. Even worse, however, was the prisoners' inability to stand united for the sake of self-preservation. Contrary to the ethic expressed in the maxim "I am my brother's keeper," Levi admits, he too looked out for his own good first. But later, affected by shame for his behavior, the survivor felt compelled to justify himself for the guilt of omission as much as that of commission.

The act of omission was unacceptable to Levi, who admits his own shame by recalling the discovery of a faucet from which he was able to draw a few drops of drinking water by manipulating it with a rock and a hammer. Crazed by thirst, he struggled to decide whether to consume all the water or to share it. His finally sharing his discovery of the water with his friend Alberto only exposed him to a more intense guilt than he might have experienced had he kept the secret to himself. Daniele, also a survivor, lets him know, some time after the fact, that he had seen both men drink and was hurt because he had been excluded. Levi admits that he can distinctly feel shame over this action, but whether his shame is justified or not, he cannot judge with any clarity. The law of survival placed self above others. It left little or no room for compassion and concern. And though there was little for which the survivors should rationally have felt shame, not only did they feel it, but it became heavier with time. Seen in retrospect, acts taken to survive reflect a breach in the wall of human solidarity. In one's own struggle to stay alive, one could ill afford to show much, if any, concern for others. Similarly, an innate sense of justice, perhaps sublimated by the circumstances, brought the realization that there were others who were dying specifically because of a commitment to human solidarity—"not despite their valor, but because of it" (83). Such was the case of "The Last One," mentioned earlier in *Survival in Auschwitz,* who is hanged because of his involvement in blowing up one of the gas chambers.

Levi maintains here and in other writings that his survival was due to nothing more than the sheer luck of not having been selected for the gas chamber. As a scientist, he can accept life as a biological fact. In these circumstances, however, death becomes almost inversely Darwinian: "The 'saved' of the Lager were not the best. . . . Preferably the worst survived, . . . that is, the fittest; the best all died" (82). The survival of the "worst" usually came at the expense of others. In other words, slyness and deceit often gave one a better probability of survival than bravery did. Understanding the implications of this regarding his own survival, Levi takes pains throughout his works about the Holocaust to clarify that he did not survive by compromising his moral values. Yet he still exhibits shame at having survived, perhaps in place of another who might have been more worthy than he and more capable of bearing witness. Thus he devotes a portion of this essay to the importance of serving as a proxy for those who perished, acknowledging that as a survivor, and therefore as the exception to the final solution envisioned by Hitler, he has not touched what he calls the "bottom," a place reserved only for those who have died, for the *Muselmanner* who will never be able to tell. These are the true victims and the only ones who have fully experienced the Lager. These are the true witnesses, and no one but they can tell the full story. With what authority, then, Levi reasons, can any survivor really speak on their behalf? No survivor knows merely by virtue of being a survivor what it was like to be dragged into that hell all the way.

This is the unpleasant, intensifying dilemma that continues to plague Levi, perhaps to the point of leading him to commit suicide. His being alive weighs on him in the form of guilt. How does any survivor justify survival, to himself and to others? Levi finds it increasingly difficult to do so and finds himself condemned to live with this guilt, heavier perhaps because his agnosticism prevents him from seeking comfort in faith. To be told by a well-meaning friend that Providence had meant for him to survive so that he could bear witness is not comforting to him. For as much as he feels he has done the best he can to bear witness to what has happened, he cannot help feeling troubled.

In quoting Donne's phrase "No man is an island," Levi points a finger at a shame of much greater proportion: the collective disavowal with which Germans mitigated their guilt. In dismissing their complicity by "deluding themselves that not seeing was a way of not knowing" (85), they succeeded in setting up a convenient screen of "willed ignorance" (86). Because of their commission or omission, millions of innocent lives were annihilated and many others psychologically destroyed. Reiterating the substance of his preface comments, Levi warns that no one can assume that a Holocaust-like tragedy will not happen again. All that is needed to allow it to happen again is to deny that it ever happened.[12] Nonetheless, Levi ends this chapter on an unusually optimistic note, commenting that in spite of much denial, there is enough remaining sense of shame to provide an "immunizational defense," an appropriately keen focus on the Holocaust. The memory of it will also bear witness.

Levi examines the possibility of a recurrence from a slightly different perspective in the fourth chapter, "Communication," in which his assertiveness reaches an emotional pitch seldom displayed elsewhere in the book. He uses this particular essay to reexamine the link between communication and survival, and he clearly unlocks for the reader the motivations behind his own need to communicate. We can now see how communication is a lifeline for the author. It is the one distinguishing characteristic between the human (outside or normal world) state of being and the animalistic (Lager) one, a state of existence that he analyses throughout his Holocaust writings. Communication is the means of reentry into the normal world and, used to bear witness, a deterrent to the recurrence of an event so devastating as the Holocaust.

Citing the attitude that was widely favored throughout the 1970s that "incommunicability" is inherent in the human condition, Levi rejects it with scorn: "To say it is impossible to communicate is false; one always can. To refuse to communicate is a failing" (89). Communication is the means through which we maintain a sense of civility and achieve mutual understanding. The ability to bear witness and to maintain civility and understanding was systematically thwarted through obstruction of cohesive verbal interaction among the prisoners. Imposed silence was in keeping with the notion that prisoners were no longer humans but animals. Ill-treated and without resort, they were subjugated by violence and abuse to a point at which speech for the purpose of communicating thought "had fallen into disuse" (91).

Performance or interaction resulting from rational communication was, of course, not something the Nazis wanted for their prisoners. In fact, Levi remembers, the rubber hose with which they were beaten was referred to as the *Dolmetscher,* the interpreter, an object that was universally comprehended without the use of words and emphasized their expendability. Communication had to be discouraged in the Lager because, being the essential means of uniting minds, thoughts, ideas, and hopes, it posed a major threat to the execution of the "final solution" envisioned by the Nazi machinery. Further, Levi defines the hierarchy that emerged as the result of one's familiarity or facility with the captors' language. This unfortunate circumstance of fate, which derides even the roots of one's origins, automatically relegated those not proficient in German to the position of barbarians.[13]

Levi, as well as many other prisoners, knew it was vital not to succumb to "incommunicability" because survival, intellectually and physically, depended on communication. Saying and understanding certain expressions often made the difference between life and death. The Germans accepted nothing other than their own language, and a very vulgar version of it at that. Levi recalls the first days in the Lager, "filled with a dreadful sound and fury signifying nothing" (93–94). Nevertheless, he continues, "foreign voices became engraved on our memories . . . the fruit of a useless and unconscious effort to carve a meaning or sense out of the senseless" (95–96), the senselessness he is still attempting to reconcile after forty years.

Many, especially among the Italians, Greeks, and Yugoslavians, lost their lives as soon they were brought to the Lager because they did not understand

German or any of the other main languages spoken in the camp: Yiddish, Polish and, later, Hungarian. To be polyglot was to have a better chance of survival. Prisoners often died because sufficient information could not be passed from one to another. If new prisoners had been able to communicate with prisoners who had been in the camp for some time, they might have been able to protect themselves from the more demanding forms of hard labor or from freezing because they had no knowledge of how to barter for a pair of shoes or additional clothing to ward off the cold.

What hybrid communication did exist, elementary but nonetheless vital, was based on a multitude of different words that, though they were devoid of any cultural value, enabled the prisoners to perform in a Pavlovian way the required daily chores and duties. These were words, to use Levi's metaphor, ingested in the same way a hungry stomach would assimilate some indigestible food. The motivation behind their use was not the need for social engagement but rather the need to function in such a way as to survive. Words acquired meanings different from their original ones. Expressions deriving from the different languages spoken among the prisoners were twisted and distorted to suit the linguistic needs of the camp. In most instances, what was being said was a mimicking of words or phrases assimilated through hearing and constant repetition, creating what Levi refers to as mechanical memory, by which, later on, he identified curses, swear words, or banalities such as "what time is it?," "Leave me alone," or "I cannot walk."

This vernacular was, in effect, a minimal and basically repulsive kind of communication, of value only in a place where all of life was lived on a minimal level. Nevertheless, it was life. Terms such as *Muselmann* came to signify weakness.[14] *Fressen,* the word applied to animal feeding, was substituted for *essen,* the term used for people.[15] The word *abhauen,* meaning a rough form of leave-taking, gives rise to one of the few amusing vignettes among all the sadder ones.[16] Levi recounts how years later, saying good-bye at a formal business meeting in Germany, with all good intentions he used this Lagerjargon expression. Realizing that it offended the people with whom he was transacting business, he politely explained its origin, adding for the reader the further somewhat ironic commentary that it was his current position and status that enabled him to "survive" this gaffe.

This contrived language, by which the Nazis reduced the current accepted one to a mix of old German used in the Prussian barracks and new expressions adopted by the SS, insured a speech with only a vague relationship to its literary norm, and this could not but offend anyone educated in proper usage.[17] But it was part of the Nazis' scheme for erecting a communication barrier against the world. It symbolized the wedge of incomprehension driven between the camp and the outside. In effect, it was a modern-day implementation of a Tower of Babel where, by creating a confusion of sounds, the Nazis denied communication at the most elementary level of linguistic expression.[18] Given the conditions surrounding Levi's exposure to these terms, it is understandable why he resented the languages from which they were drawn. He does not hide his dislike for the Polish language, and he makes no effort over time to polish and perfect his German, as is evident in his story about the use of Lagerjargon at the business meeting he attended. Showing similar contempt—and perhaps as a sign of victory—he does not have his tattoo removed, and he continues to speak German with a deliberately unrefined pronunciation. At that time, even Yiddish, a notably "Jewish" language, raised resentment in Levi. He was troubled and offended that his inability to understand and speak it made him suspect among the Eastern European Jews, who could not conceive of a Jew unable to speak Yiddish.[19]

The captors further exacerbated the prisoners' sense of alienation and loss by denying them contact with the outside world. Unlike other prisoners, the Jews were forbidden written communications such as the exchange of letters with their families and news from their countries. This made their isolation all the more painful and strengthened their perception that they were completely forgotten. Experiencing the debasement and harmful use of language in the camp brought Levi to an even greater appreciation of what it means to possess the freedom of communication. In the Lager, to accept the "eclipse" of the word signaled a "definitive indifference" toward the struggle to survive. In free society too, to accept incommunicability amounts to passive surrender to the will of others. When this will is not challenged or questioned, Levi writes, intolerance leads to reproach; censure increases ignorance; and in a grand circle, intolerance itself is increased. Herein lies the trap into which humanity falls when it fails to encourage open dialogue and accepts the premise of incommunicability. This intolerance forms the breeding ground for a future holocaust.

Thriving intolerance and fractured communication promote the "insolent logic" (106), the hateful state that condones the "useless violence" discussed by Levi in the next chapter, in which he attempts to clarify and summarize the rationale for the violence of the Third Reich. Levi admits that a certain paradox exists when violence is the by-product of an event or a deed used as a vehicle to achieve an intended goal, such as war or political assassinations.[20] The "useless" or, more accurately, "unnecessary" violence [21] of the concentration camp lacks even these excuses; it is thus horrendous and evil. The preliminary degradation and punishment of someone who was, in the case of the Lager, already marked for death were additional insults—the proverbial rubbing of salt into the open wound—that served only to heighten the sadistic delight of those inflicting the pain. This is the logic that made "unnecessary violence" a "necessary" action. It was evidently necessary for the Germans to humiliate, degrade, and insult their captives to alleviate any guilt they might have suffered from their collective participation in planned human extermination.

In a tersely written, solemn account of this humiliation, Levi illustrates how an acceptable thought process based on highly glorified German efficiency became perversely skewed when it was applied to the Lager. German efficiency, generally harmless to the populace, became an exercise in destruction through its reversed, caricatured application in the Lager. It is in this caricature that the Germans' morality "came unglued from the morality common to all times and all civilizations" (107), and the "presumed right of a superior people to subjugate or eliminate an inferior people" (115) was applied with the most despicable vengeance.

The vengeance began on the train trip to the camps. While a train trip is often symbolic of life's promise, this one was unbelievably cruel. The prisoners were transported in sealed cattle cars, often overcrowded. They were deprived of food, water, and hygienic facilities throughout the journey, which lasted four or five days. If the Germans' intent was to annihilate an entire people, Levi questions why at least the old, the sick, and the infirm were not simply left behind to die and thus spared a difficult journey that was to end in sure death anyway. He surmises that such deliberate and gratuitous malice was only a first step in the process of degradation.

The prisoners were tricked into bringing valuables and warm clothing to make life pleasanter at the next stop. One cannot but marvel that such a pretext would be necessary to appropriate the prisoners' belongings or maintain order during the fatiguing journey. Exploring further the systematic reduction of humans to an animal state, Levi inventories the methodical withdrawal of clothing, bathroom facilities, and feeding utensils upon and after the prisoners' arrival at the camp. Recording the recurrent shavings and the inspections for which the prisoners were made to remove all their clothing, he hypothesizes that these were acts of offense rather than requirements of hygiene. As in his other works, he deals with the irony of the ARBEIT MACHT FREI (work will make you free) sign at the entrance to Auschwitz, recounting the senseless, unproductive, repetitive nature of most of the work the prisoners were required to perform, which achieved little but reducing them further to an animal state. In some cases, however, a kind of professional dignity prevailed, and the resulting diligence often worked to the advantage of the captors. As Levi comments on the efficacy of long training in the work ethic, a "'job well done' is so deeply rooted as to compel one 'to do well'" (122) on any job, even those one performs for the enemy and under very adverse conditions.

Levi describes Jewish musicians who were allowed to play prohibited Aryan military marches while their fellow prisoners, in their zebra uniforms, marched at a fast pace, like puppets. Their filthy, flea-infested beds, made to the specifications of Nazi precision, were measured as a surveyor would measure the foundation of an important construction. Their shorn hair was used in the manufacture of textiles, and the ashes of their fellow Jews became swampland fill, fertilizer, and lining for the paths of the SS commando village. They had become beasts to be mercilessly eliminated. "The 'enemy' must not only die," Levi observes, but, "he must die in torment" (120). At Auschwitz, the prisoners' ultimate value was clearly implied by the scornful act of tattooing, a nullifying and offensive procedure directed at the Mosaic laws of the Jewish religion that specifically forbid this practice.[22] The tattoos served as perhaps the most lasting physical evidence of the prisoners' slave-animal status in the Lager, the most graphic historical proof of the existence of the camps and their abuses. Those who do not want others to forget wear the tattoo, as Levi says of himself, without shame, as a part of the self. It stands for an accusation to an upside-down world in which almost no one had the courage to protest in the name of humanity.

In the next chapter, "The Intellectual in Auschwitz," Levi structures a further inquiry into what physical and spiritual resources are necessary to protest and survive. He accomplishes his strongest self-assessment through a literary interaction with the work of Hans Mayer (who wrote under the pseudonym Jean Améry) about the qualities of intellectualism and its impact on survival in the Lager. Mayer, also a victim of the concentration camp, was an intellectual whose alienation from his mother tongue affected him and who subsequently committed suicide. Mayer also wrote about his Lager experiences, and it is clear that while Levi disagrees with several of the other writer's views, he has a deep respect for him. Despite their differences, he considers Mayer a potential friend because of their similar cultural backgrounds, which he discusses in the context of the Jews' long-standing assimilation in their respective countries before the enactment of the racial laws. Until these laws were promulgated, neither Levi nor Mayer had been made to feel specifically threatened or different as a Jew. Levi notes Mayer's "christianized" family and his ignorance, well into his adolescent years, of Hebrew culture.

Mayer was also ignorant of the Yiddish language, a deficiency he shared with the author. Levi's not knowing Yiddish, as has been noted, contributed directly to the other Jews' mistrust of him. Their suspicion obviously offended Levi enough for him to raise the issue here as a reference point in his examination of survival in the Lager, and he has written about it with painful remembrance in several texts, chagrined at having to prove to his fellow Jews, after all his suffering, that he too is a Jew.

Levi views Mayer as a more physically reactive person than he is himself. He attributes this to the other writer's torture at the hands of the Nazis, which, Levi believes, no doubt affected his subsequent behavior and caused him to respond to violence with violence. Levi differs with Mayer's position on violence, never having espoused it as a means of self-defense or protest. He also admires the other man's "courageous decision to leave the ivory tower and go down onto the battlefield" (136), something he himself found very difficult to do. Levi uses his and Mayer's contrasting positions on violence as a basis for measuring intellectual behavior and for considering the advantages and disadvantages of an intellectual competence in the context of survival in the Lager. Further, this contrast sheds greater understanding on why Levi felt it important to analyze "useless" violence, which, he implies, had strange effects on prisoners of a certain intellect in that its associated irrationality caused bewilderment, which in turn exacerbated their feelings of hopelessness and made it nearly impossible for them to function at a crucial minimal survival level.

Mayer, like many other intellectual prisoners, found it difficult to accept the manual labor forced on him in the camps. This placed him at tremendous risk. Levi, on the other hand, quickly understood the meaning of ARBEIT MACHT FREI.[23] In the camp, the intellectual was useless and an object of ridicule because his lack of practical skills and physical strength made him inept at hard labor and even at the simple daily barracks chores. It would have been self-endangering to refuse to work. Levi's ability to perform manual work identified him as "not intellectual enough" (133), whereas Mayer's inability to adjust to such work deprived him of dignity and therefore of identity. It left him, in Levi's words, "spiritually dead: without defenses" (128).

Levi's pragmatic sense, which is sometimes lacking in those who are intellectually endowed, helped him to learn the fundamentals of survival quickly. Rather than hold himself aloof, he understood that in the Lager he was no different from the less educated inmates and that it was useless for him to emphasize his intellectual superiority. Unlike Mayer, he adopted a flexibility of spirit that helped him avoid some of the pain and humiliation felt by intellectuals who discovered that their cultural preparation placed them at a disadvantage. It may have been Levi's pragmatic position that led Mayer to call him "a forgiver," as though by broaching the connection between violent behavior, intellect, and function for self-preservation Levi condoned what was taking place. Levi resents this accusation because his position has always been one of trying to understand, never one of forgiveness.

Schooled as Levi was to observe human behavior within the context of logic and morality, it was difficult for him to accept a reality that was both illogical and immoral and that condemned anyone who dared to ask for explanations, as the intellectual might. In a place where everything had been reduced to the most basic and savage level, reason was a useless luxury. It was generally met with scorn and physical abuse, certainly by the *Kapos,* but also by the less educated inmates. The abuse by fellow inmates was particularly traumatic for Levi because "civilized" men do not expect such cruelty from those they consider their allies. Indeed, the intellectual was more alone and isolated than the uneducated inmate because he was definitely in the minority. He was made to feel different from most of the others and had hardly anyone to turn to for comfort. This condition was all the more painful for both Levi and Mayer and those other intellectuals who entered the camp lacking spiritual faith and whose experiences there served only to further confirm their agnosticism.

Levi also draws a distinction between himself and Mayer in that Mayer's native German language eventually evolved into Lagerjargon, while Levi's native Italian remained a source of relief and pleasure for him. Mayer experienced resentment and bitterness about his distorted language, concluding (as Levi himself does in "Communication") that the bending of a language reflects the bending of mind. Mayer felt betrayed by his German-speaking fellow philosophers who, he believes, abdicated their moral responsibilities not only by failing to condemn Nazism but by actually accepting it and, with time, even praising it. They had allowed themselves to be swayed by the sweeping Hegelian notion of veneration of the state under all circumstances. The world has many monsters and it is much easier to live with them than to fight them. This was a particularly painful reality to accept, especially since it came from those whose culture was bonded to Mayer's by a common language.

Conversely, the Italian language and especially Dante's verses provided Levi with the cultural context and nurturing he so needed and sought.[24] He was more fortunate than Mayer because his was a language of which he could still be proud and on which he could rely when he felt the need to "enhance an hour" (142) in that otherwise bleak Lager environment. To keep his mind alive and healthy, Levi could escape from his situation by taking refuge in the culture and beauty of his own language. This explains why the "Canto of Ulysses" chapter he inserted at a later time in *Survival in Auschwitz* was so important to him. Mayer, on the other hand, was held captive within his own language, unable to find any solace in the desecrated version fostered by the Reich and unsuccessful at writing in French, the language he later adopted. With culture as a support, Levi could view himself in the camp as a new kind of intellectual who, unlike Mayer, drew positive signs from what appeared to be completely negative.

The definition of intellectualism is Levi's essential difference with Mayer. Mayer sees the intellectual as a person of essentially humanist philosophical and spiritual attributes, centered in abstract thought. Levi's definition, more flexible and dynamic, also includes the scientist. Stressing that his scientific training and his work as a chemist have improved his patience for assessing his environment, he cites the need as well for education beyond one's training, affirming that the Lager has been his university, a place unequaled for observation and evaluation of human behavior. Science, therefore, was and is an essential ingredient, an integral part of what constitutes an intellectual. As he notes, Leonardo, though he claimed to be a man of limited literary knowledge, was nonetheless an intellectual. There is something alive and resonant in Levi's view of an intellectual as a person who has interests beyond his daily routine, has a deep feeling for his culture, is unafraid in his struggle for self-renewal, and seeks growth and modernity. The intellectual, then, is someone who by definition cannot and must not accept death.

This point separates Levi completely from Mayer, whom Levi calls, among other things, the "theoretician of suicide" (127) and whose philosophical stance indeed seems to foreshadow such an act. Levi is uncomfortable with Mayer's static intellectual context for and obsession with death, a romanticized "odorless, ornate, and literary image" (147). Death in the Lager was a foregone conclusion, so what was left to be determined was how and when, rather than if, one was to going to die. It was a trivial, bureaucratic, daily occurrence, totally devoid of the nobility that Goethe, Petrarch, Foscolo, and other intellectual literary figures had attributed to it.[25] There was nothing to intellectualize here. Auschwitz had succeeded in removing any vestige of dignity even from death. "In the face of death, in the habit of death, the frontier between culture and lack of culture disappeared" (148). For Levi, giving in to death would have meant renouncing the struggle to survive, the right to live, and yielding to the will of the oppressors. In his youthful vigor, he found life still worth fighting for despite all the suffering. For him, purposeful action and function superseded any intellectual endeavor. To survive, he had no time to devote to death. "The aims of life are the best defense against death, and not only inside the Lager" (148), he concludes.

In the essay "Stereotypes" Levi addresses the issue of how perceptions, over time, can influence thoughts and beliefs about the Holocaust. In considering this and the public's image of how those incarcerated in the camps might have acted better, he warns of the danger of arriving at conclusions without having any real understanding of the actual circumstances, fears, or constraints in the camp environment. Using the example of the German proverb "What may not be cannot be," Levi embarks on a cogent response to some of the questions most commonly posed to the survivors: Why didn't you escape? Why didn't you fight back? Since you knew what was happening, why didn't you get away before you were captured? Levi responds to these questions with a degree of pleasure because they provide him a forum to witness, but he also notes, "Who can say that the history of human events obeys rigorous logic, patterns" (150). In speaking out, he places himself among those prisoners who are willing to talk, in contrast to those who are unable to do so because of their shame or because they are not at peace with themselves. There is, Levi adds, something cathartic and uplifting in speaking of past misfortunes. Using the Yiddish equivalent "Troubles overcome are good to tell," a sentiment that is a direct play on Dante's words in canto 5 of the *Inferno,* which tells the story of Paolo and Francesca, he reveals that for all his tribulations from not having known the Yiddish language, along the road back to the post-Holocaust world he has acquired some ability in this idiom. He seems to delight in the more positive rephrasing of Francesca's painful exposition about remembrance of sweet things in time of sorrow, even if he does play down his new knowledge by quoting it parenthetically.[26]

Placing certain events outside their proper perspective and connecting them to other incidents with which they seem to have something in common tends to render them bland and considerably alters their significance. As much as Levi admonishes against this, he sadly realizes that, as the distance in space and time increases, it will become more difficult to avoid. The passage of time after events tends to promote selective remembrance and often oversimplification of them so that they are easily relegated to "the same old story" category to which one pays less and less attention. Levi definitely regrets the apparent lack of concern for the Holocaust demonstrated by the current younger generation, particularly since his efforts to see *Survival in Auschwitz* published more broadly were stimulated by the interest that people of the postwar generation expressed in knowing more about the Holocaust.[27]

It is difficult today, forty years later, for anyone who did not go through the experience to imagine what it meant to be hungry at Auschwitz or to have had the courage to escape from Treblinka. Understandably, in trying to visualize the experience, people tend to create the kind of images they are familiar with in contemporary life. Because the "typical prisoner is seen as a man of integrity, in full possession of his physical and moral vigor" (152), the historian is constrained to clarify such inaccuracy about events of the past. This is more difficult in the case of the Holocaust since the only accounts are those of a handful of survivors, and the validity of such accounts may be questioned because those who report them may be unable to remain historically objective. These "were not 'typical prisoners,' they did not have integrity, on the contrary they were demoralized and depleted" (153).

It is absurd, however, to consider the concentration camp just another prison and those who were detained there, especially the Jews, ordinary prisoners of war. Prisoners of war are protected by international laws. The International Red Cross looked after British and American prisoners during World War II, but the Jews had no laws to protect them. For this reason, Levi believes the sociohistorical circumstances and the human conditions connected with the Holocaust must be taken into account. In essence, his point is that the questions asked about the "then" should not be measured with a "here and now" yard-stick. Those who ask questions should not do so rhetorically, and they should be open to hearing the truth, not "What may not be cannot be." The fifth-grade student who ingenuously tells Levi what he should do if he were ever taken to a camp again is a wonderful example (perhaps forgivable because of the questioner's youthful innocence) of the failure on the part of many to consider the distinctions between the stereotype and the reality.

Even if the Jews could have escaped from the camps, a virtually impos-sible feat, there was no place where they could hide. At that time Europe had travel restrictions and closed borders. The detainees were in a foreign land, despised by those inside and outside the camp. They would have been easily identifiable by their zebra uniforms, their shaved heads, and their wooden clogs. Their emaciated physical condition and their inability to speak the local lan-guage would have given them away immediately, particularly since anti-Semitic Nazi propaganda had created a negative stereotype of its own about the Jews. Harsh punishment and possibly death also awaited the inmates who were friends or mere acquaintances of the escapees. This was another cruel process for insuring a solid resistance among the prisoners. The Nazis took escape very seriously. Not only was the containment of information about the activities in the camps vital to their plans, but escape would represent a victory of the intel-lectually "inferior," thus creating a contradiction of the stereotype the Germans wanted to maintain. Simply put, escape could not be tolerated.

In addition to the misconceptions about possible escape, there was a misunderstanding, fostered by faulty historical recall, about why the Jews did not resist and fight their oppressors. Levi confirms that they did try, and at tremendous cost. He believes too that the perception that one should rebel completely ignores the emotionally demoralizing and physically incapacitating conditions in the Lager and is a further result of stereotyping.

As to why the Jews failed to leave before they were rounded up, one might say that the previously quoted German proverb—"What may not be cannot be"—was perversely and detrimentally active. An innate sense of security rendered it difficult for the Jews to believe what was actually happening, and in the presence of patent assimilation, how could a whole group of people suddenly become the enemy? Even with their atavistic acceptance of persecution, the Jews preferred to stay in what they felt was their homeland. They simply could not believe they were unsafe. This reaction is not particularly unusual; faced with a danger that may cause pain and suffering, humans have the innate ability to block sensation and emotion, fooling themselves into believing that whatever is taking place simply cannot be. As had other citizens, they too supported their country, obeyed its laws, swore to defend it, and fought for it. Some of their ancestors had died for it. It was a place in which they felt they rightfully belonged, a place where they had put down their roots and in which they had felt secure. While some did indeed leave "before,"[28] Levi acknowledges that most did not. To emigrate is always painful and not easily accomplished because one needs help from those at the destination point.[29]

More important, however, are the psychological difficulties of separation, displacement, and rebuilding. Levi compares the Jews' disbelief in events leading up to the Holocaust to conditions in Europe at the time he was writing this work. Despite the threat of nuclear attack, a threat different from that of the 1930s but of infinitely more destructive proportions, Levi asks how many have taken measures of protection by moving to safer areas such as New Zealand, Polynesia, or Antarctica? Why are they not making provisions before it is too late? Levi's overriding implication is that there always was and still is a state of "before." The more salient question might be whether there will always be an "after."

After the long and painful journey of reliving his experience of Auschwitz through writing these essays, Levi has his final word in the form of more direct confrontation through "Letters from the Germans." In this section he uses correspondence to confront the German people who, with few exceptions, demonstrated weakness and cowardice by condoning the activities of the Third Reich, either tacitly through inaction or obviously through direct participation.

More than once in the course of his literary life Levi had come face to face with his antagonists. As it turned out, this would be the last time. More than once his observations had led him directly to the German people who, in his judgment, had to bear the blame for the occurrence of the Holocaust. At a distance of some years, he was also interested in how and if the Holocaust had affected them. By focusing on the letters he has received from Germans who initially wrote to him on the publication in Germany of *Survival in Auschwitz,* he reveals in this work many of the same characteristics he had warned about. His closing this book with a discussion of the letters is significant because this epistolary exchange reflects his constant attempt to maintain open lines of communication. This is the underlying theme of his remarks in his conclusion. He now admits that though *Survival in Auschwitz* was written in Italian and for Italians, it was aimed primarily at the Germans. His revelations in that book, Levi states, were the smoking gun that called for their accountability. Though he wrote the book to gain better understanding of the Germans' behavior before and during the Holocaust, Levi does not deny his implied accusation.

Levi's apprehension at seeing this book translated into German is therefore understandable. To insure that the message was clearly and precisely imparted, he demanded and received from the publisher permission to supervise the translation closely. It was very important to him that it not distort the facts and events in any way. Fortunately, the translator achieved a faithful replication of the original version, and Levi was pleased with the results.[30] The translator was a humanist and an anti-Fascist whose sentiments had kept him insulated from the corruption of the Third Reich and its language and whose love for Italian literature led him to live and study in Italy for some time. This experience had made him particularly sensitive to the nuances of Italian. With the wider dissemination of a well-translated edition, Levi feels more secure, to use his own words, in laying all the cards on the table to see how the Germans view their past behavior. Though he is appreciative of the kind words from most of the forty or so individuals who have corresponded with him, as he says in his account, he realizes that within that group, along with those who appear to be truly remorseful, there are others who try to exculpate themselves by offering excuses and explanations of dubious validity.

Questionable, for example, are the explanations forwarded by Doctor T. H. of Hamburg, whom Levi sees as a typical example of the German middle class. He not only refuses any responsibility for Hitler's rise to power but believes he and the entire German nation were betrayed by this evil man. He finds it difficult, if not impossible, to believe that the Germans, who had always been friends of the Jews, could have hated and persecuted them during the Nazi period. This man's hypocrisy is further heightened when he states that even if more had been known about the atrocities at the time, it would have been impossible to show opposition in a totalitarian state. Levi finds these explanations despicable, and they make him angry because he sees in them the typical reasons given by those who refuse to acknowledge that Hitler left no doubt what he stood for even before he came to power. His book *Mein Kampf* made his views incontestable. As for the inability to act in a totalitarian state, Levi points out that Italy was burdened with a similar political situation, but this did not stop many Italian citizens from manifesting their solidarity with the oppressed, and some risked their lives in doing so.

This first letter is counterbalanced by the letters of L. I., the librarian in Westphalia, and W. G., the historian and sociologist from Brema. Both express a deep, somewhat excessive sense of shame. The first regrets not having done enough to comfort and protect the Jews and is now expiating her guilt by helping with the restoration of bombed cities. The second feels shame simply for being German, even though he should not share in the blame because he was too young at the time to protest. Similar sentiments are expressed by W. A., a physician from Würtemberg, who considers Levi's book a help for having given him an orientation and having made him realize and admit that he is an accomplice of those who did violence to "the destiny" of the author and other victims.

Other letters, such as the one written by M. S. of Frankfurt and that of I. J. of Stuttgart, seek additional explanations and justifications or point to the difficulty of getting the message across. M. S. questions whether the ones who committed those crimes should be called "true" Germans, while I. J. writes that, since the average citizen still finds it difficult to believe fellow "Western Christians" could have committed such evil crimes, the Germans need to gather up a great deal of civic courage to read and accept Levi's book.

The correspondence with H. L. and Hety S. of Wiesbaden offers more significant insight. Levi is much more familiar with these two because he has exchanged many letters with them and established a closer relationship with them, especially the latter. H. L., a student from Bavaria, can be regarded as representative of the German postwar generation. A part of her feels some guilt for what the Germans have done. While she condemns, she also promises that her generation will make amends and prevent it from happening again. On the other hand, she also finds it difficult to condemn her contemporaries for what Hitler did. In this she is like Dr. T. H. She too fails to see that to admit Hitler betrayed the Germans is tantamount to denying that they knew what he stood for, something that Levi finds totally unacceptable, as he has expressed in his angry response to Dr. T. H.'s letter.

H. L. seems to have fallen into the trap of contradictions. While she may mean well, she lacks the steadfastness of her convictions. For example, she fails to see the contradictions in stating that she is generally satisfied with her education even though she laments that Nazism is never discussed in depth in her contemporary history classes. In another letter she notes that the students whom she has previously accused of not wanting to discuss politics are not afraid to disagree with and attack those professors who, contrary to her earlier statement, do discuss the Nazi period and substantiate their points with some documentation of the time.

Levi realizes that H. L. sways between "documentary seriousness and childish fantasy" (189) when she sends him a kaleidoscope with a letter in which she writes that she would like to sew for him a suit that, like those worn by legendary heroes, would protect him from all the world's dangers. Just as the kaleidoscope changes its colorful images with the slightest of movements, this woman seems to have changed a reality into a fantastic image. While it may feed the vivid imagination of a young, sensitive, receptive mind, it is completely detached from the source of inspiration. Feig writes that "the struggler is not a likely hero."[31] Levi, who carries his survival bundled with a sense of guilt, as do most of the other survivors, is too modest to see himself as a hero. Though he endured "dread and hopelessness without the loss of will to carry on in human ways,"[32] he is too honest to deny that it is to fate that he owes his survival.

While Levi understands that H. L.'s wavering behavior is normal for someone her age, he must also realize that his desire to communicate with the younger generation carries its risks. This generation should have its curiosity satisfied and must be made aware of what has taken place, but its members will not necessarily understand or act accordingly to remedy the wrongs of the past.

Levi's correspondence with Hety S. of Wiesbaden provides the most intriguing but finally the most disappointing results. Hety is a contemporary of the author and one of the few Germans not to have been contaminated by the Nazi propaganda machinery. Like Levi's translator, she is, unlike many Germans, firm in her beliefs and endowed with a strong sense of right and wrong. For these reasons Levi considers her a friend and corresponds with her for over sixteen years. Hety, unlike most Germans, resisted the Nazi movement and was expelled from school as a result. She came from an activist Social Democratic family and had to endure the pressures of the Nazis. Following the 1944 attempt on Hitler's life, her father was sent to Dachau, and Hety, mainly because of her political views and the firmness of her convictions, divorced her husband, who felt that her activities jeopardized the family's welfare. After the war she worked for the Ministry of Culture of the Land Hessen, where she distinguished herself for her straightforward approach and often for her controversial stand.

More than anything else, however, Hety had always been hungry for human encounters. In fact, it was she who put the author in contact with Mayer, and she also played an essential role in helping Levi trace Dr. Müller, about whom he writes in *The Periodic Table*.[33] For Hety, human encounters were a way of opening channels of communication, which would in turn lead to more open exchanges of views and to mutual understandings and perhaps mutual respect. Evidently she believed that an open exchange of views could have led to a change in positions and even a change in thinking. She certainly sensed and hoped that this might be the case when she met Albert Speer, the so-called court architect of the Third Reich, who, in 1943, as minister of the war industry, played a major role in setting up the organization of the factories where many prisoners died of overwork and hunger.

At Nuremberg, Speer was the only defendant to plead guilty, even for the things he did not know about. His remorse seemed sincere to Hety, and this gave her the hope and courage to write to Levi about it. She had come face to face with one who had allowed himself to become the corrupt creature of Hitler, and he had impressed her with what seemed a genuine attempt to understand something that could not be understood. She saw in him a key, the symbol of "German aberration" (196) who appeared nevertheless to have some redeeming qualities. Unlike Levi, she accepted this apparent repentance without skepticism, and she was shocked when she went to see him a second and final time and heard him boast about his past. This time she realized that Speer was still stupidly taken with himself and was proud of his detestable role as "pharaonic architect" of one of humanity's most shameful periods.

To Levi, Hety's experience with Speer is another confirmation that, deep down, little if anything has changed. Despite her good intentions, Hety demonstrates that she is still in some part unwilling to believe what her fellow Germans have done. In this sense, she comes close to her own father, who, despite his experience in a concentration camp, did not believe what he was hearing about the atrocities. Hety too tries to veil the reality of what her countrymen have done by seeking comfort in what appears to be the repentance of the perpetrators. Instead, Albert Speer, the one who ironically accepts all the blame at Nuremberg, later confirms that what he and the others did, they did willingly and with full cognizance. To Levi, Speer's behavior comes as no surprise, because he would never accept the excuse that an intelligent human being could be easily duped into doing such things out of ignorance.

But Speer's conduct is indicative of something even more disturbing. Prejudice and ignorance are not easily erased, especially if the guilty refuse to acknowledge the wrong they have committed. Has society learned to distinguish right from wrong? Does it know what to accept and what to condemn? The answer to these questions is not an encouraging one. The fact that Levi still needs to write about the Holocaust forty years after it happened is proof that humanity would rather forget than learn from it.

For the most part, the Germans confirm by their letters to Levi that they have not grasped the gravity of the offense and probably never will. It is clear to Levi that, between those who barely acknowledge what happened, those who accept it but only conditionally, those who deny it outright, and those who in their ignorance and stupidity still take pride in what they have done, the German people are not willing to acknowledge the cowardice of their past behavior, whether out of shame, embarrassment, simple obtuseness, or arrogance. Sadder still, as time passes, this becomes true of society at large. The memory of the Holocaust is fading with the deaths of those who did bear witness. If the skeptical younger generations acknowledge the event, they see it as a historical dinosaur with little or no relevance to their lives.

Confronted with this reality, Levi doubts his success in having made others aware of the Holocaust and its repercussions. He realizes that this horrible event has not made any great impact in the long run on those who were not victimized by it. Those same people who claim that another holocaust cannot take place because times have changed reveal their skepticism when they say that wars cannot be avoided and that violence is sometimes needed to prevent more violence. To Levi, these are obscene statements that demonstrate complete insensitivity toward all those who have been victimized by this kind of warped reasoning, and he vehemently denies them. There is nothing, he insists, that cannot be resolved by discussion. The only thing needed is a demonstration of good faith.

As Levi says this, his tone changes to one of passion, at a level that is out of character for him. He realizes that, in order to be heard, he must appeal to more than reason. Reason has not served him well enough to make a dent in indifference; and perhaps, he ponders, reason was not the proper vehicle for describing and analyzing the Lager, which, as he has stated more than once, was the product of an evil aimed at defying human reason. For as much as Levi pleads that a heedless society sharpen its senses and not pay attention to "beautiful words" that are not supported by sound reason, the reader senses in these words a last-ditch effort to avoid the unavoidable.

Levi's desperate cry that "we must be listened to" (199) contains the pain of a man who fears that his story, and more important, the story of millions who have paid with the ultimate sacrifice, will be forgotten. He owes it more to them than to himself to make sure such a thing never happens again, even if he must resort to emotional pleas to prevent it. The younger generations must believe him when he says that the conflicts of more recent years—in Vietnam, Cambodia, Afghanistan, the Falklands, and Iran and Iraq—are all examples of how devastating a war can be in an industrialized and technological age, even if it is not carried to the point of a nuclear conflict. Society must see, through these events, that the potential of another holocaust is always there. What has happened in the past can happen again if caution and vigilance are not exercised. One must stand guard because the tormentor has no distinguishing features. He is the product of an average education and is thus no different from most civil servants who obey orders without questioning them.

The Holocaust took place because most chose not to ask questions, because most chose not to be different from the others. Implied in Levi's cry is his appeal to society to be ready to question and to hold those who govern accountable for their acts. Millions of lives were lost because an entire society refused to exercise those rights. In light of the sad events of more recent years— wars, conflicts, doubts and denials of the atrocities of the past—Levi seriously questions if today's society has the moral courage to correct what is wrong. As he bursts forth with harsh, strong words, in a tone not to be found in any of his other works, understanding now gives way to severe sentencing. His words "Let it be clear" (203) leave no doubt about the firmness of his conviction that the blame for the Holocaust lies on the great majority of Germans who, "out of mental laziness, myopic calculation, stupidity, and national pride" (203), swallowed the "beautiful words" of "corporal" Hitler. Levi's mockery is evident in the juxtaposition of the rank and name.

Levi is enraged because he realizes that, despite the collective stupidity, the Germans are about to have the last laugh.[34] In his preface to this work he writes that the SS enjoyed cynically telling the prisoners that, no matter what, the Germans would have won the war because no one would be left to bear witness. Now, forty years later, Levi realizes that time is proving them right. Those who did bear witness are dying, and, with them, so is the memory of this century's most inhuman atrocity. At this point he has to ask himself if his own efforts, which have so far kept him alive and writing, will serve any purpose whatsoever.

There is a postscript to *The Drowned and the Saved* that should not go unmentioned, though it may not have any bearing on the significance of the work. Levi died, supposedly by suicide, a year after this book's publication. Among the many who accept that his death was a suicide, there are some who feel that it is nothing more than a coincidence that this book was the last of his works to be published before his death. Were it not for other small but significant pieces of evidence from interviews and other minor works, the idea of a coincidence could be accepted without much debate. As Levi admits in *Dialogo* (63), however, the mere fact that he temporarily interrupts this work to write *If Not Now, When?* gives cause for speculation. *Dialogo,* published in 1984, provides some revealing information on Levi's attitude toward his writing. He confesses, with obvious disappointment in himself, that he feels he has exhausted his creative reservoirs and that he is writing poems he can place little value on. He admits that perhaps the time has come for him to take a new direction.

At the same time he has returned to complete *The Drowned and the Saved,* he has also discovered the computer, which has facilitated the mechanics of his writing. He admits that to live without the word processor once one has learned how to use it would be tantamount to separating oneself from society and insisting on living at its margins. What he says about the computer reveals a side of himself that seems out of character for the Levi who is familiar to his readers. He claims that it is best just to use it and "repress the humanistic desire to understand 'what's in it'" (*Dialogo* 64; my translation). The phrase "repress the humanistic desire" is perplexing. Both as a scientist and as a writer, Levi placed the need to understand above everything else. Now he seems to have altered his views. This statement, considered in conjunction with his overall dissatisfaction with his work, appears to indicate that he has reached a critical point and that whatever he is producing comes more from sheer inertia than from "humanistic desire."

Levi's emptiness and disillusionment are also reflected in his increasing references to the "black holes" that he uses as metaphors to express the dark void history was and is making of the Holocaust.[35] The pain this causes him is very much in evidence in the last article he wrote about Auschwitz, "Buco nero di Auschwitz" (The Black Hole of Auschwitz), which appeared in the Turin daily *La Stampa* (22 January 1987) less than three months before his death.[36] In it he takes issue with several German historians (including Nolte and Hillgruber) and revisionists, if not deniers, who are attempting to trivialize the Holocaust by raising inane questions concerning the accuracy of the number of deaths and, worse still, by questioning whether the Holocaust ever occurred. The title of this article suggests that nothing of importance seems to have come out of Auschwitz, no lasting lesson, and it is unlikely that any will. The "black hole," then, is a confirmation of his concern, raised in his essay "Stereotypes," that with the passing of time the mystery of the Holocaust will only increase and its impact will disappear. At this point Levi sees a bleak future ahead with little promise for any improvement.

The clearest sign of what Levi has determined for his future appears in the chapter "Shame," in which he writes that, following the liberation, many cases of suicide among the survivors occurred in a moment of reflection and depression, when a person turned back to look at the "perilous water" in which he or she had been wrecked. The words "perilous water," taken from Dante's *Inferno* (1:22–27), can be seen in their original context to elucidate more definitely the tragedy that lay ahead for Levi:

> E come quei che con lena affannata
> uscito fuor del pelago a la riva,
> si volge a l'acqua perigliosa e guata;
> così l'animo mio, ch'ancor fuggiva,
> si volse a retro a rimirar lo passo
> *che non lasciò giammai persona viva.*

> (And as he who with laboring breath
> has escaped from the deep to the shore,
> turns to look back on the dangerous waters,
> so my spirit which was still fleeing turned back to gaze upon the pass
> *that no one ever left alive*) [37]

The "dangerous [perilous] waters" belonging to that "pelago" (deep) or "pass" represent for Levi an image of sinful life. The connection is clear. The deep that God created as part of the punishment that brings the sinners into hell corresponds to the Lager itself, which, paradoxically, the Nazis created to punish the innocent. This difference notwithstanding, what the deep and the Lager share is their implacable design never to leave anyone alive. This realization will haunt Levi with increasing anguish, and eventually it will take its toll. History is proving the Nazis right. In the end, it seems, just as the Nazis had planned, there will be no survivor to tell because whatever mysterious evil force allowed the Lager to exist also willed that no one who was part of its trauma be left alive. Levi sees and knows of no reason why he should be exempted from this judgment.

On a literary plain, one would feel Levi considers it fitting that the words of Dante disclose what is to come. It was Dante who provided a hell to which Levi could compare his own, who gave him "humanistic" life through the words of Ulysses and allowed him to realize that, despite the harsh adversities, he is still a man and that as such his charge is to seek "virtute e conoscenza" (knowledge and excellence; *Survival in Auschwitz* 103). It is to Dante that he turns now to give notice that the omega point is nearing.[38]

Notes

1. Levi so defines Langbein in his book *La ricerca delle radici* (1981), his "personal" anthology, made up of a selection of excerpts drawn primarily from works on letters and sciences. Levi considers these sources fundamental to his cultural development.

2. Hermann Langbein, *Menschen in Auschwitz* (Vienna: Europa Verlag, 1972). Levi's high regard for Langbein prompts him to incorporate a section of Langbein's work, which he translates himself, in *La ricerca delle radici.* He is so impressed with Langbein's work that he expresses regret that he is not able to write with the same intensity.

4. In Turin's newspaper *La Stampa* (4 July 1986).

5. In *Conversations with Primo Levi* he states that it was the university assistant about whom he writes in "Potassium," in *The Periodic Table,* who will tell him that he had been predestined to survive.

6. His extreme sense of fairness drives him to try to understand even the behavior of the most despicable of all, the *aguzzini* (tormentors). Unless otherwise noted, all quotes from *The Damned and the Saved* are from its English version.

7. Levi discusses this at greater length in the last essay, "Stereotypes."

8. Levi also explores this premise in the chapter "With Malice Aforethought" in *The Monkey's Wrench.*

9. This was the case later in that same year, 1944, when four hundred Jews from Corfu fought back.

10. Levi writes more extensively about this man in "Story of a Coin" in *Moments of Reprieve.*

11. See the importance Levi places on bread in *Survival in Auschwitz.* He always insisted, with a degree of self-solace, that he never stole bread from anyone.

12. This is Levi's concluding statement in the RAI documentary *Sorgente di vita,* which treats his return to Auschwitz forty years later.

13. Hurbinek, about whom Levi writes in *The Reawakening,* born in mysterious circumstances of unidentified parents, was the true child of the Lager. In his almost complete inability to communicate, this child is the living prototype of the Nazi-imposed silence.

14. Levi does not know how this word, literally meaning "Muslim," acquired the meaning of the prisoner who has lost the will to survive and precipitates his or her own demise. Levi writes about the *Muselmann* in *Survival in Auschwitz.*

15. Outside the camp, this was a term used only for the feeding of animals.

16. Literally, "to cut." In the Lager it corresponded to "Go to hell."

17. On the subject of language and the concentration camp, see George Steiner's essay "The Hollow Miracle" in his book *Language and Science* (New York: Atheneum, 1967), 95–109.

18. To suggest this condition, Levi uses the same biblical phrase in *Suvival in Auschwitz.*

19. As demonstrated in the episode in *The Reawakening* in which Levi meets the two sisters who cannot believe he is Jewish because he does not speak Yiddish.

20. Levi mentions the assassination of Aldo Moro, allegedly carried out by the Red Brigades, an Italian extreme leftist group of the 1970s. Aldo Moro was a member of the Italian Parliament and one of the more distinguished figures in the Italian government. Among the various offices he held was that of prime minister.

21. The English translation has the title "Useless Violence" for the Italian "Violenza inutile." For *inutile* I prefer "unnecessary." Levi explains in this chapter that to the Nazis, this kind of violence had a purpose, so it was not useless.

22. In Leviticus 19:28.

23. Améry writes of his experiences in his book *Jenseits von Schuld und Shne* (Stuttgart: Clett-Cotta, 1980), published in an English translation as *At Mind's Limits: Contemplations by a Survivor on Auschwitz and its Realities,* trans. Sydney Resenfeld and Stella P. Rosenfeld (Bloomington: Indiana University Press, 1980).

24. In his interview in *Conversations with Primo Levi* (64), the author admits that it was in the Lager where he really began to understand and appreciate the true significance of Italian literature.

25. Ugo Foscolo (1778–1827) is one of the central literary figures of the early Italian romantic movement. He was an ardent patriot who wanted to see Italy free from Austrian domination. Among his best-known works are *Ultime lettere di Jacopo Ortis* (*Last Letters of Jacopo Ortis*), an epistolary novel; the patriotic poem *I sepolcri;* and his translation of Laurence Sterne's *Short Sentimental Journey.*

26. See *The Drowned and the Saved* 149.

27. See opening statements in this book's chapter on *Survival in Auschwitz.*

28. Examples were Attilio Momigliano and Gaetano Salvemini, noted historians who went on to teach at the University of London and Harvard University, respectively.

29. In his modesty and sensitivity, Levi prefers not to point out that most of those who did leave were internationally known figures in their respective fields and were helped by influential contacts abroad.

30. He was much less happy with the French translation of this work. In a letter in the Einaudi archives, Levi expresses his displeasure especially with the translation of the chapter entitled "Canto of Ulysses," about which he states that he is not sure whether the translator has a greater dislike for him or for Dante.

31. Konnillyn G. Feig, *Hitler's Death Camps: The Sanity of Madness* (New York and London: Holmes and Meier, 1979), 437. Also see 436–42.

32. Feig 437.

33. In the chapter "Vanadium."

34. See Cynthia Ozick's perceptive observations on Levi's rage in her essay "Primo Levi's Suicide Note," especially 46–48. While I agree with much of what she says, I do not share her view that in this rage lies a strong connection with Mayer. Nor do I see it so much in terms of "latent" rage. In my view Levi's "rage" stems more from the fact that accounts of the Holocaust seem to be falling on deaf ears.

35. In *Dialogo* he discusses the "black holes" in space at considerable length with

Tullio Regge, the co-author of this work. Regge, a noted physicist and recipient of the Einstein Prize, taught at Princeton for many years. He is professor of theoretical physics at the University of Turin and regularly contributes science articles to the Turin daily *La Stampa*. The image of the black holes has already been shown to be important to Levi in *La ricerca delle radici*. It is significant that he ends that book with an excerpt from Kip S. Thorne's *The Search for the Black Holes*. He confirmed in an interview with Giovanni Tesio ("L'enigma del tradurre" in *Nuova società* 10.237 [18 June 1983]: 61) that the black hole metaphor is not a positive one. In *La ricerca delle radici,* the black holes are connected with humanity's minuscule, weak, and lonely position in the universe.

36. This article appears in Primo Levi's *The Mirror Maker,* trans. Raymond Rosenthal (New York: Schocken Books, 1989) under the title "The Dispute among German Historians."

37. I have used Charles Singleton's translation of Dante's *Inferno* (Princeton: Princeton University Press, 1980), 5; italics mine.

38. Risa Sodi too, in her praiseworthy study *A Dante of Our Time: Primo Levi and Auschwitz* (New York: Peter Lang, 1990), 89, points out the relevance of Dante's "acqua perigliosa" to Levi's case. However, when she quotes Dante's verses, she stops short of that closing verse (27).

CHAPTER SEVEN

Stories and Essays:
Levi's Minor Works

If the need to bear witness brought Levi to the world of writing, his background as a chemist provided him with new ideas and creative outlets. Though Levi is remembered primarily for his memorial and witness writings about the Holocaust, his many short stories and essays and a collection of poems, all written over a span of nearly forty years, reveal a full range of interests that he presents with a keen sense of curiosity and a versatile and vivid imagination. His shorter compositions encompass a spectrum of subjects that include fiction, additional autobiographical reminiscences, and essays on current events and scientific and literary issues. In this material, which reflects the breadth of his vision, Levi writes with his customary clarity, accuracy, and concision and reflects moods that include the witty, ironic, funny, sad, and critical.

The vast majority of these shorter works originally appeared as single selections in journals and newspapers, primarily the Turin daily *La Stampa*. *Storie naturali, Vizio di forma,* and *Lilìt e altri racconti* were first published in compiled editions in 1966, 1971, and 1981 respectively, while *L'altrui mestiere,* largely a collection of essays, was published in 1985. The first two collections appeared in print between the Italian publications of *The Reawakening* (1963) and *The Periodic Table* (1975), which shows that Levi's interest in other subjects was concurrent with his writing about the death camps. Many of these stories have now been translated into English and gathered into volumes. *The Sixth Day and Other Tales* (1990) comprises a selection of stories taken from *Storie Naturali* and *Vizio di forma. Other People's Trades* (1989) is the English version of *L'altrui mestiere,* and *The Mirror Maker: Stories and Essays* (1989) is a translation of *Racconti e saggi di Primo Levi* (1986). While Levi would be the first to admit that these shorter works are not on a par with his major ones, they are nonetheless important to a complete understanding of his literary opus and his concerns. This study focuses on the collections of short works that appear in English translation.

Storie naturali, in *The Sixth Day and Other Tales,* contains twenty tales that border on science fiction, though none of the plots is distant from possible reality. These tales, for which Levi received the 1967 Bagutta Literary prize, were written between 1952 and 1964 with the exception of the first, "The Mnemogogues," which was written in 1946. On the whole, they denounce the social malaise gripping modern society and affecting its moral fiber.

Following the advice of one of his editors, Roberto Cerato,[1] Levi originally wrote *Storie naturali* under the pseudonym Damiano Malabaila.[2] He did so out of shyness and modesty. He conceded that he had a "vague sense of guilt" for the relatively light treatment he gave these pieces.[3] Since he regarded them as mere *divertimenti,* light pastimes of limited relevance that he jotted down as they popped into his mind, he was reluctant to give them his name, which had become synonymous with the *Lager,* or prison camp, experience he described in his somber works published earlier. Once he realized, however, that the views he espoused in these stories had been determined in great part by his experience in camp, he no longer saw any reason for using a nom de plume. In fact, he openly admitted that he agreed to the publication of these stories because he saw a continuity between them and his earlier works. In any case, readers familiar with Levi's writings would have had no difficulty identifying the author's hand. Some of the stories had already appeared elsewhere under his real name, and a statement on the book's back clearly identified the writer as the author of two earlier works connected with his experiences in the concentration camp.

The title *Storie naturali* is a paradox of sorts because, on the surface, there appears to be little content in these stories that can be deemed conventionally natural. The author's objective, in fact, is to underscore the anomalous, the bizarre, and the irrational. The title's reference to the natural is not only paradoxical but ironic, if it is viewed in light of the lapse of the natural reasoning process on the part of a large section of society that resulted in the Holocaust. This event is still unequaled as one of what Levi called on the dustjacket of *Storie naturali* "the monsters generated by the sleep of reason" (my translation). While the stories reveal on the surface a writer of lighter and more amusing disposition, beneath the levity the effects of Levi's experience in the camp are evident. The author's departure here from his earlier autobiographical mode is therefore nothing more than a subtle masking, an attempt to divert his own and his readers' attention temporarily from his awful experience. This is futile, however, because the memories of the camp cannot be erased; they continue to reveal themselves in these stories. The tragedy of the Holocaust forced Levi and all people of conscience to confront their responsibilities to humanity. These stories are the author's further attempt to effect that confrontation.

As Giuseppe Grassano notes in his biography, central to these stories is the progressive and programmatic disintegration of human sentiments, of the individual's sense of self, of his moral values, and of his psychological balance. With the Lager silent in the background as the constant reminder of one people's violation of another, Levi portrays in these stories the destruction brought about primarily by human ambitions and illusions. This progressive disintegration is clear in the cycle of stories that feature Mr. Simpson, the American sales representative of a company that specializes in the production of highly advanced machines that evolve into anthropomorphic devices, eventually controlling their maker and those who use them.

Beginning with "Order on the Cheap," Simpson introduces an innocent-looking duplicating machine that, in its capacity to reproduce surface and depth, can create "order from disorder."[4] It catches the fancy and the imagination of the first-person narrator, who immediately uses it for his own illicit purposes. In godlike but contemptuous fashion, he accurately tallies his creative achievements on a day-to-day basis, finally resting "on the seventh day" (31). To Simpson's shock, the narrator uses the duplicator to reproduce a range of things from objects to foods to small living creatures. The experiments, however, do not end here. In another story, the machine—now placed in the hands of the unscrupulous Gilberto—duplicates a human being and then the human being's wife. Because of his greed and unscrupulousness, Gilberto cannot distinguish between the legal and the illegal, and he loses all sense of morality and ethics. Thus the narrator (speaking for Levi) reveals the despicable and horrendous incapability of modern man to be "concerned about his fellow man" (43).

Gilberto, whom Levi defines as "the symbol of our century," satisfies his excessive egotism and greed by his ruthless exploitation of anything and anybody. His thirst for power and profit transforms him into "a small noxious Prometheus . . . ingenious and irresponsible, arrogant and foolish" (39). He is the type who would not think twice about making and dropping an atom bomb merely to see what effect it would have. Gilberto's shallowness is further demonstrated in "The Measure of Beauty," in which, by adding excessive narcissism to his other deficiencies, he sets himself up as the paragon against which the beauty machine, the latest product Mr. Simpson is now pushing, can make its evaluations about what women find physically desirable and appealing in men.

Even when intentions are good, something can make things go awry. In the story "Full Employment," Simpson turns his attention to hard-working insects such as bees, dragonflies, and ants, which he puts at his service with some degree of success. The initial positive quality of this project changes when Mr. O'Toole, Simpson's partner, seizes the opportunity to make money illicitly by training eels to carry cocaine on their backs across bodies of water.

Ambitions of wealth and creativity increase progressively in this cycle of stories, only to terminate in complete passivity and degradation. This is manifested by the Torec, the machine-protagonist of the book's final story, "Retirement Fund." Ironically, and with twisted justice, the last and most pathetic victim is Mr. Simpson himself, whose doubt about the might of the machines is overshadowed by his unending faith in them. The implication is that when not it is controlled, humanity's dependence on technology and science leads to damaging effects, just as addictive drugs weaken its ethical sense, moral responsibility, and social commitment. Reliance on technological inventions to escape pain and suffering can lead to tragic consequences. In the end, the real destroyer is not profit or avarice but rather a machine that, capable of producing artificial sensations, deprives people of their self-control and confines them to the void of self-destruction.

To avoid the boredom that accompanies his retirement, Simpson needs to be fed constantly by the sensations this machine can provide him. The author's warning, reflected in the view of the *I* narrator, is replicated in the solemn words of Ecclesiastes, a fitting concluding statement that contains Levi's message and the central thesis of this book. The strength of human beings, Levi sees, lies in their effort to make free and responsible choices, overcoming all odds to do so. Often such choices may lead to the realization that life can be harsh and without true happiness. "For in much wisdom there is much grief; and he that increaseth knowledge increaseth sorrow" (124). However, unlike Solomon's wisdom, which was acquired through pain and toil, the knowledge Mr. Simpson has gained comes from electronic circuits and multitrack audiovisual tapes, without any expenditure of effort on his part. This causes him to feel ashamed, but now, caught in shame's vicious circle, he can hide it only by returning to the Torec, again to apply the artificial sensations that cause his euphoria but numb his freedom. In truth, one must look to and accept experiences attained through self-examination and hard work, which lead to conquests as well as defeats, joys as well as pain. The use of machines or other artificial means of recreating the natural processes defrauds humans of their instincts and deprives them of their rationality.

It is no coincidence that the last story in the book has a clear relationship to the first, "The Mnemogogues," a piece Levi wrote before *The Reawakening*. Like Mr. Simpson, Dr. Montesanto in "The Mnemogogues" is a prisoner of an invention that helps him escape from reality, in this case by reducing all his memories and sentiments to olfactory sensations stored in vials. In his Faustian obsession not to relinquish any memory, the aged Dr. Montesanto retreats into the past to avoid facing his present state of languor and relative uselessness. His success in artificially creating smells that connect him to his past enables him to turn his back on the present and relive his dynamic, busy yesterdays. What Mr. Simpson had achieved with the help of technology, Dr. Montesanto attains through his direct relationship with nature. In both instances, however, Levi underscores the oddity of using "unnatural" methods to cope with the natural.

The taste of the past in which Dr. Montesanto seeks comfort has its counterpart in one of the two short plays included in this collection. In the futuristic one-act play "The Sleeping Beauty in the Fridge: A Winter's Tale," a clever parody of Charles Perrault's famous fairy tale with a similar name,[5] Levi pokes fun at the idea of cryogenics to preserve eternal youth. The results are not so different from those in previous stories. Preservation is dearly paid for with loneliness and boredom, passive states that Patricia, the "sleeping beauty," will reject. Tired of the frozen lethargy to which she is condemned most of the time, she welcomes the opportunity to be freed by a providential but unrewarded Prince Charming. In an unexpected ending, instead of living happily ever after with her savior, Patricia goes off to find a "contemporary" friend of hers somewhere in America.

Our human sense of self-importance, Levi seems to imply, could stand some careful introspection, something that could teach us to measure our achievements with a degree of humility and less arrogance. Another short play in this collection,[6] "The Sixth Day," addresses this point with its clever exploration of the foibles of a technologically and bureaucratically controlled environment. It takes the reader into an executive meeting room where advisors in various fields are engaged in an animated discussion about how best to achieve the creation of Man. The meeting is vividly portrayed, with the humor and sarcasm the reader would expect to find in the interaction among such a group of experts. Their competitiveness and their earnest application of time, effort, and planning prove to be completely counterproductive and embarrassingly disproportionate to the finished product. When all differences have been resolved and an agreement has been reached to create Man in the form of a bird, a curious force from "above" nixes the project and, in virtually no time at all, creates Man out of plain clay, then makes Woman from one of his ribs. This "God/Chairman of the Board," who is simply referred to as "they" (105), grows tired of the time-wasting debates, brainstorming sessions, and other bureaucratic entanglements and decides to take matters into his own hands.

Levi is underscoring in this play the danger that may arise when science and technology are pushed too far. The obtrusive intricacies that consume our time and energy without addressing our purposes for existing cause more harm than good. Intoxicated with our achievements, we allow ourselves to be carried away to a point at which we lose sight of the meaning in life. We forget that we are only human, and it is presumptuous and foolish to consider ourselves godlike.

Modern society has been so much influenced by technology and science and is so dependent on them to serve its needs that, for gain, it is disposed to bend the moral values on which it operates. The result is that what was meant to be good and useful is turned into something evil and destructive. The most glaring example of this is what happened under Nazism. "Angelic Butterfly," the most chilling tale of this collection, serves as a reminder of Nazi evil. In it, the aberration is more than a phenomenon that lends itself to an entertaining treatment of a moral point; it is carried to the most extreme level of dehumanization, and, absurdly, the story thus comes closest to historical truth.

Dr. Leeb's experiments, which transform human beings into monstrous birds that are later to be slaughtered and eaten by a hungry mob, are a frightful reminder of the atrocities carried out during the Holocaust by Dr. Mengele, known as the "Angel of Death," and other Nazis. It is no coincidence that the events described take place soon after the war, in Berlin, a city now in rubble and under the control of the Allied forces. This is the Germany that, called to account for what has happened, admits through the voice of nineteen-year-old Gertrude Enk to having indeed witnessed such cruelties and to having preferred silence because, as Gertrude's father explains, "For us Germans the less we know, the better" (24). In the face of these painful events so close to his personal life Levi's voice in the first person is noticeably absent. But in this silence lies the powerful eloquence of his accusation. Leeb, contrary to any official version or any expressed belief, is not dead. People like him "give up only when faced by failure" (25). Since Leeb does not see himself as a failure, humanity has yet to hear the last from him and others like him who are only too anxious to come out of their hiding places, if they are allowed to do so, and disseminate fear and hatred under the guise of scientific research.

The grimness of "Angelic Butterfly" is present also in "Versamina," set in a postwar Germany that is "timeless, petrified like Gomorrah" (48). The game is still that of the wish to subvert the natural order, this time with an analgesic substance called Versamina that is intended to convert all painful sensations to pleasurable ones and to heighten them to a point at which all desire is lost. In this instance, drugs have replaced the Torec in producing catastrophic results. The human subjects used for the experiment are pushed to an abnormal state of behavior, while the inventor of the substance, himself falling victim to the destructive properties of his product, commits suicide. Again Levi draws a moral conclusion: pain cannot be erased, nor should it be, because it serves as a necessary control on pleasure. Pleasure can be enjoyed only as long as it can be measured against a painful experience, and altering the balance of the two inevitably leads to disastrous consequences.

"Man's Friend" is a more felicitous story. The animal that the story is named for is nothing more than a simple tapeworm, an unlikely creature to become the voice of conscience that Levi turns it into. He takes as his point of departure the discovery made by a professor of Assyriology at Michigan State University who, with the assistance of the Flory photographs, identifies in the structure of the tapeworm's epithelial cells a "rhythmical" (34) schema resembling that of terza rima—the rhyme scheme Dante made famous in the *Divine Comedy.* Levi abandons himself to an uncharacteristic, iconoclastic position when he gives a poetic voice to this parasite and places it in the ungrateful human body from which it is about to be expelled. With the hope that people will take its message to heart, man's friend, this solitary worm, uses the "knowledge" (35) and "wisdom" (37) it has assimilated from its human host to denounce the hypoc- risy and arrogance of man's consideration of himself as a proud demigod. While the human relationship to science and technology is face-to-face in the other stories in the collection, here the lesson, significantly and poignantly, comes from a voice within.

In the stories that comprise the *Vizio di forma* section of *The Sixth Day and Other Tales,* Levi underscores what he calls the *smagliatura,* literally a run in a stocking or a sweater, but in this context the element that upsets continuity and cohesion in the flow of life. It is the "flaw in form"[7] that renders useless or inefficient some aspect of human civilization and of our moral world. This book is Levi's fourth and least recognized book. Thematically, it is so closely related to *Storie naturali* that it can be seen as its logical continuation, and Levi indeed used the term *vizio de forma* in the introduction of *Storie naturali* to acknowl- edge the absence of moral fiber as the flaw in society that disturbs the natural balance of things and turns the normal into the bizarre.

Compared to Levi's reminiscences about past transgressions in other works, *Vizio di forma* is about the harsh realities of the time when it was written. The dominant science fiction motif in *Storie naturali* is replaced in *Vizio di forma* by themes taken from the problems of the 1960s and 1970s, with a concentration on how the advancement of modern technology can contribute to the creation of a defective moral climate. In his letter to the editor, a document used as introduction to the 1987 Italian edition of this book, Levi writes that, even though the situation has changed since 1971, when he wrote *Vizio di forma,* the disquieting events of those years contributed to his "apocalyptic" vision of renunciation and defeatism. His disappointment with these events is expressed in the sadness, often tinged with irony, that flows through these pages. Con- cerned about a widespread intoxication with technological advancement and dependency on it, Levi lets his fantasy convey his anxiety. Yet his feelings are not so negative as despair. Under his pessimism, Levi still holds onto a glimmer of hope. If we are able to regain the upper hand in our handling of science and technology, he seems to say, all is not lost for the future.

This note of optimism is prominent in "The Hard Sellers," a story in which S, an entity yet to be born, opts to come into this world without the advantage of any offered privilege. This choice suggests that the wish to be measured through the validity of one's own deeds is not dead. The *homo faber,* the human who wishes to be defined and judged on the merit of personal accomplishments, rare as that person might be, can still be found. With this story as a premise of hope, Levi directs his attention toward the tension humanity has generated between itself and nature. It is a strain brought about by our self-subjugating dependency upon technology, Levi believes, and by our greed and desire for power, which stop at virtually nothing, not even at the abuse of nature and the destruction of the environment.

While the central issue in *Storie naturali* is the relationship between individual morality and technological invention, the author's concern in *Vizio di forma* centers on the effects of this relationship on society as a whole. We have become so dependent on science and technology that even their benefits may become a threat to the survival of the human species, to ecology, and to the entire planet. In hindsight, these stories have a sense of prophecy since many of the concerns they highlight have become central in our lives today.

The conflict between humans and the environment is dramatically treated in "Mutiny" and "Excellent Is the Water." The first of these stories, which Levi dedicated to his good friend and fellow writer Mario Rigoni Stern, presents the plight of the plants through the voice of Clotilde, a pastoral figure and a creature of innocence through whom they declare their mutiny against humanity for the abuses and mistreatment they have received at its hands. It is now their turn to revolt and to refuse to cooperate. Hidden in the innocence of Clotilde's voice is the plea that we evaluate our capabilities with a sense of humility and respect for the environment, of which we are nothing more than a tiny particle, as confirmed by the moon people in the story "Seen from Afar." In "Excellent Is the Water," significantly the last story of this collection, the author takes aim at the precariousness of the elements vital to our planet and our survival. At the same time he underscores the difficulty created by those in power who, driven by profit and greed, impose silence on those who have discovered the wrong and are willing to expose it. Our abuse of nature, in this case by polluting the water, poses a threat of great proportions, and we alone can remedy the situation. The population explosion and the moral implications of genetic engineering and euthanasia, issues that are creating schisms among human beings and civilizations, are also matters of concern in this collection of stories.

The distancing of the "civilized" world from that segment we call the Third World is the theme of the stories "Recuenco: The Nurse" and "Recuenco: The Rafter," in which two different views of a rafter—a kind of ship that travels on air, sea, and land—demonstrate the huge gap that exists between the members of a modern, technological society and those who are still living in primitive conditions. Our modern society is destructively indifferent, while those we exploit politically and economically under the guise of "helping" see us, paradoxically, as a godsend. While the natives view the milk-like substance delivered by the rafter as providential manna that will keep them alive longer, the operators of the rafter, concerned about their earnings and the economics that dictate the time allotted for the delivery, see it as an insignificant, almost annoying task.

It is ironic that groups of people we consider primitive are the only ones who still respect the natural processes of life and reject life-prolonging assistance, especially if it is artificial. The Arunde tribe in the story "Westward" teaches us that humans should allow the natural clock of time to tell them that the end is near and not try to prolong their stay. Levi seems to imply that, if this is the case, suicide is justifiable if the decision for it is made rationally and without moral or ethical prejudice. The natural flow of life ought not to be obstructed or tampered with. Walter, the ontologist who has created Factor L, the formula intended to renew joy in life, is deeply disturbed by the throng of lemmings headed toward their demise as he stands in their way, though the lemmings' rush over the edge is as natural an act as it is natural to the Arunde tribe to end a life that is without joy or usefulness.

In this story Levi addresses the fundamental question, no doubt raised by his personal experience at Auschwitz, of why humans want to cling to life as long as they can at any cost, even when it is not pleasant. Levi wonders what is it that makes them want to go on living, when, aware of having exhausted their usefulness, they know they will only become a burden on those around them. The Arunde prefer to die with dignity, and there is no compromise to their freedom of choice. As soon as they sense that their enjoyment of life is outweighed by their suffering, they let go. In modern societies, conversely, we are blinded by vanity and presumptuousness; we take ourselves too seriously in our belief that we are too valuable to terminate our existence. This parable is about euthanasia, which Levi seems to have approved of, and perhaps a clue to his own death. He sees a basic contradiction in prolonging a useless life, especially by artificial means. Yet he acknowledges that we have difficulty in accepting our inevitable physical demise gracefully, maybe because it is within our nature not to let go.

Humans are paradoxical creatures. We can use our inventions to elevate ourselves to masterful proportions. At the same time, though, after millions of years of existence, we can and do still behave cruelly. This is the bittersweet message in "His Own Blacksmith," which Levi dedicates to his friend and fellow writer Italo Calvino, whose *Cosmicomics* [8] evidently served as an inspiration for this story's theme and design. Adopting a diary format, Levi creates a fable based on the concept of ontogenesis, the study of the successive stages and progressive changes life has undergone over the course of millions of years, during which time the embryo has developed into its most complicated form: the human one. Yet the mnemonic id that has run the gamut over this period from an *it* to a human, and has made many discoveries in the process that have helped sensitize and civilize his character, concludes his story on the cynical and abject note that, thinking more with his hands than with his brain, he has made himself an ax with which, to protect and widen his territory, he will not hesitate to "bash in the heads of certain other 'I's'" (202) whom he either dislikes or who get in his way. Levi warns that we must proceed with caution lest we fall victim to the inventions we have created to improve our existence.

In "Small Red Lights," Levi denounces our indiscriminate use of technology by having red lights condition and control human life. In an Orwellian setting, these lights have the power even to regulate humans sex life. The picture of human enslavement to technology is carried even further in "Psychophant." In this story a group of friends play a game in which an apparatus in a box expresses the "inner image" (176) of the player who touches it. In "For a Good Purpose," a telephone network assumes a human dimension to remind people of the moral values and responsibilities they have forsaken.

Levi realizes too that we find ourselves in a precarious situation because it takes firm judgment and a strong will not to overstep our bounds when our human inclination is to constantly strive ahead. This is eloquently rendered in "The Servant," a story with a Biblical resonance in which Rabbi Arié of Prague molds clay into a golem, a servant-robot, which he endows with obedience, courage, and strength, but no wisdom. The rabbi, the epitome of wisdom and knowledge, marvels at the many human qualities he has given his creation but is overcome and almost killed by it. One Sabbath, when he forgets to extract from its mouth the silver capsule that gives it life, the golem, a servant that did not want to be a servant, turns into a destructive force. The rabbi's experience comes strikingly close to that of humankind's present condition. The cause of the problem is to be found in the contradiction arising between the order to serve the master faithfully and the order to rest on the Sabbath. Herein lies the conflict that torments us in our choices between the opposite imperatives of instinct and reason, desire and duty, responsibility toward others and egotistical drives.

In the end, Levi demonstrates, we must simply act with care, concern, and clear vision. The validity of this collection of stories lies in its reminder to us to proceed cautiously through our world of technological wonders to avoid falling victim to them. From this point of view, all the stories in *The Sixth Day* can be seen as a continuation of Levi's exorcism of the Lager.

Lilìt e altri racconti, published in Italy in 1981, appeared in a reduced English version in 1986 as *Moments of Reprieve.* It was reprinted for the first time in 1987 under that same title. Of the thirty-six stories in the Italian version, only fifteen are included in the English translation; and, with the exception of three pieces, they are all part of the first section of the work, entitled "Passato prossimo" (Present Perfect), no doubt the most interesting of the three groups of stories contained in the original volume. The second and third sections, "Future Perfect" and "Present Indicative," excluded from the English version, include science fiction, moral and religious allegories, and simple tales of uncomplicated characters entangled in everyday situations. Like most of Levi's other short stories, many of those in this book appeared first as single pieces in the Turin newspaper *La Stampa* between 1975 to 1981.[9] In the preface to the English version Levi says that he is encouraged to write these stories because his memory of Auschwitz has become not weaker but stronger over the years. His recollections have remained intact to the point that he has been able to recall the faces of the survivors he knew in the camp. Thus it is not a particularly difficult task for him to return to that experience—in fact, the distance in time may even have attenuated the pain of his memories, so that he can more easily view his experience objectively and "round out" the parts of his account that were previously unfinished.[10] He returns to some of the characters we have met in the past and introduces other characters whom he treats in a more accomplished and detached fashion than he could have managed earlier. While the episodes and characters are part of Levi's history, it is not the need to tell that impels him to write this book but rather the enjoyment he draws from the art of telling.

As in the past, Levi's main concern is understanding more fully the unpredictability and mystery of human behavior. On this premise he returns to the concentration camp because there, given everyone's common goal to survive, one would assume that human behavior could have been as predictable as humanly possible. This is not the case, however, as Levi demonstrates in "Rappoport's Testament," the first story. Through the opposite figures of Valerio and Rappoport, he gives metaphorical life to this world full of human mysteries.

Valerio, with his resigned attitude and his grayness, made more salient by association with the mud all around, manifests his unwillingness to fight for survival. Rappoport, on the other hand, shows his unquenchable thirst for survival in the Lager by being willing to fight like a tiger in the jungle and, like Capaneous in Dante's hell, by having the temerity to challenge anyone.[11]

As in other works, Levi assumes here only the role of the chronicler who gathers scattered facts and pictures, urging the reader to draw his own conclusions rather than offering an opinion himself. And at the end of each episode he only raises troubling questions. Faced with a mix of opposite characteristics within a given individual, he cannot go beyond pity and surprise in witnessing the behavior of a man who, forced by such an extreme situation as the death camp, reveals himself to the fullest. This is the case with Chaim Rumkowski, "The King of the Jews" (also called the "Elder of the Jews") and president of the Lodz ghetto.[12] In "Story of a Coin," this man is inebriated with the power his enemies have given him and does not hesitate to abuse his own people, though at the same time he defends them from the violence and mistreatment inflicted on them by the oppressors who have elevated him.

A reverse case is that of the "Cantor and the Barracks Chief." In this story, Otto, an old political prisoner who is the barracks chief, is surprised and moved by the cantor Ezra, who tells him of his decision to fast for an entire day in observation of Yom Kippur. Otto respects the cantor's wish and goes against the rules of the camp by saving him a ration of soup for the following day. Similar unexpected behavior is seen in the case of the dwarf Elias, who, despite his violence and his bullying attitude, listens to stories with the enchantment of a little child; or of Wolf in "Our Seal," who, on a rare Sunday of rest, plays the violin in this violent and dehumanizing place. Levi is also taken by the unexpected response of Eddy, "The Juggler," who chooses not to turn the author in but simply to give him a warning smack when he catches him in the act of writing a letter to his family, an act punishable by death.

The most notable moments in this book, however, occur in the stories "Lilìt" and "Lorenzo's Return." From very different perspectives, they reveal the culminating point of the search for a reason for the evil in the world. In "Lilìt," the story for which the Italian version of the book is named, the problem of evil is observed from the standpoint of the religious faith of the Eastern Jew, in the person of the Polish carpenter who tells Levi the story while the two of them take refuge in a giant iron pipe during a rainstorm and are joined by a woman whom the carpenter sees as a temptress. It is the story of the feminine form God created along with man—not from man—which has been conveniently deleted from the Bible but survives in the oral tradition in a constantly changing form.

In the strength of his faith, the carpenter sees the evil in the legend in a clearer way than the evil around him. It is equally interesting how this story gets mixed in with all the other stories that use the camp as a background. Because of the place where it is told, there is irony in the combination of the Lager's mud with the mud of creation.

In "Lorenzo's Return" the focus falls on the good, as Levi resumes the story of the bricklayer to whom, as he writes in *Survival in Auschwitz,* he may owe his life. The story of kind Lorenzo, who walked all the way back to Italy, has a sad ending reminiscent of the Arunde tribe in the story "Westward": Lorenzo allows himself to die once he feels he has outlived his usefulness. Although saddened, Levi cannot but admire this man's constant dignity. Lorenzo's fate is counterbalanced by that of the title character of "Cesare's Last Adventure," who achieves his wish to arrive triumphant back in Italy by plane and continues on his picaresque ways with unending zest for life. Perhaps this same Cesare, who was so vital in helping Levi pull away from the ordeal of Auschwitz in *The Reawakening,* however briefly, comes to Levi's aid again with his reminder by example that life goes on and can still be enjoyed. This seems to be true especially in Italy, whose spirit Levi hails in "The Story of Avrom." Though the Italians too have reasons to be ashamed, Levi admires their courage and humanity during the more difficult moments of the war. Avrom owes his survival to the help of some Italians, and there seems to be little doubt that Levi sees a part of himself in this character.

In its presentation of the different facets of Levi's literary interests, *Moments of Reprieve* serves as a unified confirmation of his vision.

The variety of subjects Levi addresses in the essays that constitute *L'altrui mestiere (Other People's Trades)*, the final work to be considered apart from his writings directly about the Holocaust, derives from his "roaming about as a curious dilettante" for nearly ten years.[13] During that time, he wrote on subjects that, he modestly claims here, were beyond his limited expertise. This explains the title of the book, and the variety of the writings it contains mirrors Levi's belief that it is erroneous to see science and literature as two detached and incompatible cultures. The range of topics he discusses—as diverse as zoology, astronomy, linguistics, and literary criticism—supports his premise that cultural one-sidedness is detrimental and dangerous.

The apparently indiscriminate order in which the pieces are arranged in the book suggests that Levi wishes not to create a hierarchy of importance among his topics but rather to return to the tradition in which literary people and scientific ones thought it natural to venture into each other's field. The essays "The Language of Chemists," "The Ex-chemist," and "The Chemist's Mark" appear next to the essays on literature: "To a Young Reader," "Writing a Novel," "Aldous Huxley," and "François Rabelais."

Other pieces include "The Moon and Us," written in 1968 on the occasion of the Apollo 8 flight. In this essay Levi expresses regret that the accomplishment of demystifying a mystery provides also an inherent opportunity for disillusionment. Now that the moon has absorbed the human footstep, can its poetic and romantic image stay the same as it was in the past? The circumstances of Levi's death have triggered the interest of some critics in his first essay, "My House."[14] In it the author gives a detailed description of the ordinary house where he was born and from which he was taken to be sent to Auschwitz. Notable mainly for its lack of character and its anonymous and impersonal appearance, this house witnessed Levi's professional and artistic development throughout his life as well as his disappointments and his violent death. In this sense it is a microcosm of a man's existence.

Finally there is the essay "Il buco nero di Auschwitz," which may have been Levi's last piece, written in 1987 just months before his death. This work, which appears in its English translation in *The Mirror Maker* under the title "The Dispute among German Historians," serves as evidence of the author's steadfast commitment to keeping the memory of the Holocaust alive, even though, at this point more than ever before, he had serious doubts that his words and those of the other survivors who had written about their experience would have much impact on generations to come. The metaphor of the black hole, one that often appears in his work, shows that, as in the black holes in space from whose gravitational pull nothing ever escapes, no amount of evidence seems to satisfy the historians and the revisionists who raise questions about the actuality of the Holocaust. Because it is a black hole, from which nothing exits, they refuse to look at the evidence objectively. After so many years, they still fail to recognize the harm that has been done, and they hinder the truth by raising points of, at best, marginal relevance.

This position appears to be Levi's final one on the results of his efforts to witness, and it implies his belief that he has failed to call to the world's attention the irrationality of the Holocaust. It is sad that only since Levi's death is his impact being truly recognized.

Notes

1. Letter written to the author on 1 August 1966 (in the Einaudi archives).
2. In an interview in *Il Giorno* (12 October 1966), Levi claims his attraction to

this name was purely coincidental. He often saw it on a shop sign he passed on his way to work. But he was pleased with it because "Malabaila," he claims, can mean "bad wet-nurse" in the Piedmontese dialect—a fitting name, he believes, because there is a meta-phorical "vague odor" of milk gone bad that emanates from several of these stories. He insists, however, that he took this pen name not to hide his identity but to keep the autobiographical current of his first two books and the fantastic (and, in his view, less serious) content of these stories separate.

3. Levi calls these stories *racconti-scherzo*—tales told in jest. He seems to be raising the question whether this genre is the proper vehicle for the issues he is treating.

4. Levi wrote this story even before he wrote *The Reawakening.*

5. Charles Perrault (1628–1703) was a Frenchman who put into written form the old folk tales of Sleeping Beauty, Little Red Riding Hood, Cinderella, and Mother Goose.

6. The original version contains three short plays. The English translation does not contain "Il versificatore" (The Versifier), the play with which the author opens the cycle of stories about Mr. Simpson.

7. The term *vizio di forma* is a legal one that has no close correspondent in English, especially as Levi intends it. This may be the main reason the American version has a different title.

8. Trans. William Weaver (New York & London: Harcourt Brace Jovanovich, 1968).

9. The stories and essays printed between 1982 and 1987 appear in a later book.

10. *Moments of Reprieve,* trans. Ruth Feldman (New York: Penguin, 1987), 11.

11. See the *Inferno,* canto 14:63 and canto 25:15.

12. Levi has written at length about this man in "The Grey Zone" in *The Drowned and the Saved.* He is also referred to as "The Elder of the Jews."

13. *Other People's Trades,* trans. Raymond Rosenthal (New York: Schocken Books, 1984), 9.

14. See Franco Ferrucci, "La casa di Primo Levi" in *Primo Levi as a Witness* (Fiesole: Casalini, 1990) 43–52.

BIBLIOGRAPHY

Works by Primo Levi

Se questo è un uomo. Turin: De Silva, 1947. Rev. ed. Turin: Einaudi, 1958. [*If This Is a Man.* Trans. Stuart Woolf. New York: Orion, 1959. *Survival in Auschwitz.* Trans. Stuart Woolf. New York: Macmillan, 1961. Reprint 1987. With afterword "Primo Levi and Philip Roth: A Conversation." New York: Macmillan, 1993.]

La tregua. Turin: Einaudi, 1963. [*The Truce.* Trans. Stuart Woolf. Boston: Little, Brown and Co., 1965. *The Reawakening.* Trans. Stuart Woolf. With afterword "The Author's Answers to His Readers' Questions," trans. Ruth Feldman. New York: Macmillan, 1987.]

Storie Naturali. (Originally published under the pseudonym Damiano Malabaila.) Turin: Einaudi, 1966. Reprint 1979. [Appears with *Vizio di forma* in *The Sixth Day and Other Tales.* Trans. Raymond Rosenthal. New York: Summit Books, 1990.]

Vizio di forma. Turin: Einaudi, 1971. Reprint 1987. [Appears with *Storie Naturali* in *The Sixth Day and Other Tales.* Trans. Raymond Rosenthal. New York: Summit Books, 1990.]

Il sistema periodico. Turin: Einaudi, 1975. [*The Periodic Table.* Trans. Raymond Rosenthal. New York: Schocken Books, 1984.]

L'osteria di Brema. (Poetry.) Milan: Scheiwiller, 1975.

La chiave a stella. Turin: Einaudi, 1978. [*The Monkey's Wrench.* Trans. William Weaver. New York: Summit Books, 1986.]

Lilìt e altri racconti. Turin: Einaudi, 1981. [*Moments of Reprieve.* Trans. Ruth Feldman. New York: Summit Books, 1986. Reprint, New York: Penguin Books, 1987.]

La ricerca delle radici. Turin: Einaudi, 1981.

Se non ora, quando? Turin: Einuadi, 1982. [*If Not Now, When?* Trans. William Weaver. Introduction by Irving Howe. New York: Summit Books, 1985.]

Ad ora incerta. Milan: Garzanti, 1984. [*Collected Poems.* Trans. Ruth Feldman and Brian Swann. London: Faber and Faber, 1988.]

"Beyond Survival." Trans. Gail Soffer. *Prooftexts, a Journal of Jewish Literary History* 4.1 (1984): 9–21.

With Tullio Regge. *Dialogo.* Turin: Einaudi, 1984.

L'altrui mestiere. Turin: Einaudi, 1985. [*Other People's Trades.* Trans. Raymond Rosenthal. New York: Summit Books, 1989.]

Racconti e saggi. Turin: La Stampa, 1986. [*The Mirror Maker: Stories and Essays.* Trans. Raymond Rosenthal. New York: Schocken Books, 1989.]

I sommersi e i salvati. Turin: Einaudi, 1986. [*The Drowned and the Saved.* Trans. Raymond Rosenthal. New York: Summit Books, 1988.]

Opere. Vol. 1 (autobiographical texts). Introduction by Cesare Cases. Turin: Einaudi, 1987.

Opere. Vol. 2 (fiction and poetry). Introduction by Cesare Segre. Turin: Einaudi, 1987.

Opere. Vol. 3 (tales and essays). Introduction by Pier Vincenzo Mengaldo. Turin: Einaudi, 1990.

Other Works

Biasin, Gian Paolo. "Till My Ghastly Tale Is Told: Levi's Moral Discourse from *Se questo è un uomo* to *I sommersi e i salvati.*" *Reason and Light. Essays on Primo Levi.* Ed. Susan Tarrow. Ithaca: Cornell University Press, 1990.

Camon, Ferdinando. *Conversations with Primo Levi.* Trans. John Shepley. Marlboro, Vt.: Marlboro Press, 1989. (Original title: *Autoritratto di Primo Levi.* Padua: Edizioni Nord-Est, 1987.) One of Levi's last and most penetrating interviews before his death. The English version contains an essay in which Camon questions whether Primo Levi's death resulted from suicide.

Cannon, Joann. "Canon-Formation and Reception in Contemporary Italy: The Case of Primo Levi." *Italica* 69.2 (Spring 1992): 30–44. This study looks at the emergence of Primo Levi as a writer and the various uses to which his texts may be put.

Dante Alighieri. *The Divine Comedy.* Ed. and trans. C. S. Singleton. Princeton: Princeton University Press, 1970.

Dini, Massimo, and Stefano Jesurum. *Primo Levi. Le opere e i giorni.* Milan: Rizzoli, 1992. An informative study of a biographical nature based on an interview by Levi, comments by his friends and acquaintances, and information drawn from some of his works.

Epstein, Adam. "Primo Levi and the Language of Atrocity." *Bulletin of the Society for Italian Studies* 20 (1987):31–38.

Feig, Konnillyn G. *Hitler's Death Camps. The Sanity of Madness.* New York & London: Holmes and Meier, 1979. Of particular interest are the pages that focus on Auschwitz, 333–69.

Frassica, Pietro, ed. *Primo Levi as Witness: Proceedings of a Symposium held at Princeton University.* Fiesole: Casalini, 1990. Contains essays by G. P. Biasin, C. Cases, G. Einaudi, F. Ferrucci, L. Fontanella, C. Segre, A. Stille, G. Tesio, and G. Lagorio.

Gilman, Sander L. "To Quote Primo Levi: 'Redest keyn jiddisch, bist nit kejn jid' ['If you don't speak Yiddish, you're not a Jew']" *Prooftexts, a Journal of Jewish Literary History* 9.2 (1989): 139–60. This study concentrates on the artistic values Levi attributes to the Italian, Yiddish, and Hebrew languages.

Grassano, Giuseppe. *Primo Levi.* Florence: La Nuova Italia, 1981. An extensive study, with a rich bibliography, of Levi's works up until 1980.

Gunzburg, Lynn M. "Down Among the Dead Men: Levi and Dante in Hell." *Modern Language Studies* 16.1 (1986): 10–28.

Howe, Irving. Introduction. "Primo Levi: An Appreciation." *If Not Now, When?* New York: Summit Books, 1985. 3–16. An instrumental document for general information on Levi, as seen from the perspective of an American writer.

Hughes, Stuart H. *Prisoners of Hope.* Cambridge: Harvard University Press, 1983. A significant study on the Jews in Italy and on the literary contributions of prominent Italian Jewish writers such as Italo Svevo, Alberto Moravia, Giorgio Bassani, Carlo Levi, and Natalia Ginzburg.

Michaelis, Meir. *Mussolini and the Jews.* Oxford: Claredon Press, 1978. Useful document for a clearer understanding of the historical and political situation of the Jews in Italy during Fascism.

Mitgang, Herbert. "Authors Newly Make the Holocaust Connection." *New York Times,* 17 March 1990, sec. "Words and Image." The author, in a review of a book on the Holocaust, states that a Mr. Kazin calls Levi "one of the two greatest postwar writers (with Italo Calvino being the other) Italy has produced."

Motola, Gabriel. "Primo Levi. The Auschwitz Experience." *Southwest Review* 72 (Spring 1987): 258–69. An interesting, although brief, analysis of *Survival in Auschwitz* and *The Reawakening.*

Ozick, Cynthia. "Primo Levi's Suicide Note." *Metaphor & Memory.* New York: Knopf, 1989. 34–48. Of particular interest are Ms. Ozick's comments on Levi's "anger" evidenced in *The Drowned and the Saved.*

Patai, Raphael. *The Jewish Mind.* New York: Scribner's, 1977. A study of Jewish traditions and historical information on the Jews.

Roth, Cecil. *The History of the Jews of Italy.* Philadelphia: Jewish Publication Society of America, 1946. An indispensable document on the Jews in Italy.

Roth, Philip. "A Man Saved by His Skills." *New York Times Book Review,* 12 October 1986. Possibly the most important interview with Primo Levi in English.

Sodi, Risa. "An Interview with Primo Levi." *Partisan Review* 54.3 (1987): 355–66. A revealing interview in which Levi tells much of himself as a writer.

———. *A Dante of Our Time (Primo Levi and Auschwitz).* American University Studies Ser. 2, Romance Languages and Literature. New York: Peter Lang, 1990. A thorough and intelligent study of Dante's influence on Primo Levi.

Steiner, George. "The Hollow Miracle." *Language and Science.* New York: Atheneum, 1967. An outstanding essay on the Holocaust's effect on language.

Styron, William. "Why Primo Levi Need Not Have Died." *New York Times,* 19 December 1988, sec. A:17. An essay in which the author speculates on the reasons why Primo Levi may have commited suicide.

Tarrow, Susan, ed. *Reason and Light. Essays on Primo Levi.* Cornell Studies in International Affairs/Western Societies Papers 25. Ithaca: Cornell University Press, 1990. Essays on Primo Levi by G. P. Biasin, J. Cannon, R. Feldman, S. Gilman, L. Gunzberg, I. Klein, F. Girelli-Carasi, N. Harrowitz, and C. Segrè, and a testimony by Ruth Feldman and J. Wolsky.

Vincenti, Fiora. *Invito alla lettura di Primo Levi.* Milan: Mursia, 1984. A valuable analysis of the life and works of Primo Levi until 1982. This study does not include *The Drowned and the Saved* or *Moments of Reprieve.*

Zuccotti, Susan. *The Italians and the Holocaust. Persecution, Rescue, Survival.* New York: Basic Books, 1987. The most extensive study, with ample data and statistics, of the events surrounding the plight of the Jews in Italy during the years of Fascism and subsequent German occupation.

INDEX